HARLAN ELLISON'S ENDLESSLY WATCHING

AN EDGEWORKS ABBEY OFFERING

Harlan Ellison's Endlessly Watching
is an Edgeworks Abbey® offering in association with Jason Davis.
Published by arrangement with the Author and The Kilimanjaro Corporation.

**Harlan Ellison's
Endlessly Watching**
by Harlan Ellison®

This edition is copyright © 2014 by The Kilimanjaro Corporation.
All rights reserved.

Harlan Ellison and Edgeworks Abbey
are registered trademarks of The Kilimanjaro Corporation.

No part of this book may be reproduced or transmitted in any form or by any means electronic or mechanical—including photocopy, recording, Internet posting, electronic bulletin board—or any other information storage and retrieval system, without permission in writing from the Author, except by a reviewer who may quote brief passages in a critical article or review to be printed in a magazine or newspaper, or electronically transmitted on radio, television or in a recognized on-line journal. For information address Author's agent: Richard Curtis Associates, Inc., 171 East 74th Street, New York, New York 10021, USA.

All persons, places and organizations in this book—except those clearly in the public domain—are fictitious and any resemblance that may seem to exist to actual persons, places or organizations living, dead or defunct is purely coincidental. These are works of fiction.

**Harlan Ellison website: www.HarlanEllison.com
To order books: www.HarlanEllisonBooks.com**

Publisher & Editor:	Jason Davis
Assistant Editor:	Cynthia Davis
Cover Layout:	Bo Nash

ISBN: 978-0-9895257-7-0

First Edition

Copyright acknowledgments appear on pages 186-187, which constitutes an extension of this copyright page.

290914

How Could *This* One
Not Be for
LEONARD MALTIN
& Alice & Jessie?

TABLE OF CONTENTS

1	*Psycho*
3	Total Impact: *The Terminal Man*
13	3 Faces of Fear
35	35: In Which the Phantasmagorical Pales Before the Joys of the Mimetic
43	36: In Which, Darkly and Deliciously, We Travel From Metropolis to Metropolis, Two Different Cities, Both Ominous
53	37: In Which Not Only is No Answer Given, But No One Seems to Know the Question to Ask
61	38: In Which, Though Manipulated, We Acknowledge That Which All Men Seek
69	39: In Which We Hum a Merry Tune While Waiting for New Horrors, New Horrors
77	40: In Which We Scrutinize the Sedulousness to Their Hippocratic Oath of Troglodytic, Blue, Alien Proctologists
85	41: In Which an Extremely Nervous Fool with His Credentials Taped to His Forehead Tacks Trepidatiously Between Scylla and Charybdis Knowing that Angels and Wise Men Would Fear Even to Dog-Paddle This Route
97	42: In Which It Waddles Like a Duck, Sheds Water Like a Duck, and Goes Steady With Ducks, But Turns Out to be a Tortoise
107	43: In Which We Lament, "There Goes the Neighborhood!"
115	44: In Which the Good Ship Coat-Tail-Ride Sinks, Abandoning Hundreds in Treacherous Waters
129	45: In Which *Tempus* Fidgets, *Fugits*, and Inevitably Omnia Revelats
137	46: In Which We Bend So Far Over Backwards To Be Unbiased That You Can See The Nose Hairs Quiver With Righteousness

149	**47: In Which Artful Vamping Saves the Publisher $94.98**
157	**48: In Which the Wee Child's Icons are Demeaned**
165	**49: In Which the Old Man of the Sea Bites the Head off Yet Another Chicken**
171	**50: In Which the Playroom of the Prodigal Gives One Last Gasp**
173	I Saw *Ghost Rider* Today at the Galeria
177	*12 Years a Slave*
179	**Death To All Hollywood Award Shows!**
181	***Bram Stoker's Dracula*** a previously unpublished review
183	***Honey, I Blew Up the Baby*** a previously unpublished refusal to review
185	A few words on ***The Mask***

Psycho

Now, to begin, let's set the ground rules: you're a guy who makes his living writing, you know all the clichés, all the phony starts, and you can usually second-guess the movie scripters every time out. You are over twenty-one, find the mockings and mewlings of Lugosi and Chaney more pitiable than frightening, and the last time you were really scared was when the platoon leader wakened you for guard duty at four in the morning out on bivouac. Further, you've read the book, know the author is a greater wit than weirdie, and you're all set to be bored. Ground rules set. Witness in point: this reviewer. I went to see the Bloch-Hitchcock *Psycho*.

Frankly, I had the shit scared out of me.

No two ways about it, Charlie, this time they've pulled off the Indian rope trick. It starts out like a below-par chapter of *Stella Dallas* and pretty chop-chop leaves all reality behind as the fist of terror wraps around your windpipe. If you've read the book, be assured the moom pitcher follows pretty faithfully (they've extended the opening to give you some drool-invoking scenes of Janet Leigh in her bra and half-slip, and they've taken literary license with the character of Norman, the son who runs the motel). (As to the license taken with Norman's character, I feel it is all to the good as warmed-over by Tony Perkins: brooding, pensive, darkly intense, engaging, altogether terrifying in its simplicity and naturalism.)

If you haven't read the book, the gravest disservice will be done you by the trap-mouth who spills the plot. Far be it from me to kill the goose. However (he said, remembering how annoyed he used to get in high school when oral book reports were concluded,

"And if you want to know what happens, you'll have to read the book."), the scene is the Southwest, the opening gun gets fired as Miss Leigh, full in the midst of an affair with a young divorced cat from a small town somewhere, heads out with a bagful of her employer's loot. She stops, in her mad flight, at a rundown motel operated by a likeable but lopsided Tony Perkins, who has nasty fights with his mother, seen as a shadow through the window of their brooding, Addams-like mansion on the hill...under the scud-filled cadaverous-gray sky.

That's it. That's all you get. From there on out, you had better bring the Miltown out of your weskit pocket. Because at that point Hitchcock uncorks some of the most brutally gagging detailwork ever to grace the screen. Consider: on tv and suchlike, murder is a fairly uncomplicated matter. You want someone dead, you stab or shoot him...once...and down he goes. Life just ain't like that, Charlie. In the real world (the one where you have to carry out the garbage or it begins to smell faintly bad) murder can be mucho difficult. Just consider again: the guy doesn't want to die. He fights you as you try to stab him. He grabs your arm. You struggle. He throws you off balance. You get in slight slashes to the arms in an attempt to land a fatal blow. Blood begins to splatter. The struggle goes on. Reality.

That's right, Charlie. That's what Hitchcock has given us in *Psycho*. And this, this grotesque pathological attention to the sensational aspects of reality combined with obscure camera angles and stream-of-consciousness music leaves the viewer in a state of debilitation and shakenness.

It was so painful...the suspense, the horror of it all...that twice I felt compelled to get up and leave the theater. I *literally* could not stand it. And to top it off, the ending is in the finest tradition of the macabre. If *Diabolique* with its eyeball-thumbing scene scared you, this picture will stop your pump permanently. I can say with all sureness that *no one* will escape terror at this show.

It was filmed the smartest way possible (for this sort of flick) in black and white, and the cast is brilliant. They all have dimension and purpose, and what befalls each of them (even the unseen mother) matters—to you.

Go then, Charlie, with my best wishes and my condolences. Because after you've seen this film, you'll be scared to ever take a shower in a motel again. And that, Charlie baby, is a promise.

Total Impact:
The Terminal Man

"Madness has become man's possibility of abolishing both man and the world—and even those images that challenge the world and deform man. It is, far beyond dreams, beyond the nightmare of bestiality, the last recourse: the end and the beginning of everything. Not because it is a promise...but because it is the ambiguity of chaos and apocalypse..."

Michel Foucault
MADNESS AND CIVILIZATION

On an unseasonably sweltering evening in May of 1966, Baton Rouge was jolted out of its personal discomfort by one of the strangest murders ever recorded in that city. A thirteen year old boy named Judson Lagrange, for no apparent reason anyone could discern, murdered his mother. Not simply in an act of passion, but over and over again as though driven by a terrible, inexplicable compulsion: using a .38 S&W Webley English Service Revolver left behind by the father who had deserted him and his mother six years earlier, the boy had fired the first shot, utterly and finally fatal, straight into his mother's heart; the woman died instantly, but the boy—as he recalled the event later—felt as though he was emerging from a long dark night—he was unable to recall the events leading up to the slaying—and he stood there, swaying, ever so slightly, as something within him compelled him to notice the revolver was now empty, though only one shot had been fired, compelled him to go to the drawer where the gun had lain unused for years, compelled him to reload the chambers of the weapon, compelled him to carefully check the gun for readiness and, finally, compelled him to stand over the corpse and fire six more shots into the dead woman.

When the firing pin clicked on an empty chamber at last, he set down the revolver, went to the sofa across the room from the corpse, sat down, and quietly waited for the police to come for him. He was unable to give a reason for his act.

In no way connected to the life of Judson Lagrange save by a formidable thread of mental illness, four years and two months later, halfway across the continent in New York City, a fifty-two year old man who had signed the guest register of the cheap midtown hotel into which he had checked the week before as Walter M. Dickinson, awoke with a scream of terror and disorientation. Awoke, as he put it later, "like I was coming out of a long, dark sleep." He lay in the bed, wrapped in sweat-soggy gray sheets, staring up at an unfamiliar ceiling, staring around at unfamiliar walls, staring out a window on a city he had never before seen. He did not recognize the room in which he had lived for a week, did not in fact recognize the hotel, the city, the name he had signed, or even the clothes he had clearly been wearing.

An entire week had been erased from his memory.

Shaking with disoriented fear, he remanded himself into the custody of the New York Police Department and, through the Missing Persons Division, he learned that for seven days he had been gambling heavily, living on his meager winnings, had been frequenting Times Square movie houses till the small hours of the morning, and had been frequenting Times Square prostitutes when he was not clothed by the darkness of the theaters.

None of this was consistent with his past. His real name was Paul Robinson, he lived in Columbia City, Indiana, he had a wife and three children, and for thirty years had been a salesman of religious articles throughout the Midwest. He had never touched a pack of cards in his life, had been a faithful husband and father, had been a regular churchgoer, and was not particularly fond of motion pictures.

He was never able to explain why or how he had gotten from Indiana to a flophouse in Manhattan, nor why he had done it, nor what had transpired during that vanished week.

He was sent home to his family and the pattern never repeated itself.

Both of these unfortunate human beings, the teenaged matricide and the fiftyish amnesiac, were finally diagnosed as suffering from a strange, little-understood affliction known as psychomotor epilepsy.

Even in a time of bypass surgery, transplants, artificial stimulation of brain centers, and pacemakers, this comparatively rare offshoot of the group of diseases most commonly termed "epilepsy" is singular as a baffling, mysterious and potentially dangerous ailment known to medical science. And though its dramatic symptoms have drawn widespread attention in medical journals both here and abroad, still...with case histories like the above reported regularly...virtually no breakthroughs have occurred in diagnosing and curing. Truly, those suffering from psychomotor epilepsy are the damned of our time.

And with that peculiar exhuming of minutiae in the various sciences (that has fascinated writers of the imaginative since Wells first supposed "what if") it has fallen to the genre of science fiction to come up with the first extrapolative consideration of psychomotor epilepsy in human terms.

First as a brilliant and suspenseful sf novel by Michael Crichton—whose THE ANDROMEDA STRAIN and BINARY have placed him in the forefront of mainstream novelists utilizing the rigors of the sf idiom to full effect—and now on film in a startling adaptation of the Crichton book, psychomotor epilepsy becomes more than a conversation piece for idle conjecture at medical conventions. In *The Terminal Man*, science fiction blends with a deep concern for the human condition to produce a film that *aficionados* cannot help but view with admiration and excitement.

As set forth in Crichton's bestselling novel, an experimental technique for treating the disease is postulated that would control the devastating symptoms utilizing futuristic surgical techniques that, at present, exist nowhere outside the fertile imagination of Crichton (who was educated at Harvard College, Harvard Medical School, received his MD in 1969, and is currently on leave of absence from the Salk Institute for Biological Studies in La Jolla, California). Brain controlling mechanisms implanted inside the body are only one element of this fantastic therapy.

And even as adventurous as Crichton's original conception may have been in the novel, it is Warner Bros.'s film of the novel that most perfectly examines this extrapolative consideration of the consequences inherent in combining man and machine to solve an insoluble human dilemma. With the rare magic that the motion picture idiom brings to certain special works of the Imagination, *The Terminal Man* not only scintillates with the suspense and drama of the pure sf "hard science" story, but probes deeply into the aspects of what Faulkner termed "the human heart in conflict with itself."

Judgment of the sf community on the implied classic stature of this film is yet to come, but from preliminary screenings and examinations of the sketches for the hardware used in the motion picture, it seems safe to say that Crichton, producer-director-scenarist Michael Hodges, and Warner Bros. have brought forth a visual feast that will rank beside *2001: A Space Odyssey*, *The Day the Earth Stood Still*, *The Time Machine* and *Things to Come* as a milestone of memorable science fiction.

"The electromotive force, such as arises when tides of ions play across magnetic lines, like the bowing of violin strings, has its counterpart in the human brain and nerve cords where comparable vibrations create 'brain waves' that can be tuned in on, measured and interpreted by man. The electroencephalograph, for instance, records the brain's tides and weird melodies: the alpha rhythms 'resembling a scanning device,' the delta waves' 'billowy rhythms of sleep,' the theta rhythms evoked by repulsion and disappointment, the kappa waves that are most active when cerebral 'wheels are grinding' in a conscious effort to remember. Can it be of less ultimate meaning that epilepsy is being successfully treated as 'a temporary electrical storm in the brain,' a cross-circuit of billions of neurones?"

Guy Murchie
Song of the Sky

If it be true, as it has been said, that the history of human civilization is a record of the diseases with which humankind has had to contend, then epilepsy is surely as old as recorded civilization itself.

Perhaps even older: the earliest chronicles of western culture frequently refer to men being possessed by gods, demons, devils, imps...behaving oddly...the legends of soul-stealing, demonic transference, the "amok"...and a general acceptance exists among historians that these are bastardized accounts of men, women and children stricken with epileptic seizures.

Even the sophisticated Greeks associated epilepsy with the supernatural or paranormal world; and thus the disease, totally misunderstood, was integrated into much of their religious rituals.

What amusing little creatures we are, always seeking some new and all-encompassing overview that will explain the ethical structure of the universe. From Anaxagoras's belief that the world was round, through time to Nietzsche's theory of the *Übermensch*, to Darwin's origin and descent, to Velikovsky's colliding worlds, to the space visitors of Von Däniken and Duncan Lunan's alien space probe that's supposedly been in orbit with our Moon for thirteen thousand years…not to mention the world-views of the Maharishi, Guru-ji and the John Birch Society…humans have always sought to explain away the unknown with wild fantasies. Usually paranoid.

So, too, did the ancients try to explain epilepsy.

One of the most familiar was the Delphic Oracle, to whom kings and conquerors and commonfolk went to learn of the future. Because of the supposed liaison between epileptics and gods, "the epileptic may be felt to have gained supernatural insight into the future as a result of his intimate relationship with the supernatural," according to Isaac Asimov, in THE HUMAN BRAIN. Thus, if the poor Oracle had an epileptic seizure, it would be unarguable proof positive that the prophecy of such a seer was direct from the Fates themselves.

The first person to rebel against such nonsense was, not surprisingly, Hippocrates of Cos, the father of medicine. Hippocrates ventured that, far from being of spiritual origin, epilepsy was organic in nature. Of Hippocrates's conviction, essayist Gustav Eckstein wrote: "Epilepsy, he insisted, ought not to be called divine. There was no divinity in it. It was a disturbed brain."

It was a disturbed brain.

With a single sentence, Hippocrates stripped away uncounted centuries of superstition and inhumanity and ignorance, thus striking in the direction that has led to the modern medical practice of applying inquiry, logical thought processes, and a heightened sensitivity to the problem of bodily ills.

But the first successful treatment of the disease had to wait till the early part of this century—until which time epileptics were thrown into Bedlams so "the madness would not return to the village"—and with the rise of pharmaceutical technology sophisticated surgical techniques and advanced forms of drug therapy were brought into common use.

Modern medicine now recognizes three forms of epilepsy: *grand mal*, where seizures manifest themselves as bodily convulsions and loss of consciousness (a plot pivot in Crichton's THE ANDROMEDA STRAIN); *petit mal*, marked by very brief unconscious periods; and...*psychomotor epilepsy*, in which various kinds of "automatic actions" may occur during extended amnesia, or long blackouts like "a long, dark night" of troubled sleep.

Clearly, the psychomotor variety is the most difficult to treat. It is generally resistant to anything but the most powerful chemotherapy, or drastic surgery, such as the prefrontal lobotomy. However, while both forms of treatment render the patient "acceptable" to the society in which he must live, imprisoning his sociopathic tendencies, they also have the most undesirable and repellent side effects. Drugs able to unravel the twisted processes of a disturbed brain cause total impotence. Old-style lobotomies result in a "flattening of the mind, a bleaching" to use Eckstein's vivid phrase. The lobotomized become *overly* tranquil, frequently too free of ambition or motivation to compete with others in even the smallest fashion. They sink into apathy. They become zombies, little better than living vegetables.

Recently, an updated method of lobotomization was proposed to cure a "John Doe"—confessed rapist and murderer—held in the Ionia State Hospital near Detroit for eighteen years. Early this year, several doctors secured permission to operate on "John Doe," utilizing a special surgical technique that was alleged to destroy only the minute brain structure known as the amygdala, a switching point for sexual and aggressive impulses. The prevailing opinion was that this operation would reduce the patient's violent sexual tendencies while avoiding the gross side effects resulting from a normal lobotomy in which relatively large areas of the brain are excised.

Before the "John Doe" operation could proceed, however, a legal battle developed over the ethics of the experiment, eventually lengthening into an extended debate over what was seen as blatant "mind control." The concurrent revelations at that time of ghastly experiments using blacks in illegal studies of venereal disease in Alabama prisons only served to deepen concern over the propriety of the operation.

A court decision killed the operation and, apparently, any future attempts at altering personalities by removal of portions of the brain. Accordingly, research is now concentrated on the control of antisocial behavior stemming from organic brain dysfunction not by tinkering with the physical structure of the brain, but by reorienting the impulses that cause such malfunctions.

But even the most liberal proponents of corrective brain surgery admit that in terms of success with the unknown terrors of psychomotor...we are no better off than the primitives who believed epileptics were struck by the Arrows of Apollo or the thunderbolts of Zeus.

And it is at this juncture, into this *terra incognita*, this domain of fantastic speculation, that *The Terminal Man* plunges, beginning with a startling projection of a method for humanely restraining the dangerous seizures of Harry Benson, the terminal man.

Harry Benson. Perhaps Michael Crichton's most outstanding character creation (including the many in his suspense novels written under the pseudonym "John Lange"). An acting plum requiring the most careful casting perceptivity.

And though Crichton may be unhappy with the rewritten script by Michael Hodges—the novelist-turned-film director has removed his name from the script—he can certainly have no sorrow about Hodges's selection of George Segal to play the hag-ridden Harry Benson. George Segal was the perfect choice. If there is an actor currently working in front of the cameras who can match the amazing performances of Segal in *Ship of Fools*, *King Rat*, and *Blume in Love* (three films undistinguished save by Segal's charismatic presence), not to mention such triumphs as *Who's Afraid of Virginia Woolf?*, *No Way to Treat a Lady*, the unsung classic *Bye Bye Braverman*, *A Touch of Class*, and the now-famous *Where's Poppa?*, then I cannot think of his name. Segal has such a range, such a formidable yet relaxed manner, that his very presence in *The Terminal Man* makes the film a must-see.

Screenings of clips of the soon-to-be-released film fulfill the expectations Segal's very name promises. He *is* Harry Benson, and his story is a contemporary parallel of the Jekyll-Hyde dilemma fraught with humanity and helplessness.

Like most good sf stories, the plot is complex and utterly fascinating.

Benson, a computer technician working with advanced forms of machine intelligence, has been afflicted with extended "blackouts"—times when he develops a Hyde-like personality that replaces his normally gentle behavior, when he brutally attacks both friends and total strangers. Increasingly, Benson has come to believe that computers are taking over the world, replacing human beings. In that respect he is one with the millions in our society who feel ever more and more alienated, threatened, dissociated by the onrush of rampant technology. His paranoid fantasies remain submerged, smoldering, during his everyday life, but they burst loose when he has a seizure. At such times he is apt to attack anyone he suspects of collaborating with the enemy machines. His problem is more twistedly heightened by his awareness of himself as working in collaboration with the machines himself: he is a computer expert, one of the fifth columnists.

Benson's condition, referred to throughout the film in its shortened form as "para-epilepsy," has reached the stage where it is correctable only by an extremely debilitating drug treatment or by a radically new form of experimental surgery.

Despite protests from Benson's psychiatrist, Dr. Janet Ross (a role assayed with extraordinary skill by Joan Hackett), Benson agrees to undergo the surgery. A special medical team at a Los Angeles hospital's Neuropsychiatry Research Unit plant a dime-sized computer and a tiny nuclear powerpack in Benson's body, and a series of wires to electrodes implanted in the amygdala, the posterior area of the limbic system in Harry Benson's brain.

In Crichton/Hodges's extrapolation of this startling new technique, the electrodes have a double-edged function: they detect the distinctive electrical imbalance in Benson's brain that immediately precedes a seizure, and shunt that data to the miniaturized computer. The computer than decides which of the forty electrodes to shock, thereby having the effect of canceling out the seizure before it can take effect and manifest itself as sociopathic behavior.

One of the most fascinating aspects of the superlative and authentic production of *The Terminal Man* is the operation itself. Sparing no expense, Warner Bros. constructed a gigantic set of the operating theater at a cost of over $30,000 and then furnished it with actual electronic and surgical equipment valued at nearly a quarter of a million dollars.

Everything from the gleaming laser X-ray machine to the multipositional operating chair to the special computer that oversees the hundreds of surgical sequences that must be followed precisely to successfully conclude the implantation, are either actual devices already in use, or the next closest thing. From start to finish the authenticity of the entire surgical sequence is not only as accurate as exhaustive research can make it, but carries with it an ambience of reality that forces the viewer to suspend all disbelief and for the duration of the film accept that such operations are possible.

But if the truth be told, the computer/electrode/powerpack assembly is nowhere near a reality. It is once again the creation of the fertile science fiction mind of Michael Crichton and the amazing talents of the Warner Bros. production team. And it is yet another example of the added dimension that can be brought to works of the imaginative by the miracle workers of the contemporary cinema. It is, in very special ways, a realized dream any sf writer would give his royalties to realize.

But if the harnessing of Harry Benson's crippled brain is only a sf dream, it is certainly the next step in mind control experiments that have been proceeding for several decades. All are based, as is *The Terminal Man*, on the principle that electrical stimulation of specific portions of the brain can bring about specific actions and reactions. A tiny, five millivolt jolt of electricity on one matrix of cortical cells may produce intense pain, while a stimulus a thousandth of an inch away might induce ecstatic pleasure.

Another jolt in a still different location might summon up a neutral image—such as the taste of ham on rye, to take an example from the film.

Although no one has yet planted a closed circuit control device in a human (as far as we know…peculiar rumors come to us from behind the Iron Curtain), that day cannot be far off. As recently as 1969, Yale researcher Jose Delgado implanted radio sets in the skulls of animals and transmitted signals that caused them to perform in as Pavlovian a manner as Dr. Delgado might have wished, even to the point of distinctly altering their emotional states from rage to calm.

The gap between radio-controlled cattle stimulated to graze in productive patterns over vast pasture lands and computer-guided people ordered to and from routine production line jobs is narrower than we might think, and closing with every advance in biochemistry and electronics. A terrifying thought. Perhaps only a wry and vagrant vision of a fantasist, or perhaps an ominous shadow on the horizon. Are you keeping your eyes open?

Little over a year ago, Dr. Delgado, rather a busy man, announced that he was developing "something like a cerebral pacemaker" with the ability to constrict the functions of some portions of the brain in the same manner that cardiac pacemakers control the rhythms of the heart.

How great a leap is it from Dr. Delgado's developments of a cerebral pacemaker to the computer planted in the terminal man, Harry Benson?

Which the greater danger? A society in which the potentiality for mind control exists with the existence of the technology and hardware—history proves: to have it, is to use it—or a society in which a Harry Benson can walk the streets beside us, a human bomb waiting to explode?

Beneath the sheer entertainment and speculation of a film as memorable as *The Terminal Man*, there is a disturbing subtext we must all, every one of us, eventually consider.

Even as we consider the total impact of the word *terminal*.

3 Faces of Fear

1

Chill beneath a cadaverously gray Autumn sky, the tiny New Mexico town. That slate moment in the seasons when everything begins to grow dark. The epileptic scratching of fallen leaves hurled along sidewalks. Mad sounds from the hills. Cold. And something else:

A leopard, escaped, is loose in the town.

Chill beneath a crawling terror of death in the night, the tiny New Mexico town. That thick red moment in the fears of small people when everything explodes in the black flow of blood. A deep-throated growl from a filthy alley. Cold.

A mother, preoccupied with her cooking, tells her small daughter to go down the street to the bakery, get a loaf of bread. The child shows a moment of fear...the animal they haven't found yet...

The mother insists, it's only a half block to the bakery. Put on a shawl and go get that bread, your father will be home soon. The child goes. Hurrying back up the street, the bread held close to her, the street empty and filling with darkness, ink presses down the sky, the child looks around, and hurries. A cough in the blackness behind her. A cough, deep in a throat that never formed human sounds.

The child's eyes widen in panic. She begins to hurry. Her footsteps quicken. The sound of padding behind her. Feet begin to run. Focus on darkness and the sound of rapid movement. The child. The rushing.

To the wooden door of the house. The door is locked. The child pinned against the night, with the furred sound of agony rushing toward her on the wind.

Inside, the mother, still kitchened, waiting. The sound of the child outside, panic and bubbles of hysteria in the voice, Mommy open the door the leopard is after me!

The mother's voice assumes the ages-old expression of harassed parenthood. Hands on hips, she turns to the door, you're always lying, telling fibs, making up stories, how many times have I told you lying will—

Mommy! Open the door!

You'll stay out there till you learn to stop lying!

Mommy! Mom—

Something gigantic hits the door with a crash. The door bows inward, and dust from between the cracks sifts into the room. The mother's eyes grow huge, she stares at the door. A thick black stream, moving very slowly, seeps under the door. Madness crawls up behind our eyes, the mother's eyes, and we sink into a pit of blind emptiness…

…from which we emerge to examine the nature of terror in the motion picture. Fear as the masters of the film form have shown it to us, and fear as the screen has recently depicted it, with adolescence and cheap thrills. Fear in three guises, with an attempt to understand its value, note its proportions, taste it, sink a hand into it and draw out a vital organ if possible. First, a memory of fear from a childhood spent in the dark, watching Lugosi, watching Lorre, watching Richard Dix as the Whistler, watching—among others, and most notably—the films of Val Lewton.

The scene depicted at the outset of this examination, a scene shot in small screen, in black and white, with a minimum of production values (as currently conceived by the LARGER film-makers), with unknown actors, shot by indirection and subtlety rather than the sound of hands clapping sharply in your ear to startle you, that scene was from a 1943 RKO Radio Picture, *The Leopard Man*.

I may have recalled it completely inaccurately. I wouldn't know. I saw the picture only once, when I was nine years old, at a Saturday afternoon matinee in the Lake Theatre in Painesville, Ohio.

That scene, that thick, glutinous flow of little girl blood beneath a heavy oak door, has stayed with me for twenty-two years. It scared me. It scared me at the time. It scares me now. I was afraid, and when I recount this scene to listeners today, I can impart the same fear to them, merely in the retelling.

When was the last time you were frightened by a film? Truly frightened. Frightened enough to worry about it much later, when your thoughts were elsewhere, and suddenly *that* came back to you? The shower sequence in *Psycho*? The unmasking in *Phantom of the Opera*? The discovery of the bloodless sled-dog in Hawks's *The Thing*? Bette Davis serving Joan Crawford her canary in *Whatever Happened to Baby Jane*? or possibly a fillip from Polanski's *Repulsion*? If it was this last, part three of this examination may annoy you. If it was any of the others, then perhaps you have already thought the thoughts I will offer next.

But it is a progression. Before a dissection can have any worth, we must examine the whole organism, and for the first part of this discussion of the anatomy of fear, I offer as the finest example of terror in its most natural, unsullied, incarnation, the *oeuvre* of Val Lewton.

To *aficionados* of all that is worthy and touched by glory in the film medium, the name Lewton will be no great surprise. To those who play at understanding movies, who ride with the tide, or who take their cues from slickpaper yellowsheets such as *Time* or *Newsweek* (and I level this derogation with calculation to be elaborated upon later), I would better have struck the responsive *kitsch* chord by citing the early Dassin, or Hitchcock.

But as a truer barometer of the centigrades to which horror can inflame a filmgoer, I find no contest with what Lewton produced in merely eight films from 1942 to 1946, with budgets so ludicrous, achievements so startling, and studio intentions so base that they stand as some sort of landmark in the landscape of cinema.

Lewton began as a story editor for Selznick and shortly thereafter was placed in charge of a new low-budget production unit at RKO, expressly created to specialize in cheapjack horror films. It was born out of the need for lower-half double-bill films to accompany big-budget vehicles, with a sort of antediluvian "exploitation" approach and very little else to recommend its product. But RKO had no idea of the nature of the monster they were creating. Lewton was given titles such as *Cat People*, *I Walked With A Zombie*, *Isle of the Dead*, *The Ghost Ship*. He was then set to the (supposedly) inglorious task of making *schlock* fit only for Times Square scratch-theatre gleaners.

In his first film, *Cat People*, Lewton explored the psychiatric and emotional implications of lycanthropy through the medium of a beautiful young girl who thinks she has inherited the taint of animal transvestism—her alter-ego a panther. It is the foremost of only three films Simone Simon made in this country that can stand today as having been worth the doing. Many have called it a classic.

In *The Body Snatcher*, made in 1945, Lewton used the incomparable Karloff to full advantage in a thinly-veiled retelling of the Burke & Hare grave-robbing story. (How did that old tot-terrifier go? "Burke's the butcher, Hare's the thief; and Knox the boy who buys the beef." Well, *how*ever, it was the strange story of the doctor who needed cadavers for autopsy purposes, who bought his meat from a pair of unsavorys not above catching the anatomical visual aids while they were still very much alive and kicking.)

In *Bedlam*, 1946, Lewton opened with a full-screen medium closeup of Hogarth's famous painting of the Eighteenth Century English madhouse, dollied in on it to extreme closeup and then did a wax-dissolve to a letter-perfect real life scene, precisely as the painting showed it. The credits on the film nodded to Hogarth, possibly the only time in the history of film that a painting (rather than a play, a novel, a song, or a title) inspired a motion picture. Lewton went on to explore the conditions in lunatic asylums with Karloff, and what later institutional liberals exposed about the criminal conditions in our asylums, was all there for them to see, years before the hue and cry for reforms.

Of *I Walked With A Zombie*, Lewton is reported to have said, "They may never recognize it, but what I'm going to give them in *I Walked With A Zombie* is 'Jane Eyre In The West Indies.'" (The author must at this time bow in the direction of scenarist De Witt Bodeen, from whose article in the April 1963 issue of *Films in Review* that quotation—and much of the minutiae of this section on Lewton—emanates.)

To show the incredible broken-field-running of Lewton as a producer, against odds calculated to produce nothing but *merde*, *I Walked With A Zombie* was inspired by a Hearst Sunday supplement series. If you don't think what he brought forth was remarkable, catch a re-run of this film on a Saturday afternoon tv showing, and compare it (bearing in mind what inspired it) with what horrors of an entirely different stripe have been produced by movie-makers with acromegalic budgets, e.g., *Moby Dick*, *Cleopatra*, *Mutiny on the Bounty*, *King of Kings*, *55 Days at Peking*, *Circus World*, *Ship of Fools*, the list goes on with truly terrifying overpopulation. (I refer, of course, to the most recent incarnations of each of the foregoing films.)

Praising Lewton has become, in recent years, an "in" game of the "in crowd." There is no great bravery on my part to single him out as the perpetrator of the *ne plus ultra* in horror films. Yet in all of these huzzahs, there has never been a satisfactory explanation of precisely *what* it is in those films of fear that makes them perfect models for the sluggards currently infesting the genre. Nor has there been a rationale for why these films are always referred to as "*Lewton's* films" rather than Karloff's films, or Jacques Tourneur's films—though he directed three of the finest—or Mark Robson's films—though he directed four—or Robert Wise's films—though he did two, of which one, *Curse of the Cat People*, remains today as one of the most original plumbings of a child's mentality. They are always called *Lewton's* films, and therein lies the secret not only of successfully producing films of fear, but of the art of *producing*, itself.

Lewton's role as producer was anything but that of the stereotyped fat-cat, thumbs hooked in the pockets of his velvet vest, cigar masticated between gopher teeth, eyes on the till and heart of blackest anthracite. He was a creator.

In a recent conversation with actor Robert Blake (incidentally, another immense talent Hollywood has done ill to ignore), the point was made that in every successful production, whether television or feature film, the presence of one strong man can be seen: whether the lead actor, or the head writer, or the director, or the producer, if there is one man with balls enough to swing his weight in the cause of artistic integrity, what emerges, nine times out of 9.89, is worth viewing, while the reverse proportion holds for those efforts born of Art by Committee Decision. This, I think, is the secret of why Lewton's films were always *Lewton's* films, and why they bore an unmistakable stamp of continuity of talent.

What he thought about his work, and how he conveyed these thoughts to men like Tourneur (still another fine talent who, while he works regularly, has been denied access to top production directorial chores that would have placed him with the best in the field), was the cornerstone of Lewton's success, the vitality that brought more than animation to his creations—that brought *life* to them. One example:

In *The Bad and the Beautiful*, Kirk Douglas, playing a producer who has been advised his first film will be a horror film (very much like *Cat People*) convinces his staff that blatant visualizations of horror must be avoided by the simple expedient of flicking off the lights in his office, and telling them the story in the dark. It is a remarkably effective scene, and the strongest cinematic argument ever made for subtlety and indirection in film-making. He is thoroughly convincing, of course.

This incident was precisely what Lewton did with his staff on *Cat People*. The story became Hollywood legend, and has now been preserved as fiction. Thus, portrait of a *producer*.

Producing, I submit, is not primarily a matter of budgets, schedules, manipulations or politics (though in the latter stages no producer succeeds in this arena without knowing how to move them pieces around the board). It is, in the gestation period, a matter of instincts, insights, the eye of Art—and I'll damned well use the cap "A" every time—and gonads. The producer whose sole concern is "product" is doomed merely to make money.

Pause, while the fat-cats chuckle on their way to the bank. Yeah, we know that bit.

Nice talking to you, fellahs. Move on, so we can get back to the business of *creating*, as opposed to producing.

Lewton typifies the creative producer, with an instinctive love and appreciation of form, grace, direction, and message. His films were never polemics, nor were they studiedly "arty." But they were always meaningful, had something important to say about people and the Times, and they were always artistic.

Much of this, I contend, came from the fact that Lewton was filming fear and terror and horror, and that way lies a touchstone for the motion picture audience.

Since the first night of Man, hunkered down hairy and hungry by the primeval lightning-borne food fire, fear has been the prime mover. Forget momma love and posterity and man's unquenchable curiosity. Fear is the primary mode of locomotion of *homo sapiens*, as Mel Brooks suggests. Show hairy Man a pair of yellow eyes just outside the ring of light thrown by that first fire, and within twenty minutes he'll have invented the crossbow, the arbalest, the mace, Thompson submachine guns, and klieg lights to chase that mother away.

We walk through all the days and nights of our lives terrified. Of the world that surrounds us, of one another, of the unknown, of ourselves. Fear is the hammer that leaves us stunned and speechless. Fear is the goad that sends us to places we fear to be in, to find out things we're scared witless to know. Fear.

Of this simple fact, Lewton was a master.

He knew there was more monstrousness in the *sound* of a killer cat slinking through the branches of a tree that brushed the top of a graveyard's stone wall, than all the Godzillas or Rodans ever pulled by puppet strings. He played like a Landowska on the stops and keys of the psyche. He let you build the monsters in your mind, in that terrible nightland of individual torment no studio special effects man could ever visit. It was the visual application of the secret of old-time radio. (What some call the sense of wonder. The reason why no tv can ever rival a radio program for opulence of sets.)

It was *suggestion*, the use of the power of the mind, that made Lewton's films so terrifying. It was an instinctive regard and respect for the imaginations and mentalities of his audiences—as he respected his own imagination, intellect, and originality—that led Lewton surely and surefootedly to the one infallible path of fear. He thought he could make intelligent films for intelligent people. This is a concept largely ignored in Hollywood, these days, by producers of the Stanley Shapiro/Ross Hunter cadre, who make movies as intellectually demanding as a Giant Golden Book, and who seemingly visualize their audiences as microcephalics fit only to salivate over the constantly-imminent deflowering of Doris Day, or the shade of puce in a Jean Louis gown.

Lewton did not merely invite the filmgoer to use his gourd, he *demanded* it. He led them up to the door of terror and commanded them, **"KNOCK!"**

As with all work that either approaches or becomes Art, there is a specific and enormous demand on the observer, *by* the very nature and dimensions of the work *itself*, to commit; to participate; to bring something very individual and personal *to* the *work*, to expand it, in effect. To add to it. To enlarge it. To color it and intensify it, to personalize it, if you will.

Fear is undeniably a *subjective* affection. It is personal. What scares you may not scare me. Fear of spiders. Fear of drowning. Fear of immolation, being buried alive, suffocation. Fear of snakes. Fear of needles. In NINETEEN EIGHTY-FOUR, Orwell's Winston Smith is finally broken by being led to Room 101 of the Ministry of Love, the room containing that which most easily can break a man—the thing he secretly fears most. In Smith's case...rats. Each of us has his own Room 101 (which was, in many ways, what Orwell was trying to say in his novel) and each of us can find himself as insensible, as useless as a bag of shattered toys, if the proper subjective stimuli is employed. This was Lewton's secret for terror.

He was, in many ways, a consummate student and applicator of gestalt psychology. He opened all the doors to all the rooms numbered 101.

But Lewton employed a much more mature and subtle approach to the concept of fear. His was a second-level psychology, different from the typical "sharp noise" or "sharp movement" of most horror films, where you are momentarily frightened by a (for instance) hand suddenly jumping into the frame. He must have had knowledge of the reversal-of-impulse concept, either unconsciously or by study. To explain:

From Köhler on fear: "When a sudden event is felt to cause fright, a very strong impulse to move away from the event arises at the same time...Does anyone believe that the child feels his fear of the object, and the impulse to withdraw his hand, as two unrelated experiences? Or that, in his fear, the child might just as well feel a tendency to *embrace or to swallow the disturbing object*? [Italics mine.] ... Just as an impulse of withdrawal arises directly from certain situations, so the opposite tendency is felt to be adequate in other situations."

Thus, when confronted by Lewton's horrors, we cover our eyes. And peek.

In *Cat People* the fiancée of the hero is trapped in a swimming pool by a creature we do not see. It circles the pool, and she screams again and again. We are petrified with fear, but we are drawn to the scene inexorably. For long moments as the *very* long scene is played, we do not breathe. And not once do we see what it is we fear. The child in us walks to Room 101 and stares in numbed terror at the darkness beyond.

This was Lewton's secret, and the thread that made of his tapestries works of Art rather than just momentarily amusing cartoons. The fears inside us, the fears of the dark, of youth, or of the unknown. The modern terrors that outstrip all the werewolves, vampires, and ghouls Transylvania ever exported.

Explaining what terror *is* becomes a bore. It is akin to dissecting humor or honesty or love. Easy enough to cite examples of each, but murder trying to explain why they work.

Lewton's films worked. Nothing more need be said. They were the heartmeat of fear. The apotheosis of true mortal terror. What we get these days is something that exists elsewhere, and does not work in the same way, nor nearly as well. I have gone into some detail on Lewton, to set the reader up for the tirade that follows, for without knowing what a critic stands *for*, it is impossible to validate what he is *against*.

I am *for* Lewton's brand of terror.

I am *against* what Polanski did in *Repulsion*, in many ways. But between the two poles, there lies a no man's land of films that *should* have employed terror, and did not, and before we reach Polanski, I beg your indulgence for a brief detour through counties not generally considered haunts of terror.

For in the traveltalks we may suffer through these unfamiliar counties, we may discover something not only of the nature of failure in current Hollywood fear-films, but of the general nature of boredom and failure in much of the cinema we get these days.

Onward.

2

Let's shake 'em up a little:

King Rat, as a film, is a failure. *The Loved One*, as a film, is also a failure, but for entirely different reasons. *Bunny Lake Is Missing* is the biggest failure of the three, again for different reasons.

And all three fail because they were lousy films of fear.

Fear? *King Rat* a film of fear? *The Loved*—what the hell is he talking about? Are they reeling? Let's hit them a little harder.

Bunny Lake is a cheat, from start to finish. *King Rat* is a wretched bore. *The*

Loved One not only cheats and bores, but is in execrable taste, but not in the way its campy makers intended. It's just a very sick series of private jokes, and misses vivisection of the horrors it originally intended by at least six feet deep. And all three of them could have profited from Lewton's rules of terror. From which point—as we departed from section one of this triptych—we invade the Country of the Blind. Namely, the big fear moviemakers.

King Rat was taken from an excellent novel by James Clavell. It should never have been a movie. The fat-cats live in constant trepidation; it is the climate of Hollywood. You are only as good as your last film. Ergo, insure the next one. Pick something that was a success on the legitimate stage, or a best-selling novel, or a remake of something popular. (Because of this last, we have been "treated" to such displays as new versions of classics like *Mutiny on the Bounty*, *Three Coins in the Fountain* and *Rashomon* [as *The Outrage*; a film made purely for money, so plagiaristic in execution that it could not even be redeemed by calling it the sincerest form of flattery]. And we can look forward to a remake of *Stagecoach* with current lightweights of the Ann-Margret school mocking parts made memorable by Claire Trevor, John Wayne and Thomas Mitchell. One day soon we must discuss the venality and stupidity of producers who have the temerity to revamp films done to perfection the first time, merely to cash in on their perennial popularity.)

Thus, every novel that sells over sixteen copies becomes a film, without artistic regard for the suitability of a property for translation to the visual medium.

(And occasionally we get winners like *Sex & The Single Girl*, made from a title. How lucky we are.)

There are some books that were born to be *read*, not filmed. LORD JIM was one of these. SHIP OF FOOLS was another. Even Welles, in filming *The Trial*, came a cropper; and though he produced a film of excellence in his own vision, the mass of criticism leveled against him was based on the fact that it was not *Kafka's* version or attitude. That's tough, for the critics. They were not flexible enough to understand that THE TRIAL was not a book to be filmed, but a book to be *read*, as conceived by Kafka. But of the recent crop of "sure-fire money-making properties" translated by emasculation and amputation into second-rate films reaping box-office disaster, and deservedly so, *King Rat* is the prize example. It was a helluva book; it was a terrible film. Terrible, because it commits the one crime no work of art or entertainment should be allowed to commit unpunished.

It bores. It bores! Jeezus, to tears, it *bores*!

Now *how*—he asks, with incredulity in his voice—could a film about men suffering privation and each other's basest moralities in a Japanese prison camp, be boring?

The element of fear was missing.

Ah. Back to the point. Roundabout, but back, nonetheless.

The scene is Changi Prison, 1945. A prison whose bars and locks are invisible, yet no less binding than those of cast iron, for Changi's topological features are such that to escape is to die. There is no place to go. In the compound live ten thousand men who eke out a minimal existence by their wits and the tenacity to go on breathing just one breath longer, chiefly because it's built into the machine. But there is King. He lives high. He is an entrepreneur, he is a mover, he is a provider, and in that strange way that only asserts itself in times of deepest tribulation, a leader and molder of men. But King wants only to make it for himself. He wheels, he deals, but he does not crawl on his belly like a reptile. He trades with the enemy for favors, and for the best of all reasons, Bryan Forbes's intention to make him loathesome to us fails completely. He is the only smart one in the pack. He wants to do more than subsist, he wants to live with a certain style, and a great deal of comfort. Most of the men (if not all) hate him, but they serve him, for the residue favors that are left behind when King has had his fill. Now from this intrinsically exciting and emotionally ineluctable situation, it would seen impossible to derive anything but a film of tension and passion and importance.

But it was a novel of complex inner motivations, on a personal level, and to portray merely the outward, physical actualities of these dark drives was to strip a story of psychological imperativeness down to the level of a shadow-play. All chiaroscuro. For in playing the story at the skin-level, Forbes and his cast eliminated the one thing that was dominant in the book: fear.

Because of the fact that Changi was a prison in which no one could contemplate escape, there was never the omnipresent fear of the brutal Japanese guards, nor of imminent death. It became a study of men merely trying to hang on. Now that is a reasonable subject for a novel, in which we penetrate the skulls of the principals, and experience the terrors to which they were heir, day by day, moment within moment. But eliminate that *internal* fear, all the Room 101's, and we are left with a landscape devoid of motivated, fearful particulars. All we have is an empty carcass.

Had Forbes understood the nature of fear, the nature of terror, he might have been able to save the film. But—and I will expect those of you who have not already seen the picture to see it, rather than accept my theory as some sort of *Obiter Dictum*—he had not studied his lessons; Lewton's lessons, mind you; and so all those heavy areas of light and dark were moved around like so much earth and gravel. This was a potentiality for a film of fear, in the same category with Lewton's subjects, but it was passed over in favor of more dubious "quality" elements. Nowhere in *King Rat* do we get the feel, the heft, the *weight* of trepidation, from anyone in the cast. Not even by cinematography or sets or direction is there the suspense of fear, the clutch of abiding terror. We have placidity, we have torpor, we have boredom.

And that is why *King Rat* fails.

Bunny Lake Is Missing, however, deals in fear and suspense and a kind of psychological horror that Lewton would have understood and approved. Yet as baldly as *King Rat* misses its impact-points for lack of fear, it is a modern classic compared with the stumbling, falling-down silliness and ineptitude of Otto Preminger's latest carcinoma.

(Note to my mother, in Miami Beach: Dear Mom, I *know* I work in the industry, and I *know* they won't hire me, but there are times when the sensible writer in me finds himself outshouted by the Ivory Tower writer who deplores bad movies and the men who continue to make them on the strength of reputations ill-deserved. On the other hand, Mom, I've always had a tendency to bite the hand that feeds me. Check your own. Much love, Disraeli.)

Because of the total misapplication of the strictures and freedoms of the implement fear, *Bunny Lake* becomes an exercise in hoodwinkery. We are led down all the wrong garden paths, without even the justification of a valid denouement.

Given: a pretty young woman and her pretty young brother, who have recently arrived in England. The young man attends to his journalistic employment, and the young girl (whose husband is confusedly referred to on occasion, but, it is made clear, is no longer on the scene in any way) puts her child Bunny in a day nursery. When she goes to pick her up, the child is missing, and no one remembers seeing her at any time. The police Inspector who handles the case is forced further and further toward the conclusion that the girl is hallucinatory, and the child never existed.

Given: a mounting strain of hysteria on the part of the girl, who fights to convince the Inspector and the world at large that Bunny does, indeed, exist, and is in terrible danger. The brother continues to drop inadvertent hints that Sis may be around-the-bend, despite his reiteration that Bunny does exist, and he will stand by his sibling come what may.

Given: a long, drawn-out crawl toward fifteen minutes of madness at the end of which we discover the brother is the whack, and has kidnapped the child himself, to keep his sister beside him, keep her love and attention for himself. A case of arrested adolescence. Or something.

Taken from a suspense novel by Evelyn Piper (which I must confess I have not read), this would seem to be a fulsome subject for a film of fear. Yet no one I know who saw this picture, myself included of course, felt anything but cheated when it was done. Why? I submit it was in the misunderstanding of the tenets of fear, and what is permissible in directing the logic of an audience in this area. If there was an internal consistency in the novel, it does not show up in the film.

Rather than merely solidify the points I am about to make by my own instinctive reactions, I approached the cornerstone of the structure of *Bunny Lake*—the madness of the brother—with an open mind, and consulted several texts on abnormal psychology. Everything I found led me to believe the character had been twisted to serve Mr. Preminger's ends. Even so, it seemed feasible that in the swampland of the deranged mind such a syndrome *might* be possible, and so I consulted an expert in the field, Dr. Eugene A. Levitt, Clinical Psychologist of the Peterson-Guedel Family Center, in Beverly Hills. After a lengthy discussion of the motion picture, and the aberration as delineated by Keir Dullea in the part of the brother, Dr. Levitt came to the following conclusions:

"Given a deviant personality structure as grossly pathological as that of the brother in *Bunny Lake*, it would seem highly improbable that it would be manifested solely in the area of his feelings *about* his sister. One would certainly expect to see signs of deviancy in his behavior *toward* the sister; not just at the dramatic moment when it best suits the purposes of the plot-makers of the film, but *consistently*, throughout. And possibly more important, because of the clearly psychotic personality with which we are presented at the final stages of the film, indicating an aberrant childhood relationship to his parents, additionally there should—reasonably—be visible symptomatology in his relations with *all* adults, most particularly with such authority figures as the Inspector, who in this situation most specifically parallels a father-image. The absence of these 'clues,' if you will, connotes an intentioned deceit on the part of the story-tellers."

Thus, we come to another pillar that must be present in the superstructure of the fear film, lest it fall down about the makers' ears, as does *Bunny Lake.* Fear must carry with it, its own internal consistency and logic. It is not merely enough to say *The Martian carries off the beautiful girl, kicking and screaming.*

If the Martian's body chemistry is completely alien to that of an Earthwoman, if he is a methane-breather, with a reproductive cycle closer to that of a chicken than to that of a human, then by all rights he should be raping a Rhode Island Red, not Kim Novak.

We are more terrified by the plight of Dorian Gray than all the Creatures who ever bubbled up from Black Lagoons, because we see reflected in Gray the terrors to which we are heir. The logic prevails in the one, and flees in the other.

We are led by the hand, by Mr. Preminger and his group, down a dark hallway toward a Room 101 that promises to hold unspeakable horrors. But when the door is opened, we find someone else's terror there, and we feel we have been subjected to flummery. Had Preminger wished to make the film honestly, he would have carried the psychotic nature of the brother through the film, but obviously that would not have been dramatic enough, and the shock ending would have been pre-revealed. So Preminger lied to us. He altered the logic, made it inconsistent, and hoped that the pyrotechnics of the denouement would blind us to the cheat.

He failed, and with the failure comes the inescapable logic that if the film could not be made honestly, it should not have been made at all. We see in the stance of commercialism herewith adopted by Mr. Preminger, a similarity to the posture adopted by those who made *King Rat*. A neck-craning attitude, much like that of a flamingo, on one foot, precariously arching toward the money. It is an undignified stance.

Now we seem to be getting somewhere. We have set up a model of successful fear, the *oeuvre* of Lewton; we have established several seeming truths about fear's application in the visual medium: it must not bore, it must reflect the personal terrors of the audience, it must contain its own internal logic and consistency, it must employ the imagination and powers of expansion of the audience, and it must view (ideally) through new or original visions.

We have examined a film that failed in that it did not use fear when it should have. We have examined a film of fear which completely misunderstood and misused the tools of terror it needed to succeed. Now we will go all the way to the far wall and examine a film of humor that somehow strayed into the Country of Cold Chills when it should not have done so; and failed thereby.

The Loved One, based on a novel of biting satire by Evelyn Waugh. Which I have read. (Two out of three is pretty good.)

No one who has even scanned Jessica Mitford's incredible study of the funeral industry, *The American Way of Death*, can be oblivious to the horrors passim the trade in coffins and coagulants. It would seem impossible to produce a film around Waugh's shredding dissection of these latter-day ghouls that would not bring forth raves of delight, and kudos for honesty. To even *contemplate* a motion picture in which the saccharine sanctity of the down-the-hole boys is stripped away (revealing them as used car salesmen in mourning rags), automatically incurs the not-inconsiderable wrath of the Funeral Lobby and its local leech-lines. The question of honesty would seem not even to arise. The question of suicide, perhaps, but not honesty.

How, then, is it possible that Tony Richardson and his high camp followers made such a dishonest film, such a disastrously unsuccessful film, such a depressing and off-the-mark film? A film about as funny as an acrobat in a polio ward? A film about as funny as a turd in a punch bowl?

The answer, from this corner, lies in the intrusive shadow of fear that Richardson and his cast found themselves unable to dispel. Under a constantly-darkening veil of horror, the bizarre and the ludicrous intermingled with the hilarious and the hideous. In an attempt to make a film of humor about something basically ghastly, Metro-Goldwyn-Mayer's *The Loved One* wandered slantwise into the Country of Terror and could not find its way out. Trapped on a landscape of gore and grue, dealing with the carrion-flesh of those who live off the dead, Richardson was forced to the outer edge of sanity and visual imagery, in a frenetic attempt to stave off the encroaching phantom of horror that permeated the film.

He was not able to escape. The picture was forced to adopt advertising that proclaimed, SOMETHING TO OFFEND EVERYONE! and I suppose in Coshocton, Ohio, they will be offended. But we are not dealing with the chauvinism and naiveté of the Bible Belt in these pages. (The presumption that first-level film criticism and fan magazine goshwow need not enter into our considerations *may* be unwarranted, but if that is what you, gentle reader, are seeking herein, one of us ought to be elsewhere.) The picture *is* offensive, but not in the way the producers intended.

As I said earlier, it is offensive because it substitutes cute for cutting, weird for witty, and camp for clever. If MGM wishes to cop-out, it may well save its critical bacon by proclaiming this one of the first of the pop art films. (Though I contend Godard's *Alphaville* is the front-runner in that category.) But that fear and terror permeated this film, in a way surely no one could have anticipated, is something Metro cannot deny.

Snap! We see Bobby Morse and Sir John Gielgud lunching in the studio commissary. Gielgud orders "the breast of Chicken, Lolita" and Morse orders "a Goldwater nut flip." Funny. Snap! Morse discovers Gielgud's body hanging grotesquely from the diving board of the weed-infested pool. Not funny. Snap snap!

The juxtaposition is alarming. We are made to laugh, then to shrink back in horror.

Snap! Anjanette Comer (surely one of the comeliest creatures God ever set down on this weary cinder to delight our eyes) wrestles about on the lawn with a salivating Morse, hellbent intent on invading her underwear. Amusing. Snap! Anjie Comer jams a pair of tubes of embalming fluid into her veins and dies slowly, slowly, very slowly. Oh-migod, not funny at all. Snap snap!

We are shown beauty, and it is tainted with madness. The juxtaposition is ghastly in its spectacle, in its roiled commingling of pure and foul.

The vomity obese mother of Rod Steiger. Steiger's muscular faggotry. (There is sufficient reason to call it such, despite Steiger's obvious lust for Miss Comer, because of the almost rampant homosexuality of almost all of the other principals in the cast, in every scene, in every gesture, in all of the private jokes so blatantly put on display for the gay crowd. I'm not knocking it folks, I'm merely saying that it served to deepen the unconscious strains of unrest and nausea for those of us who don't happen to ride that particular hobby horse.) The Air Force romp with the tarts in the coffin room. The grotesqueries after grotesquerie piled one atop another. The dead dogs in the ice boxes. The very scent and smell of the funeral industry that reaches us through celluloid, through soundtrack, through flickering posturings of the players.

There is brilliance here, no question about it. But it is the deranged brilliance of a de Sade, the mad joy of an Octave Mirabeau or a Rimbaud. It is thoroughly decadent and debased brilliance. It is the invoking of the demons of fear and insanity, the creation of monster that, like a lynch mob, went berserk and devoured its makers. Consumed by their own creation, Richardson and his company now must exist in the blazing belly of the horror, knowing they somehow inadvertently cast the runes and read from the grimoire of terror, and brought forth they knew not what.

Here, in *The Loved One*, we see the incalculable power, the torment for producer and audience alike, the numbing quality of the implement fear. This was a partial awakening of the demon, and it managed in its somnambulistic sleepwalk to destroy a film of some importance. Loose, unfettered, uncontrolled, the fear Richardson came to work with can be a juggernaut that lays waste the most honestly-intended film.

But with full knowledge, with the chains of understanding firmly wound in place, fear can be used to woo and capture the elusive mind-balance of an audience. In what particular areas Richardson's helplessness before the mad face of the god he unleashed can be observed, lies a vivid warning to other film-makers who would toy without understanding with the single most potent implement a film-man can employ. Richardson played with it, tried to tame it with guffaws and outrage, but it destroyed his film.

In part three of this survey, I will attempt to analyze the struggle of yet another St. George, who may not have slain the Dragon Fear, but certainly dealt it a helluva bruising. And in that direction, I suspect, lies the hope not only of the film of fear, but of the entire motion picture industry.

Room 101 is just ahead of us. After you.

> How interesting: many years ago when I wrote this essay about Roman Polanski I said "*This* is a young man to watch." Now years have past and events are current. "He *was* a young man to watch; now he is an old man to watch...especially around your daughter."

3

Roman Polanski's *Repulsion* is the closest thing to a Lewton-oriented film of fear to which we have been treated in recent memory. Many there may be who will cite *Psycho* and others who will say segments of *Charade* suit better the appellation. (Most noticeably in the latter, the frightening scene of James Coburn tied to a radiator, his face blue and distorted from suffocation, head gently wrapped in a common plastic clothing sack, of the type we are warned to keep away from children.)

There is validity in their points, but for overall terror—albeit flawed, as I will delineate further on—the Polanski vision of a beautiful young girl's progressive psychopathia is monumentally right for our attention here. I cannot quibble with the horror of the shower sequence in *Psycho*, nor of the final scene in which Tony Perkins talks with the voice of his mother (though I think the subliminal flashing of the death's head was a bit much), but match these against the subtle horror of Catherine Deneuve's performance, her sudden start of fear as the walls symbolically rend asunder overhead, the vagrant mad rubbing of the nose as she walks down a street in daylight, the head of the rabbit in her purse, the casual murders, the slatternly deterioration of the lovely girl...all of it, in totality, a numbing portrait of insanity in our times, laid out bare and quivering as the severed arteries of her victims.

Polanski is a man to watch.

It is entirely possible we have with us in the person of this young Polish director, another Lewton. From what we have seen of his first two films, it is obvious that Polanski's interests lie in the area of human motivations and interpersonal relationships. In *Knife in the Water* Polanski brought tension and originality to the time-worn theme of the eternal triangle. Alone on a small yacht, two men and a woman act out a drama of hate and frustration, of decadent lives and brutality, all on the most subtle of levels, all inextricably involved with the symbolic search of each man for his masculinity. This, told in the framework of a love/sex story as simple as any folk tale. In *Repulsion* we go very much into the mind of a girl going insane.

These are the topics Lewton might have explored, had he lived longer. In point of fact, the similarities between *Cat People* and *Repulsion*, each with a heroine living with delusions and murder, are uncanny. It would be interesting to know if Polanski is familiar with Lewton's work.

But whether consciously aware or otherwise, what Polanski does in his films, to a marked degree, is what Lewton did. The movement, the easy manipulation of great masses of light and dark, the emphasis on the dark mind of the contemporary man and woman, the force of study on the terrors that beset us all...these are the trembles and trinkets Lewton found indispensable to the production of small classics of fear.

Polanski seems unerringly to find the way of most terror, in the same vector of talent that was Lewton's. But there are differences—both in motivation and technique—between Polanski and Lewton. Differences that occasionally mar and blight what Polanski has brought forth, and against which Polanski hurled his talent, not always successfully.

Earlier I snapped at *Time* and *Newsweek*, and promised I would elaborate on the attack. My reasons are simply considerations of honesty and the inherent values of serious criticism. When I am manic, it is my belief that we *need* critics: sober and dedicated men and women who will remind us of the heritage of the past in the Arts, who will try to keep our level of attention and achievement at highest tide. (It hardly needs more demonstration than a flicking on of the tv set to prove that if left to its own devices, the taste of the mass—per Sturgeon's Law—will inevitably sink to the lowest possible common denominator.) Both *Time* and *Newsweek*, and the soporific little journals that imitate their approach to reviewing, debase the act of criticism. They become exercises in cleverness; turns of the phrase with tongues in cheeks...admittedly making for garble. They are first to follow the trend of what is "in," and first to condemn what they do not understand. The shabby need to appear street-smart, cutting edge, in the know, *au courant*, hip...at all costs; and the spiteful vengefulness when they realize they don't understand the film, that they are dunce-cap befuddled! They turn their reviews into something like popularity contests, and where the function of constructive criticism is most needed, it is absent in their approach. Both *Time* and

Newsweek praised *Repulsion* outrageously, without taking the time or indulging the cerebration that would have recognized its flaws, and thus enriched the lessons Polanski might have learned, thus benefitting his methodology in future films. Thus, my fury at the newsmagazines. They chose the way of the cop-out, the line of least resistance, the dazzlement of technique that should not have kept the serious critic from his craft. For Polanski pulled a rabbit out of a hat, and no one so far has bothered to notice that the rabbit was dead.

And in their hurry to add another film to the *Recommended* listings, the clowns failed to serve the artist who needed their comments, needed their attention, needed the benefit of their critical faculties.

It is altogether too easy to say that *Repulsion* is the closest thing to a perfect film of fear we have had since Lewton. Too easy, because of the obviousness of the comment. It *is* a fine film, a close-to-perfect film. But as I noted earlier, I am *against* what Roman Polanski did in *Repulsion*, in many ways. For he chose to substitute effect for logic, he chose to substitute adolescent fear for mature fear, he chose to be blatant rather than subtle, and in the final analysis, his genius carried him when he should have been relying on skill and craft.

What follows, these observations, are made in a spirit of camaraderie, with honorable intent. For it is my belief that Roman Polanski is one of the most adventurous and stimulating directors in the world of the cinema today. What they like to call a "promising" director. It is entirely possible that he bears within him the seeds of authentic greatness. And to the end that he not be whiplashed by sycophants, that he escape the too-soon adulation of those who toss away all critical objectivity in the sack-race to praise him soonest, that he not sacrifice growth for easy success, these comments are offered with respect and gratitude for bringing to the screen an individual and important talent.

But a talent that still needs comment.

Repulsion functions almost entirely on two levels. The first, a purely physical level of progression of events that sends the heroine through a series of emotional and psychological ambivalences. The second, a completely subjective fantasy-world that is reflection and refraction and distortion of the mental state of the girl. Where these two impinge, where they bisect each other, we have the most stunning and successful moments of the film. When we are helplessly drawn into the mind of the young girl and find ourselves staring down at the severed head of a raw rabbit in her purse we are assaulted by an admixture of nausea and horror. Like the child-in-fear to which Köhler referred in Part

One of this article, we are both repulsed and attracted. We cover our eyes when Catherine Deneuve grapples with the lecherous landlord, but we peek between our fingers to see the moment she will slash him across the neck with the naked straight-razor.

Polanski plays on our feelings of fear toward sharp instruments, blades, knives; on our loathing of slippery men who attempt rape; on our ambivalent pity for the girl assaulted and trepidation for the man whom we know cannot stand for a moment against the assault of her insanity. We are tossed and turned by our own fears and the conditioned impulses of our upbringing.

In these areas, Polanski is a master.

But in the areas of motivation and logic, he opts rather for scintillation and pyrotechnics than for plotting.

We must line-out the basic story first, however, before we can explain where Polanski did not do a full job: Catherine, a Belgian manicurist working in a Harriet Hubbard Ayer-type beauty salon in London, lives with her highly-sexed sister, who in turn shares bed-space with a rather hairy salesman. They make it frequently, and on the night silence comes the off-screen moaning and panting that sends sleepless Catherine under the covers in the next room. We understand almost immediately that the pretty Dresden figurine that is Catherine conceals a mind that is torn with ambivalence at the thought of sex. She is attracted to, and repulsed by, the sight of her sister's paramour. Catherine has a boyfriend. He is a gentleman, but she is so strange, so distant at times, that he suffers the ribbing of his pub-crawling friends with ill humor. Finally, Sis carts off to the hinterlands on holiday with her Lothario, and Catherine is left in their small flat with an uncooked coney on a plate, and the stench of encroaching lunacy. As she exists there in the somnolence, we see her illusions—great cracks suddenly ripping down the walls, hands thrusting out of a hall corridor that has turned to mud, rapists breaking down her doors, lurking under her bedsheets. Finally, as her mind disintegrates before our very eyes, she uses the razor on the landlord who comes to get the rent and stays to paw her shape. (Prior to this she has clubbed her boyfriend to death and dumped him in the bathtub, when he broke down the door to find out if she was all right or not. Hell of a way to find out.) In the end, the sister and lover return, to find Catherine in a catatonic state, and the joint surfeited with dead meat, not all of which is rabbit. Final shot, we dolly slowly in on an old photograph of the family, and we see Catherine-the-child. Her eyes. Quite mad. A twinkle of lunacy as she sees the world.

In his overwhelming impulse to show us the progression of Catherine's madness, the rapid overtaking of her mind by a desire/revulsion of sex, Polanski handles the delusions with startling facility, presenting them so realistically, that for *moments* after they are over, we have to reorient ourselves that they were only wraiths of Catherine's mind. In this, he employs the Lewton technique with great facility and impact.

But it is all demonstration, without motivation.

Questions, never asked, much less answered:

- Why is Catherine afraid of men?
- If she is so terrified of men, how did she get a boyfriend, and why does he persist in following her?
- Is her sister so dense that she has not noticed this obvious aberrant behavior previously?
- What was Catherine's relationship with her parents, most specifically her father (as subtly hinted in the final shot of the family photograph), that brought on this derangement?
- Why didn't Polanski either tell or suggest the answers to these questions, and many others, of motive and personality?

Which brings me to my final point, on the nature of fear in films, its use, and the dangers therein present.

Fear in the hand of a motion picture maker, like a shotgun in the hands of a baby, need not necessarily be properly aimed to make a helluva bang. But to hit the target dead-on, requires maturity and thought.

Polanski, to my mind undisputed heir to the throne left vacant by Lewton, is a master of technique and hoodwinkery. He substitutes effects for the deeper logic of the situations his stories imply. Fear in his hands is a weapon that he uses to stun the audience, to reduce them to adolescent trepidation. But when the theatre has been left alive, the fear vanishes. Instead of making us understand the nature and impetus of the horrors that grip Everyman, he has dazzled us, and when the sparklers fade, we depart untouched and our sight restored.

To be entirely successful, a film of fear must deal with logic and the explanations that logic demands.

Polanski came closest to the superlatives with which Lewton dealt. Closer than Hitchcock, closer than Dassin, closer than anyone who has attempted the film of fear in many years.

There is a lesson to be learned here. Not only for Polanski who, god willing, will persist in improving himself and create finer films of fear, but for the entire motion picture industry, currently glutting its production schedules with vapid comedies, senseless extravaganzas, and ludicrous spy dramas as improbable as the Loch Ness monster. The lesson is simply that the intelligence of film audiences is a fine-honed tool, an additive that can be used to enrich any film. Moviegoers are ready to laugh, ready to shriek, ready to involve themselves to the eyeballs with films that demand something of them, as Polanski and Lewton demanded something of them.

They are saying, in the way they spend their money at certain box-offices, "There is nothing to fear but the lack of fear."

A word to the wise ought to be sufficient. Ahead of you lie all the corridors with all the Room 101s, numbered. All that is required is that you knock.

35 In Which the Phantasmagorical Pales before the Joys of the Mimetic

Call me madcap, if you will, but I do not think it was an act either desipient or devil-may-care when the Hal Roach Studios selected *Topper*, a film made in 1937 in black and white, as the first motion picture to suffer the depredations of Colorization, Inc. in 1985. As the first toe immersed in the market waters, to see how the public responded to "classics" in this corrupted-for-tv-viewing form, they desired a film that had everything going for it. *Topper* filled that bill. It was bright, brash, still amusing after almost fifty years; it had enchanting performances by Cary Grant, Roland Young, Billie Burke, and the breathtaking Constance Bennett; it had an urbane screenplay by Jack Jerne, Eddie Moran and the then-popular though now sadly-undervalued novelist Eric Hatch, based on a sprightly Thorne Smith fantasy; and it was directed by one of the great "lost" comedy talents, Norman Z. McLeod—he of *Monkey Business, Horse Feathers, If I Had a Million, It's a Gift,* and *Panama Hattie* fame...to recall a mere sprinkling of his more than forty credits.

Yet given even such values, it is my guess that what made *Topper* the exactly right choice to be the *vade mecum* of color-blighted films, over all other possibles, was the subject matter.

Topper is a ghost story.

And we do love our ghost stories.

From the classic *Outward Bound* in 1930 and *Berkeley Square* in 1933, the ghost story has been treated with evenhanded results ranging from sensitive (*Portrait of*

Jennie, 1948) and romantic (*The Ghost and Mrs. Muir*, 1947) to coarse (*High Plains Drifter*, 1973) and imbecile (1966's *The Ghost and Mr. Chicken* and the unforgettable *Ghost in the Invisible Bikini*). The epic ectoplasmic has received no better treatment at the hands of the inept and venal than any other genre, but has at least logged its fair share of genuinely important entries:

• *Kwaidan* (1964): a stunning quartet of supernatural Japanese folk tales based on the classic writings of Keisumi Yakumo and extravagantly directed by Kobayashi. Outstanding among the four segments is "The Woman of the Snow" in which a frost demon comes upon a pair of travelers, freezes one to death with her breath, and spares the other on condition that he never reveal what he has seen. His fate, resting on a kept promise, becomes chancey when, later in his prosperous life, he betrays the frost demon's largesse by shooting off his mouth about the fateful night to his beautiful wife.

• *Here Comes Mr. Jordan* (1941) won Oscars for Harry Segall's original story and for Sidney Buchman's and Seton Miller's smooth as butter screenplay about a prizefighter (Robert Montgomery) who is taken to heaven before his appointed time, and the Celestial Comptroller has to correct the error by sending Montgomery back to Earth in another body. Claude Rains as the priggish angel stuck with the overseer's job is, as ever he was, no less than memorable. And if the plot sounds familiar, it may be because the movie was remade in 1978 as *Heaven Can Wait* with Warren Beatty and James Mason and Julie Christie. The '78 version is okay, but is merely a walk to '41's canter. The major difference between the versions is that the original shows none of the cynicism and smartmouth contemporizing of the Beatty-Buck Henry remake. Words like *graciousness* and *kindness* attach themselves to the original; I suppose because in 1941 we were a more naive people, and the film reflects a gentler attitude toward the spirit. Life after death still had its innocence in our view. There was not the smarmy captiousness and sardonic manipulation of televangelists and scam-artists like J.Z. Knight and her trance-channeling "entity," the ever-popular ectoplasmic blabbermouth, Ramtha. (Just as a sidelight, and *absolutely* coincidentally, Ms. Knight is a multi-millionaire who raises racehorses. Ramtha is known to give advice to Ms. Knight's clients on how to buy racehorses...from Knight. Strictly a coincidence.) Oh, yes, of course, we've long been afflicted with charlatans and sleight-of-hand "spiritualists" who gulled the jejune and unworldly with promises of occult contacts to access the Beyond. To be sure, the history of psychic flapdoodle is chockablock with examples of unbelievable booga-booga bunco games run on the credulous: from the French dowser Aymar in 1692 who, through use of a swinging pendulum, "proved the guilt of a murderer"—a retarded nineteen-year-old hunchback, pathetically unable even to defend himself against the charge—who was subsequently "broken on the wheel," to the famous 19th Century child mediums, the Fox sisters (Kate, 6 and Margaret, 8) of Hydesville, NY, who, in 1848, not only earned more than a hundred dollars a night by contacting the dead through "rappings" that awed immense crowds (in 1888 Margaret Fox confessed in a newspaper article that she and her sister had produced the spiritual raps by cracking their toe joints, an amusement they had innocently been practicing for years till they'd conned adults into believing their rap-seances conveyed messages from The Other Side), but almost single-handedly—or more accurately-footedly—created the Spiritualist movement, to the current crop of outright fakers like Uri Geller and the hordes of New Age spiritualists called "channelers" who derive their credentials from the gibberish of Shirley Maclaine. But never before in history have these scamming descendants of Cagliostro had such unlimited entree to the public consciousness, such wild-eyed cooperation from mass media. Television, supermarket tabloids, several major publishing houses devoted to the promulgation of New Age lunacy, university-sponsored seminars, uncritical reports and articles in otherwise responsible newspapers…we are awash in a floodtide of occultism, obscurantist beliefs, fundamentalist-backed faith in primitive superstition. And the kinder, gentler attitude toward Travelers from the Spirit Domain has been bent into the hands of the slasher-horror novelists, the cynical film producers, and those who pick the pockets of the troubled, the desolate, and the gullible.

(It occurs to me that I've lurched away from my main point. I beg your pardon. That which purposely keeps people stupid, in order to fleece them and manipulate them, drives me more than a little bugfuck. For those of you similarly passionate, I urge the buying and reading of James "The Amazing" Randi's excellent FLIM-FLAM! Available in trade paperback from Prometheus Books, with an introduction by Isaac Asimov, 234 pp., $8.95. And now, sucking my thumb in embarrassment, let us return to matters of lesser consequence.)

• *The Haunting* (1963): Shirley Jackson's impossibly brilliant THE HAUNTING OF HILL HOUSE, scripted by Nelson Gidding and directed by Robert Wise, remains to this day, devoid of all the special effects crutches required by a generation of wise-guy film-makers raised on television, more terrifying than but one or two of all the films ever made. It towers above the mass of shockers and knife-kill treacheries that today inveigle the droolers and brutes who slouch out to get their daily requirement of grue.

• *I Married a Witch* (1942): A film that knocked me out when I was eight years old and saw it as a first-run B feature at a Saturday matinee at the Lake Theater in

Painesville, Ohio...that I have been enchanted by dozens of times since...that I taped off cable six or seven years ago because it *continues* to knock me out. If you don't know it, you are more the barren for that lack of familiarity. Not, strictly speaking, a "ghost" movie, it nonetheless features a pair of witches, father and daughter, who were burned at the stake and whose spirits return to bedevil the descendant of the Puritan who fried them. So I don't think I'm stretching the definition too much. Based on a Thorne Smith-Norman Matson confection, condignly showcasing the exquisite performances of Fredric March, Robert Benchley, Susan Hayward and the delicious Cecil Kellaway and infinitely more delicious Veronica Lake (my very first cinema crush, petite and breathtakingly sensual with that peekaboo hairdo, the image in later years of my character Valerie Lone in "The Resurgence of Miss Ankle-Strap Wedgie") as the ghostly hexers, this was one of two saturnalian directorial outings by René Clair that should be straitjacket-and-fetters viewing requirements for any contemporary director attempting similar material. The other Clair wonder, of course, is *The Ghost Goes West* (1936) written by Robert Sherwood and starring Robert Donat, whose performances in *The 39 Steps* and *Goodbye, Mr. Chips* tend to dim the memory of how endearingly he assayed the dual roles of Murdoch and Donald Glourie.

- *The Ghost and Mrs. Muir* (1947), *The Legend of Hell House* (1973), *The Horn Blows at Midnight* (1945), *Blithe Spirit* (1945) and *The Canterville Ghost* (1944) are, in no particular order, further evidence that in years past the treatment of revenants was more gracious, was kinderhearted.

In recent memory both *Ghostbusters* (1984) and *Poltergeist* (1982)—and to a somewhat but not much diminished degree, despite a general opinion that it was a fragmented failure—an opinion I do not share—*Poltergeist II* (1986) meet the standards of invention and believability and common decency toward ghosts set at such a lofty level by the noble predecessors I've noted above.

But after that recent trio (and *Foxfire*, which I forgot), we find that the telling of the ghost story in film has fallen on fumblefooted times. Even if we discount all the films allegedly set to terrify us with spectral villains and supernatural menaces, what we are dealt these days are what is called, in gin rummy circles, no-brainers.

O'Hara's Wife (1982), *Kiss Me Goodbye* (1982), *Maxie* (1985), *The Heavenly Kid* (1985), *The Wraith* (1986) and *Hello, Again* (1987) are about as dismal a collection of crap, in *any* genre, as one could possibly hack up after a lost weekend of the d.t.s and flying pink elephants.

(I purposely omit 1981's *Ghost Story* and 1988's *Beetlejuice*. The former because it is *so* wrongheaded and inept that it skews everything I want to say here; the latter because—don't ask me how—I simply missed seeing it.)

Each member of that sextet of relatively current filmic grotesqueries manifests similarities that, taken in sum, codify an attitude...a tilt of the head...a way of looking at...what has formerly been a rich, hearty, memorable and honorable medium for cinematic storytelling. An attitude better suited to lummoxes and simps.

All of which similarities, cresting the wave of ghost movies that has swamped us recently, glare forth in one consummately forgettable film, *High Spirits* (Tri-Star). A film that originally I intended as the focus of this essay; a film that, I realize, as I reach this point in my ruminations, is a film so ephemeral and pointless, that merely the comparison between it and the classics I've named, says it all. Here are the maddening similarities, all present in *High Spirits*:

1. Most evident in *O'Hara's Wife*—but present in plenitude in four of the five others—is the slow-witted behavior of the protagonist(s) who can see the ghost where others cannot. You or I, confronted by a spectral manifestation, would not continue to talk to the entity others keep demonstrating by their shock at our behavior...they do *not* see. In *O'Hara's Wife*, a fine actor, Ed Asner, is visited by the spirit of his dead wife, played by an excellent actress, Mariette Hartley. Within minutes of her first corporeal appearance, we *and her husband* know damned well that no one else can see or hear her. Yet throughout the stupidly written script, Asner keeps talking aloud to her, in the presence of others, causing everyone to think he's nuts, causing idiot slapstick contretemps that embarrass him, get him jailed, infuriate those trying to be sympathetic to him, and in general cause him to be looked on as a moron or mental defective. We are asked to identify with the protagonist, but his behavior is unworthy of a bright ten-year-old. And so everyone in the film comes off looking like jerks, because the scenarist and director think it's cute for people to act like schmucks.

2. The ghosts have variable powers. They can do, or are unable to do, things common and uncommon, in no set pattern. There is no internal consistency, no schema that sets up a logic of spectrology that makes any sense, even in supernatural terms. Sometimes they can walk through walls, and sometimes they splatter against the walls. Sometimes they can be touched, and sometimes the hand passes through them. Sometimes they leave physical evidence of themselves, and sometimes they don't. Here now, gone in a moment. But never with any degree of logic that tells us the powers of a ghost in that specific film were thought out with any degree of rationality above the level of highschool hijinks and sophomoric sight-gags.

3. The ghosts are as purposeless as the people they're haunting. In *Poltergeist* we were given a touching moment in which we see the shimmering, transparent ectoplasms descending a staircase and, heart-wrenchingly, one of the women says of them, "They're lost. They don't know how to find their way out." There is a purpose, thus, to *why* the ghosts are there, doing what they're doing. Not so in these six crippled efforts. And because we can empathize with the still-mortal hunger of these spirits, we come to care what happens. Not so in *High Spirits* where the *raison d'être* of ghostly presence is never rationally or even *echt*-fantastically explicated. They seem to gibber and caper for no more sensitive purpose than to satisfy the whim of a writer-director—Neil Jordan of *Mona Lisa* and *Company of Wolves*—in way over his head. (Because it's been done so well, so many times, even those not up to the job batten on the ego-feed that they can whip out a ghost movie with one hand jammed up the anus.)

4. The ghosts act as dippy as the live folks. They seem to have acquired no insight or sense from having gone through one of the two most traumatic experiences an entity can experience. (Birth is the other one, of course.) They seem to be creatures somehow trepanned in transmogrification, their commonsense aspects to have been lobotomized. They are idiots. The pranks they play, the way they speak, the directions they give, the things they demand...none of it rises above the level of Keystone Kops in sheets.

5. Everyone visited by a ghost in these films behaves in a loopy manner that tells us if they act like this in everyday life, unhaunted, they must be part of the hardcore unemployable. Steve Guttenberg in *High Spirits* and Shelley Long (fast becoming the female version of Chevy Chase, which is not intended as a compliment) in *Hello, Again* and Mandy Patinkin in *Maxie* and Sally Field in *Kiss Me Goodbye* are so goddamned discombobulated that to identify with them makes the filmgoer feel imbecile and scatterbrained. Loopier than Billie Burke in her dippiest moments in *Topper*.

Which brings us full-circle. *Topper*, it seems to me, is as good and as durable a film as it is, a true classic, because it manages to seem real. To appear mimetic, despite the ghostly conceits that lie at its core. The same goes for the other films I praised. Even *Ghostbusters*, as over the top as it goes, somehow has a firm grasp on reality, and plays it off against the fantasy without insulting our intelligence, our sense of balance, or our common knowledge of how human beings (and by extension, ghosts) act.

Perhaps, at last measure, it is that proper sense of reality that makes a good ghost story work. If we are asked to believe in the unbelievable, for the duration of a film, then we have to be moored tightly to the mast of rationality by verisimilitude.

When that line is cut, we are cut loose; and we are buffeted by insincere plotting, by expedient action, by unmotivated and unbelievable fumblefootedness.

Perhaps, at last measure, a ghost story is only as good as it is real. Which is a strange thing to wind up saying about an artifact as non-real as a story about voyagers from the Beyond.

36 In Which, Darkly and Deliciously, We Travel from Metropolis to Metropolis, Two Different Cities, Both Ominous

Like quite another creature of the night, *Batman* (Warner Bros.) is a hoot!

It is the first multimillion megabuck "summer spectacular" blockbuster film—

—that traditionally mindless outpouring of saturation-hype movies intended as visual junk food for tots, teens, and the terminally sophomoric of all ages, during the summer months when they seek momentary surcease from such wearying and emotionally holocryptic activities as wet t-shirt contests, spraying graffiti, and downing brewskis till they belch'n'barf—fit fare for gongoozlers—

—the first E Ticket cinematic rollercoaster since *Raiders of the Lost Ark* and *Who Framed Roger Rabbit?* that is worth every dollar of its admission ticket, worth every hour you will have to stand in line to see it. The first in several years that pays off more than even heightened expectations have promised.

It is masterful in every particular.

And if, like me, you are an admirer of that which is exemplary in comic strips and comic books...if, like me, you were weaned into the world of reading and the super-imposed precontinuum of literature by that original American art-form called the comic book...if, like me, as a kid you adored Batman and, like me, recognize the Batman as one of the great fictional detectives, worthy of enshrinement with Nero Wolfe, Sherlock Holmes, Dick Tracy, Philip Marlowe, Sam Spade, the Continental Op, Hercule Poirot, Miss Marple, and Charlie Chan...

Then you will revel in this extravagantly imaginative rendition of the Darknight Detective as cinematic magic realism. Because the hundreds of men and women who created this film have pulled off what is only the second true, honorable, satisfying transmogrification of a funnybook creation in live-action motion picture terms. The first was *Superman* (1978).

But not even *Superman* could suck you in as totally as *Batman* does. The Metropolis of Clark Kent, Lex Luthor, *The Daily Planet*, and The Man of Steel was only New York *avec* sight-gags. It worked nicely, and we all look on the movie with affection; but it was more-or-less mimetic reality with one or two fantastic elements dropped in. Like exotic slices of spicy Creole andouille sausage in an otherwise s.o.p. gumbo.

The Gotham City of *Batman* is at least fifty per cent of the success of this film. It is a designer's dream, a pedestrian's nightmare. It has the stunning, all-enthralling power of Giger's paintings for *Alien*, of Syd Mead and Lawrence Paull's Los Angeles as seen in *Blade Runner*, of William A. Horning's Wicked Witch of the West fortress in *The Wizard of Oz*. It is the most exuberantly extroverted elements of classic Art Deco melded with the grittiest aspects of the Casbah, Birmingham (the sooty one in England), Back O' The Yards in Chicago, Prague and Hell's Kitchen, by way of Quatermass's Hobb's Lane; and all of it subsumed into the vision of Fritz Lang's *Metropolis*. It is a city of fog, like London or Seattle every once in a while; it is a towering beast like Chernabog unfolding his leathery wings at the summit of Bald Mountain, his fecally-grimed buttocks hunkered in darkness at curbside; it is what lies just beyond what horrors we can see in any of Gustav Doré's engravings for Dante's *Divine Comedy*; it is concrete hell; urban paranoia personified; an evil rivet-studded poison mushroom of a megalopolis; something only Fritz Leiber could capture in narrative: the urban bad dream every *American Gothic* mom and dad shared of the corrupting city to which their innocent farmboy son was journeying for a factory job. It is Pleasure Island as all those bad little boys are mutated into screaming jackasses. It is perpetual midnight in Tiananmen Square, all killing shadows and bursts of cold light and dried blood. It is Johannesburg for whites; and if Goodness can survive there, it is only as a fitful, trembling cripple.

It is everything we read into fifty years of Batman stories, conceived in 1939 by Bob Kane and Bill Finger, embellished through the decades by Jerry Robinson, Neal Adams, Marshall Rogers, Alan Moore, and, most significantly for the heightened awareness of today's moviegoing audience, refurbished and made more dangerous than ever before by Frank Miller's 1986 *The Dark Knight Returns*.

In this dreadful dungeon of a Gotham City, abhorrent abattoir erected without building codes, Red Hook interpreted as Dresden after the fire-bombing, the idea of a vigilante who dresses like a giant bat rings absolutely true. Not for an instant, from the first moment his liquid shadow slithers across a rooftop, till the final instant in which we see him poised against the night, would any but the catastrophically grown-up doubt that *this* Batman is precisely the sort of Naderesque Zorro that would find birth, sustenance and purpose in *this* Gotham.

Unlike Superman, the Batman has appealed to generations of hero-worshipping kids precisely because he is not superhuman. We always understood that he was merely a man, without the ability to leap buildings in a single bound, to outrace a crack streamliner, to move faster than a speeding bullet, or to destroy evildoers with a blast of heat vision. Clark Kent was always a wimpy dweeb false identity of The Man of Steel. Kent was a put-on, a purposely inept red herring. But Batman is, and has always been, Bruce Wayne. Just a man. A consummate athlete, yes; a multimillionaire, yes; a philanthropist and playboy, yes: but always just as human as any of us. He can be beaten, he can be maimed, he can be killed.

But his obsession to fight crime, to go out every night, year after year, to avenge the senseless murder of his parents in Crime Alley, the murders he witnessed as a terrified child, was always a paradigm of vengeance that we understood as a dark otherside of human nature. He was, in those pre-*Death Wish* days, a symbol of balanced scales. We understood that it was a part of us that responded to the howls of the lynch mob, to the fears of city life that the NRA continues to feed, to a bloodlust that is despicable, *however* understandable. And in him, as symbol, we found catharsis.

All of that, without sermonizing, we get in *Batman*.

But more, much much more, we get an *artful* interpretation of that negativity in our souls. We get to see the violent Avenging Fury that bubbles up in us when we listen to the news and tremble at the terrors that infect our cities; and only the most deranged among us could fail to be turned away from that kind of vigilantism, even as we are captivated by his soul-crippling lust for justice, as opposed to the civilizing power of Law.

The balance is struck, in the smooth and literate screenplay of Sam Hamm and Warren Skaaren (rewritten, I am advised by numerous sources who wish to be unnamed, by the *Baron Munchausen* scenarist Charles McKeown), in the characterization of Bruce Wayne.

If the key to our willing suspension of disbelief is the persona of Gotham City—itself an active player in the superlative cast—then the codex for our acceptance of these images as having some relation to Real Life is the way in which Bruce Wayne has been written, and in the way he is played by Michael Keaton.

A year and a half ago, I was asked by *The Los Angeles Times* what I thought of the upcoming *Batman* film being directed by Tim Burton—he of *Beetlejuice* and *Pee-wee's Big Adventure*—and of Burton's seemingly-nepotic casting of Michael Keaton in the title role. That inquiry was precipitated by the deafening howls of outrage coming from the fans. Fans of the campy, counterproductive mid-Sixties crash-pow-zap television series; fans of previous comics-into-film disasters like *Supergirl*, *Swamp Thing*, *Captain America*, and *Howard the Duck*; fans of the Batman canon as accreted through the years in comics.

The din was hysterical. How could they sign someone like Burton, whose work at Disney had been less than memorable, to shoulder in any serious way this most delicate production without descending into flummery and ridicule? How could Burton so cavalierly flout the requirements of Rambo-esque physicality necessary to presenting a "proper" Batman, by hiring a skinny comedian like Keaton? The fans *knew* it would be a disaster!

And I said to the *Times* (though later misquoted for purposes of yellow journalism by a nameless semi-pro journal minimally read in the world of comics fandom) that, after all, it was only a movie. The course of Western Civilization would not be deflected by a micromillimeter even if the film were the worst thing ever made. That the rights had, after all, been bought by Warner Bros. from people whose eyes were wide open, and they had the right to succeed or fail as they chose. I said, finally, that if I had any concern, it was that perhaps the selection of Keaton—strictly on the basis of his physique—seemed to me capricious, even though Keaton was certainly a box office draw.

Three minutes into the finished film, even that concern vanished. As Batman, Keaton performs as heroically as the most demanding fan could wish. He reifies the character. But as Bruce Wayne, he transcends. Keaton plays Bruce Wayne as if he were Robin as an adult. He is sweet, yet tormented; unassuming, yet a solid presence; everything that Batman is not, yet a human being of genuine passion. When Christopher Reeve played Clark Kent, he was always demonstrably acting. His Kent was a bumbler, a bit of a dolt, a thespic cul-de-sac we endured till he hit the nearest phone booth to change clothes.

But Bruce Wayne, as assayed by Keaton, is someone we would enjoy knowing. It is not hard to understand why Kim Basinger's Vicki Vale falls for him. He is a decent man whose secret agenda may have twisted him emotionally, even as his great wealth has bent him, but like the best in all of us he continually struggles to live that non-Batman part of his life as a rational, kindly human being.

It is an aspect of this film that no one in the clamoring lynch mob pre-release could have (or did) countenance. It makes everything else work.

(A side-bar: I'm not much one for lynch law, or the strident demands of the groundlings, but it's possible that the most important element in the success of *Batman* was the manipulation of the prattling of the fans for a year and a half. I am led to believe that the film as we see it is *exactly* what Tim Burton intended all along, and that early on he had to fight the demented input of studio executives[1] who continued to believe—in the face of facts—that what was needed was a movie that echoed the idiocy of the tv series. Much *pow*, some *zap*, and a lot of *whappola*! But Burton and the Warner Bros. publicity department took that firestorm of public outrage, and fed it back effectively into the "creative sessions," and the execs bowed to Burton's vision, and stayed out of his way, to their credit, and to the excellence of the finished product. In this case, perhaps for the first time in a way that had superb results, the fan audience caused a dream to be realized as they wished. It's just an observation, and I could be wrong; but at least the Warner Bros. pr *apparat* must be lauded for turning an angry rabble into a Designated Hitter that walloped a homer.)

Which brings us to the third major player in the cast. If Gotham City and Michael Keaton form two legs of the tripod of excellence on which *Batman* solidly stands, then Jack Nicholson as that madcap mountebank of mayhem, The Joker, is a third leg as muscular as Atlas.

Nicholson was *born* to play The Joker.

---

[1] From time to time, I am accused of using too-florid language, inflammatory verbiage as purple as the desert sands of the Kalahari 'neath a gibbous dragon's-eye moon. For those who would take me to task for referring to the pre-Burton attitude of Warner Bros. executives as "demented," I offer the following intelligence. The director originally slated to direct *Batman*, the one WB thought proper to encompass their vision of what a Batman movie should be, was Ivan Reitman. Credits: *Foxy Lady* (1971), *Cannibal Girls* (1973), *Meatballs* (1979), *Stripes* (1981), *Ghostbusters* (1984), *Legal Eagles* (1986), and *Twins* (1988). Further credits: he produced *National Lampoon's Animal House*, *National Lampoon's Vacation*, and *The Heavy Metal Movie*. Nothing, it seems to me, in those credits to allay the shakes of the fans who feared *Batman* would be filmed as a drunken, dopey comedy. And if casting Keaton seemed ill-advised, know that it was only because he was considered too young to play the role, that Charlie Sheen didn't get it; know that Warners was seriously responding to Sylvester Stallone's desire to play Batman ("Yo! Robin boy!"); and know that WB's directorial choice, Mr. Reitman, cast in the lead roles...Bill Murray as Batman...Eddie Murphy as Robin. Don't talk to me about deranged. I said demented, and I *mean* demented!

Everything in his professional career has led to this characterization. When the time for Oscars slinks toward us, it is hoped that the Academy will not—as it usually does—disregard this incredible performance because it does not appear in one of those heavy-breathing *muy serioso* films of artificial angst and motheaten social conscience. Nicholson's Joker, *née* Jack Napier, is a chilling construct that makes Freddy Krueger, hockeymask-faced Jason Voorhees, and *Halloween*'s Michael Myers look as malevolent as Larry, Shemp, and Moe. All of the psychotic mugging that crippled *The Shining*, *Heartburn*, and other films in which Nicholson was permitted to run amuck, becomes (strangely!) just a subtext here. You would think this would be the arena in which all of that lunacy of Nicholson's would be set free, to splatter and dominate every scene in which he appears. But (oddly!) Nicholson seems to have understood in his bone-marrow that he had to use it as pentimento, the song only subtly heard beneath the orchestral theme. It is bloody frightening.

And as we seek balance between Good and Evil, between Responsibility and Carelessness, between Ethic and Amorality, we unconsciously require a balance between Hero and Villain. For a creature as powerful and frightening as Batman to face-off with punks and pushers and thugs would be to present a struggle that is flaccid and predictable. Superman must meet foes equally (at least) as godlike. It took a President, the U.S. Army, the power of television, and a gentle but clever country lawyer to bring down Senator Joe McCarthy. Hitler took on the whole world. And it is meet that Batman faces The Joker.

It is one of the cinematic mano-a-mano duels that will live in the annals of knockdown dragout confrontation. I will not spoil the ending for you.

Additionally: Michael Gough as Bruce Wayne's faithful friend and butler, Alfred, is splendid. You will find it hard to keep memories of John Gielgud in *Arthur* from your view, but if it is not an entirely unseen rendition of the manservant as mordant Jeeves, it is nonetheless expert and correct and endearing. Jack Palance's cameo is lip-smackingly what we know this fine actor can do when he's reprising the role he created in *Shane* in 1953, though we have seen his cornucopial abilities in offbeat casting from *The Big Knife* to *Monte Walsh*. Basinger is just fine, and if one considers her performance as counterpoint to that of the vain and ultimately tragic Alicia, as played by Mick Jagger's girlfriend, model Jerry Hall, it becomes all the more freighted with support for the foreground jousting between Keaton and Nicholson. Pat Hingle as Commissioner Gordon, and Billy Dee Williams as D.A. Harvey Dent (pre-Two-Face), don't have a lot to do—we expect to see them filled out more richly in the second and third films—for which Williams has already signed the contracts—but what they're given, they handle with skill and professionalism. They could hardly do less in a film that makes no missteps. I was not impressed by Robert Wuhl as crime reporter Alexander Knox. For a character so omnipresent—if not actively pivotal—lines less bombastic and a player more charismatic might have better suited. But that ain't no cavil.

If you seek cavils, illogicities in the total film, they are there for the nit-pickers. Cops blasting away at chemical tanks clearly labeled TOXIC in an enclosed space is kinda dumb. The gratuitous sexism of Nicholson's Jack Napier, intended to make frat boys guffaw, might have been deleted. Having Batman blow up a deadly chemical plant in the middle of a crowded city, where the winds can blow death to the suburbs, merely for the sake of a spectacular special effect, defies rationality. Dropping fifty storeys on a Bat-arang wire without ripping one's arm out of the socket does tend to defy the laws of the physical universe. But...

Who the hell cares!

This is one of those films that defies criticism of such a sort. If one starts to say, "Well, the trajectory of that missile from the Batwing should have taken out The Joker as well as the float behind him," then one should stop and say, "This is a movie in which a guy dresses up like a bat, in which a guy falls into a steaming vat of toxic chemicals and lives, in which caves under a mansion house all sorts of vehicles and no one seems to notice it's there..." and you realize you're being a fool for letting common sense get in the way of your enjoyment.

The bottom line as regards any sense of social conscience is this: you can go from first frame to last, and any connection between Serious Message and what we are given... is strictly accidental. But also on that bottom line labeled *purpose of film* is the pre-printed truth that this is an urban fairy tale, a darker-than-Grimm's fable intended to a) wow you with fantasy and b) make millions for the studio.

And there is no doubt in my mind that *Batman* will do precisely that. Had you been clever enough to buy Warner Communications stock last year, you would be looking at a tsunami ride today. The film cost thirty million to make (not counting prints and advertising), and the estimated take on just the licensing of Batman *tchotchkes* is well over $200 million. I expect that the June 23rd opening (as I write this) will outgross even the bloated box office takes of the new *Indiana Jones* and *Star Trek* killers. For the next six months no one will be able to go out on the street without seeing someone wearing a Batman artifact.

Which is as it should be. For *Batman* sets a new standard in the making of super-spectaculars. If you can remember back that far, consider what your expectations for BIG films were, right up to the moment you sat there waiting for the opening shot of *Star Wars*; and how your level of expectation for every film that followed, of any kind, was hurtled to a new pinnacle as those spaceships roared overhead. You were changed, and the film industry was changed. Not even *Fantasia* or *Pinocchio* had prepared us for the look, the feel, the sensory blowout of technical miracles in *Star Wars*.

And we held at that level, despite all the impressive films that came after, till *Raiders of the Lost Ark*. And, like junkies pumping the blood/dope mixture back again and again for a higher high, we were booted to a new plateau of technical wonderment. And we held there till *Roger Rabbit*; and we held there till *Baron Munchausen* by way of *Brazil*. And now, gasping for breath, our eyes no longer equipped to take it all in first viewing, we are flung higher yet. *Batman* makes every James Bond film look like something shot by a talented film school student with a Camcorder on a weekend. (I warn: we may not be able to take many more of these narcotic fixes and still remember how rich and re-warding can be little films like, say, *Miracle Mile*.)

Yet even as stunningly reminiscent of Fritz Lang's *Metropolis* as the design of the film may be, even as satisfying as are the lead performances by Keaton and Nicholson, even as breathtaking as are the special effects, it may well be the small moments in the film that stick with us longest. I hesitate to spoil even one second of your pleasure, but as I imagine you will all have seen the film by the time you read this, I must tell you of *my* favorite moment. If you don't want it revealed, skip the next paragraph.

It is 3:15AM. Vicki Vale has just had sex with Bruce Wayne. She wakens from deep sleep, alone there in the bedroom at Wayne Manor. The other side of the bed is empty. Groggily, she looks across the darkened room and there, backlit by the night sky, is Bruce Wayne, hanging upside-down on a grav-boot muscle toning rig, naked, flexing his shoulder muscles, slightly (ever so slightly) spreading his arms. Upside-down. Like a bat hanging from a cave ceiling. And she goes back to sleep.

I only *loved* that moment! It was a directorial touch, as opposed to something carefully scripted (even though it may have been in the screenplay), that indicated to me that Tim Burton was a wise choice for director. (Burton, I am told, directed very little of the main action sequences. The knockabout extravaganzas were ordered up, I am told, by Peter MacDonald, who directed *Rambo III*. And very well done they are, too; with an occasional sense of disorientation as to who is where, doing what to whom. But it is in the *non*-action sequences that the film comes most to mean something; and *that* is Burton.)

One final comment. In only three particulars does the film depart from the Accepted Canon of the comic book version(s) of Batman. One is the ending, which I will not comment on. The second is the absence of Robin, which doesn't bother me at all. Call it pre-Robin, if you will. And the third is in the portrayal of the murder of Bruce Wayne's parents. I cannot, without screwing it up for you, go into more detail than that. But I go on record here as championing that change. It makes the film an Apollonian-Dionysian whole, a snake-swallowing-its-tail configuration of poetic justice. And it is an *improvement* on the many-times-revamped origin of Batman.

To the end of addressing those changes, I respond to the alleged comment of scenarist Sam Hamm, who viewed these departures from cant by Charles McKeown as "vulgarities," as follows:

When one is dealing with a commercial property owned lock, stock, and trademark by as ruthless and cynical a parent as DC Comics, a plantation-mentality taskmaster that offers readers the chance to kill or keep alive Robin by use of a 900 call-in number, that turns the characters over to one flash-in-the-pan writer or artist after another, to debase and corrupt as whim or ego dictates, it seems to me the height of mendacity to pillory *any* sub-contractor for revisionism. The savaging of the Batman mythos every month at the hands of some DC wage slave, is far more offensive to me than the rational—if filmically self-serving—changes we encounter in the movie. I have considerable respect for Mr. Hamm's work on the film, and the writing he has recently done for DC, but I think his comment ill-advised.

And for those who shrieked in horror at the employment of Tim Burton and Michael Keaton—whose slight physique has been innovatively integrated into the reasons Bruce Wayne *became* the Batman, and dovetails with his use of body-armor, pulling the fangs of those who say Batman should *only* be an acrobat without gadgets—I suggest that *next* year, when they announce that the second film will be directed by someone else, starring someone else as Batman, that those will be the same howlers who'll babble that it would be un*think*able to employ anyone *but* Burton and Keaton.

But then, those will probably be the same ones who liked Prince's music in this first film. And what is there to be done with people like that?

Don't ask me...I just go to the movies.

37 In Which Not Only Is No Answer Given, But No One Seems to Know the Question to Ask

So this woman stands up in the Q&A audience during the second hour of this lecture I was giving at a Major American University—for which appearance guaranteed to warp the malleable and essentially tabula rasa minds of about eleven hundred students I was being paid a fee the scope of which one usually associates with deficit financing of nations the size of Burundi or that which is paid to genuine cutting-edge experts in arcane subjects—and she's doing the arms akimbo thing, and she says in this extremely snotty tone of voice, "Mister Ellison—"

(Already I know I've got problems when they start off with that *Mister Ellison* shit, drawing out the *Mister* with a whole lot of attitude, exactly the way one of those IRS twerps asks, "And pray tell, sir, how is it that you have deducted fifty-three thousand dollars for entertainment on your return, when your total earnings for the year were fourteen thousand?")

"—*Mister* Ellison, we've been listening to you decry the System for more than an hour, and we've yet to hear you offer a coherent, all-encompassing solution to the problem. Do you *have* such a solution, sir?"

To which set-up I respond in the only manner I've found, in twenty-five years of public speaking, that has any hope of satisfying someone who's been lying in wait for you. I say to her, "I didn't realize that it was incumbent upon one who perceives the problem to have a pat solution, as well. I am not Ronald Reagan, ma'am; I do not have all the answers to the questions that torment humanity. I am not an expert. It is more than my dear, late mother ever thought I'd be capable of achieving, that I'm even capable of stating the *nature* of the problem. Sadly, you have caught me out: your university has paid me a know-it-all sized honorarium, and I'm only a know-some-of-it. You should have booked Edwin Meese or Donald Trump; they seem to know the answers."

And I proceed with the lecture, doing the best I can.

Which is a great disappointment to the students, who have been conned and conditioned to expect that every speaker who struts his or her stuff will have some rigorously worked-out plan to repair the ozone layer, settle the pro-choice/pro-life conundrum, balance the federal deficit, feed the starving multitudes, or end white collar crime in a drug-free society.

In fact, though I come on like a know-it-all (which literary demeanor seems to drive some of you absolutely up the wall, heaven knows why), I do not know the answers to even a tiny fraction of the Great Questions.

It occurs to me that this sudden revelation, without easing you into it, might cause severe psychic trauma. I'm sorry for that; but I cannot, simply cannot, continue to live this lie. Despite the cheap sham so many of you have accepted for decades now, I must admit that there are a few things I do not know.

Like, for instance, the meaning of a phenomenon I have recently stumbled upon, the subject of this essay.

I haven't the vaguest idea what it means. I've taken note of it (as perhaps a few of you may likewise have done), and I'm prepared to describe it in detail. But what it means... well...I haven't the faintest. It will take the analytical skills of you, my faithful readers, to explain what it means.

I confess to feelings of inadequacy about this. Not to mention that it does seem to transgress the sacred lines of covenant between a know-it-all columnist and his audience, seeking your insights like this. If it were a more momentous matter, believe me, I'd figure it out myself.

What it looks like to me, is this:

Charles Fort, that unparalleled amasser of "excluded phenomena," inexplicable everyday mysteries that orthodox science cannot fit into a rational universe (what he called "damned" facts), posited a theory he termed *Steam Engine Time*. "When it's time for the steam engine to be invented," Fort more or less wrote, "even if Watt doesn't invent it, someone *will*, because it's Steam Engine Time." (With a nod to Papin, Newcomen, and Savery, who were there before the Scot, Watt.)

The concept of Steam Engine Time is a useful rule of thumb. Not only in science—Pons and Fleischmann may not have actually stumbled across a cheap, clean fusion method, but it's certainly *Fusion Time*, so don't take any bets that out there somewhere is someone who *hasn't*—but in the arts, as well.

For instance, for no reason anyone can codify, last year we were "gifted" with a feckless congeries of movies in which kids switched bodies with adults, or narrow variations of that transmogrification. Foreshadowed by 1977's *Freaky Friday*, in which momma Barbara Harris switches body with daughter Jodie Foster, last year, of a sudden, whambam and splishsplash, we got *Like Father, Like Son* (late 1987), Dudley Moore into Kirk Cameron and vice versa; *Dream a Little Dream,* Jason Robards, Jr. into Corey Feldman &vv; *Vice Versa*, Judge Reinhold into Fred Savage &vv; *18 Again!* with George Burns into Charlie Schlatter &vv; and *Big*, with Tom Hanks just phumphing out of kidness into grownupness. And all of them in 1988. For why?

Well, though this is not the phenomenon of which I will speak in a moment, it is a *similar* oddity; and about *this* one I do have a theory. As opposed to the other one, coming up, about which I haven't a clue.

Steam Engine Time happens when the *need* for a Steam Engine is generally felt by the masses, even if they don't know that it's a Steam Engine after which they're hungering. There's a vacuum created, and this unspoken necessity becomes mother to the invention that rushes in to fill the unarticulated need.

In Hollywood, this last decade or so, we've seen the shameless pandering to the youth market become so oppressive that writers over the age of thirty cannot even get hired. The same goes for older actors, directors, techs in virtually every area of cinematic expertise.

CEOs, snowed by MBA grads from Harvard Business School, put these arrivistes into positions of power. They cannot write, they cannot direct, they cannot hang a light, speak a line, design a set. But they have "input." And they all have the power to say no. They are young, and they understand flow charts, debentures, amortizing rolling stock, and best of all they lay their oblations directly on the bottom line.

And like the members of any group, they prefer to deal with their own kind. Immigrants flock to certain neighborhoods already tenanted by those who speak their native tongue. It's human nature. We trust our own. We are suspicious of outsiders.

The young executives prefer to deal with young men and women like themselves, who share their values and history...or what little of the eternal flow they perceive as history. They do not like dealing with older people, because in those persons they detect the judgmental over-status of Mother and Father. But they, the young execs, are now the power figures; why should they act as if Mother and Father are worth listening to? Isn't that why they got the MBA, so *they* could inherit the wisdom that equates with power? They develop their own Accepted Wisdom.

And one unshakeable conviction of that Accepted Wisdom is: old farts who've been at the game for decades cannot possibly be hip enough to produce a product that will inveigle the Nintendo Generation. The Accepted Wisdom is that not even multiple Academy Award winners—if they happen to be, say, forty-nine years old—can properly, effectively, intuitively relate to kids who seem unable to get enough sequels to *Friday the 13th*, *Meatballs*, *Police Academy*, *Revenge of the Nerds*, and *American Ninja*.

This certain knowledge comes to us from what were formerly hyped as the Baby Moguls, who are nothing more than very young guys, raised on tv sitcoms, coughed out of film schools all over America, steeped in the validity of the *auteur* theory and business school tactics, but oblivious to the niceties of the Creative Act (and when cognizant of it, disdain it as ju-ju), who have conned and shouldered their way into executive sinecures at studios, networks, and production companies. And they know nothing. But they know nothing *arrogantly*.

The emblematic anecdote of this situation, a story currently going the rounds out here, is of uncertain origin: I've heard it repeated featuring 77-year-old actress Natalie Schafer (she who lists among her extensive credits the exquisite portrayal of Mrs. Thurston Howell III on *Gilligan's Island*), 80-year-old screenwriter Julius Epstein (who won an Oscar for writing no less a classic than *Casablanca*, as well as screenplays for *The Man Who Came to Dinner*, *Mr. Skeffington* and the 1983 Oscar-nominated script for *Reuben Reuben*), and 83-year-old writer/director Billy Wilder (two-time Oscar winner, among whose breath-taking credits one finds *Ninotchka*, *Hold Back the Dawn*, *Double Indemnity*, *The Lost Weekend*, *Sunset Boulevard*, *Stalag 17*, *The Spirit of St. Louis*, *Witness for the Prosecution*, *Some Like It Hot*, *Irma La Douce*, and *The Apartment*). The other featured player in this anecdote has been, variously, Jeff Brickmont of HBO; 29-year-old MBA and Senior VP of Columbia Pictures (formerly at Orion), Rob Fried; Michael Levy, formerly of 20th Century Fox, currently president of Joel Silver Productions (who brought you *Lethal Weapon* I and II); and Sr. VP, Programming, Fox Broadcasting Corp., the ever-popular just-turned-30 Rob Kenneally, one of those Fox execs whom David Letterman refers to when he says the company is being run by "explorer scouts." Probably doesn't matter which cast is the accurate one, because in the case of this anecdote, they're interchangeable; and it's the thought that counts. Anyway, story goes like this:

Billy Wilder is solicited by this young exec, to come in and "take a meeting" about some project or other they want Billy to write and/or direct. So he is ushered into the ostentatiously understated office of this big *macher* who still secretly uses Oxy-10 for his zits, and he shakes hands with the guy, and he sits down. Now, the *pezzonovante* smiles smarmily and says, "I'm a little embarrassed. I've heard your name a lot, of course, but I don't, well, er, I'm just not very familiar with your credits; could you run a few of the most important ones for me?" And Billy Wilder, who was a supertalent forty years before this clown was born, stands up and says with dignity, "You first."

In 1987, the Writers Guild of America, west commissioned UC, Santa Barbara sociology professors/researchers William and Denise Bielby to prepare an exhaustive survey and study of the problems of discrimination as related to writers in the film/tv industry. The first report, covering the years 1982–85, was released two years ago and documented—from hiring records and studio reports as well as other sources of raw data—a pattern of non-employment that was not only dramatic in terms of the expected prejudices—against women, blacks, latinos and latinas, the physically handicapped—but nailed down with shocking statistics the widespread non-hiring of a new "protected class" of writers…those over forty. The WGAw membership is approximately 7,500. 53% of that number are over forty years of age.

The second Bielby Report was released on May 24th of this year, covering 1985–87. It suggested that things have grown even worse in the last two years. Of the 3,395 writers in the WGAw who are over forty, only 47% saw employment of any kind in 85–87. And the pattern of non-hiring gets significantly more obvious by the decade. Over fifty. Over sixty. And so on.

(In the event you are not now attending one of the many schools of film at an American university, where this report can be read, and if you're morbidly curious about what the economic arena is really like in Hollywood, you can send a stamped, self-addressed envelope to: Mr. Jeff Wallace, Human Resources Coordinator; Writers Guild of America, west; 8955 Beverly Boulevard; West Hollywood, California 90048 and ask for a copy of Unequal Access—Unequal Pay, the 1989 Hollywood Writers Report. The supply is limited. You can mention this column when you make your request.)

So having accorded you the background, my theory of why we suddenly saw a clothes-line-hanging full of kids-switch-bodies-with-adults movies last year, my theory as to why Tom Hanks as a child suddenly gets *Big*, is obvious. The kids in charge of the industry, and the kids who write to order for them, crawled into Steam Engine Time where there was an inarticulate emotional need for the tots to *become* Mother and Father. Not just to sit there in the offices and demean adults when they come in looking for work, but to *become*, physically and actually, the adults against whom they wield their power. It was an acting-out of the child's need to "play house." To show how much cleverer a kid can be with his adolescent mind, if miraculously shunted into a big person's body. It is a manifestation of the Me Decade's version of the Love Generation's dumb dictum *Never Trust Anyone Over 30*.

Think about it. The parallel is seen in all the tv spots for computer games and electronic gadgetry that they try to sell to kids on Saturday morning. Check out those ads. In virtually all of them, Dad (usually, because Mom is a girl, so what the hell can *she* possibly know?) and his son engage in some kind of vague competition at the keyboard. And Dad invariably dweebs out, and the kid either outscores him or solves the problem or makes Dad look like a retard.

Kids! Be the first in *your* neighborhood to make your old man look like an asshole! Screw the New Math, here's a sure-fire way to put that arbitrary power-broker, your FATHER, in his place. He may ground you for getting into his Jack Daniels, he may not let you use the car because your manner around the house lately has been appreciably more insolent than usual, he may scream to turn that goddam MTV crap down but... you're smarter than he ever was, or ever could be...and if *you* were *his* size, you'd kick the crap outta him!

Ergo, a rash of films in which precisely and exactly that happens. Dad is turned into a floundering, babbling pre-pubescent imbecile, while Sonny somehow manages to pull it all off as he masquerades in Dad's body, gamboling through the Adult World.

That's my theory. I like it. It's nasty.

But of the topic for this essay, I haven't a theory, a hint, a clue. And here it is. I call it the *Phenomenon of the Ichabod*.

Formerly, the male protagonists of motion pictures, with whom we've been asked to identify, have been the Humphrey Bogarts, the Gary Coopers, the Sylvester Stallones, the Robert De Niros, and Paul Newmans. Subsumed as Robert Redford.

Tall-seeming. (Redford is actually only an inch or two taller than your columnist at 5'5", but he's always *filmed* lanky.) Good-looking. Competent. Graceful under pressure. Inventive. Well, hell, simply *heroic*.

That's the way it's always been, with the occasional Edward G. Robinson or James Cagney or Paul Muni to break the monotony; but even *they* had such a high wattage of charisma and toughness that you overlooked in what deep shadow they stood when John Wayne or Randolph Scott towered over them.

But of late I've noticed how many of what I've come to call "Ichabods" (after the Washington Irving character, of course) are being cast as the heroes of dramatic or action movies. And when they're in comedies, they manage to *act* like heroes. I can describe the somatotype so you'll know what I mean. (There will be minor variations from person to person, of course.)

Tall, thin, loose-limbed like Buddy Ebsen dancing or Ray Bolger as The Scarecrow. Thatchy hair, usually parted in the middle and blow-dried, almost always a colorless brown. Goofy faces best suited to expressions of consternation, confusion, embarrassment, chagrin. The kind of expression you see on the face of a guy who doesn't know how to screw in a light bulb. Physically, they're in the somatology of Alan Alda.

Jeff Goldblum used to be the perfect example of that Ichabod image, when you saw him in, say, *Buckaroo Banzai*. But all that changed when he met Geena Davis and made *The Fly*. Now, as you can see again in *Earth Girls Are Easy*, as you saw in *The Fly*, he emerges from the transformation chamber buck naked and festooned with great traps, lats, and delts. An insouciant curl of matinee idol hair falling over his forehead. Intense looks. A hero. No longer an idiotic Ichabod.

The roster of Ichabods currently starring in everything from *Batman* to *The House on Carroll Street* includes the following:

Alan Ruck, Judge Reinhold, Ed Begley, Jr., Michael O'Keefe, Jeff Daniels, Lance Guest, Michael Keaton, and Tom Hanks (though superhuman efforts are being made to convert these last two into the new Jeff Goldblum image). And, of course, the most extreme case, the king Ichabod of them all, Steve Guttenberg.

Don't ask me why the Ichabod has become the protagonist of choice among casting directors, producers, and *auteur* directors. They're all over the place, and you'll have no trouble visualizing the guys I mean, or the parts they're playing. They're not quite geeks or spazolas or nerds. They're more like Dagwood Bumstead falling over the postman. They're omnipresent, to the degree that they're even showing up in tv commercials: look at the guy in the currently-airing Sizzler commercials. So help me, he's a perfect Jeff Daniels clone. Herky-jerky, babbling, falling over his feet, utterly discombobulated.

What, in the American psyche, has altered? What, in our view of ourself, has brought about Steam Engine Time for the deification of the Ichabod?

Are we simply surfeited with Stallone, numbed by Norris, shut off by Schwartzenegger, and filled with ennui by Eastwood? Or is there something more interesting happening?

Hell, gang, I wish I could give you My Theory. But, as I said, there are just some things I note, that don't make sense to me. I know it'll shatter those of you who've dismissed me as a smartass who thinks he knows just everydamnthing, but I come to that place where I'm forced to cop to it: I'm just as often befuddled as the rest of you.

So if there's a perceptive student of social trends out there in the readership who can figger this one, drop me a line and I'll attempt to cobble up some sort of rationale for a future update.

Until that time, and until next installment, when I sing its praises, crawl hop swim fly to a theater to see *Field of Dreams*, based on Kinsella's gorgeous, tenderhearted book SHOELESS JOE. It may be the best film you'll see this year.

Till then...confusedly yours...

38 In Which, Though Manipulated, We Acknowledge That Which All Men Seek

I've written of this elsewhere, but if I repeat myself, let it be risk of repetition in an eternal cause of enrichment.

Some nights ago, after a book signing for the collection of these film essays recently published by Underwood-Miller under the title HARLAN ELLISON'S WATCHING (I felt calling it PAULINE KAEL'S AND JAMES AGEE'S FILM OBSERVATIONS might be a tad duplicitous), a group of us retired to a Thai restaurant to reify our spirits; and during the course of the meal a writer named Larry DiTillio responded to my enthusiasm for the film *Field of Dreams* (Universal) with the remark, "I enjoyed it, too; but can somebody tell me what it was about?"

Like dumping a bucket of chubs into a thrave of Thresher sharks.

I went for it then, and began to write this column verbally. Pulled up short, and said, "No, better still, the next column will be for you, Larry." And so, this one is for all you good readers *en passant*, but is primarily an Essay for DiTillio.

Because I have written of this elsewhere.

Field of Dreams is based closely on W.P. Kinsella's lyrical and unforgettable 1982 novel, SHOELESS JOE, winner of the Houghton Mifflin Literary Fellowship Award. The first section of the book is called "Shoeless Joe Jackson Comes to Iowa" and this is how that splendid novel begins:

My father said he saw him years later playing in a tenth-rate commercial league in a textile town in Carolina, wearing shoes and an assumed name.

"He'd put on fifty pounds and the spring was gone from his step in the outfield, but he could still hit. Oh, how that man could hit. No one has ever been able to hit like Shoeless Joe."

Three years ago at dusk on a spring evening, when the sky was a robin's-egg blue and the wind as soft as a day-old chick, I was sitting on the verandah of my farm home in eastern Iowa when a voice very clearly said to me, "If you build it, he will come."

The voice was that of a ballpark announcer. As he spoke, I instantly envisioned the finished product I knew I was being asked to conceive. I could see the dark, squarish speakers, like ancient sailors' hats, attached to aluminum-painted light standards that glowed down into a baseball field, my present position being directly behind home plate.

In reality, all anyone else could see out there in front of me was a tattered lawn of mostly dandelions and quack grass that petered out at the edge of a cornfield perhaps fifty yards from the house.

Anyone else was my wife Annie, my daughter Karin, a corn-colored collie named Carmeletia Pope, and a cinnamon and white guinea pig named Junior who ate spaghetti and sang each time the fridge door opened. Karin and the dog were not quite two years old.

"If you build it, he will come," the announcer repeated in scratchy Middle American, as if his voice had been recorded on an old 78-r.p.m. record.

A three-hour lecture or a 500-page guide book could not have given me clearer directions: Dimensions of ballparks jumped over and around me like fleas, cost figures for light standards and floodlights whirled around my head like the moths that dusted against the porch light above me.

That was all the instruction I ever received: two announcements and a vision of a baseball field. I sat on the verandah until the satiny dark was complete. A few curdly clouds striped the moon, and it became so silent I could hear my eyes blink.

Our house is one of those massive old farm homes, square as a biscuit box with a sagging verandah on three sides. The floor of the verandah slopes so that marbles, baseballs, tennis balls, and ball bearings all accumulate in a corner like a herd of cattle clustered with their backs to a storm. On the north verandah is a wooden porch swing where Annie and I sit on humid August nights, sip lemonade from teary glasses, and dream.

When I finally went to bed, and after Annie inched into my arms in that way she has, like a cat that you suddenly find sound asleep in your lap, I told her about the voice and I told her that I knew what it wanted me to do.

"Oh love," she said, "if it makes you happy you should do it," and she found my lips with hers. I shivered involuntarily as her tongue touched mine.

Only two pages later (in the 1983 Ballantine paperback edition, which I bought new and read so many times it fell apart, forcing me to scrounge through used bookstores till I found half a dozen more copies, some for me, some to give away to friends...it's that kind of book), only two pages later, the narrator—Ray Kinsella—talks about his father: "My father, I've been told, talked baseball statistics to my mother's belly while waiting for me to be born."

The fictional narrator's father "settled in Chicago, inhabited a room above a bar across from Comiskey Park, and quickly learned to live and die with the White Sox. Died a little when, as prohibitive favorites, they lost the 1919 World Series to Cincinnati, died a lot the next summer when eight members of the team were accused of throwing that World Series."

We are dealing here, right from the soupbone, with mythic icons of a high order: the Black Sox Scandal, the great Shoeless Joe Jackson who was suspended from baseball for life, "Say it ain't so, Joe" and the power of this perfectly American competition that still, to this day, despite the popularity of football, golf, tennis, wrestling, *any* damn other sport, can shag fungoes with the media and imprison a nation's attention as a Kirk Gibson hobbles around the bases or as a Pete Rose goes down in flames.

But not even the intensity of resonance with the trope baseball lies at the heart of

Field of Dreams's impact on audiences that have come to think of it so quickly as one of the great fantasy films of our time. What burns at the core of writer-director Phil Alden Robinson's adaptation of Kinsella's soulwork answers Larry DiTillio's question: *what is it about*?

And what it is about is that about which I've written before.

It is about my father.

Many of you may know that my father—Louis Laverne Ellison—died on a Sunday morning in 1949, in Painesville, Ohio, of a coronary thrombosis; as I watched, descending as I was from upstairs; seeing him in his favorite chair, keeling over; and I helpless at age fourteen, to do anything but stare.

I did not cry. I loved and admired my father more than I can say, more than you need to know. But I was already a loner, had run away from home and been faraway on the road two years earlier, and had long since begun to wear my face, the one I wear today. So I did not cry. Not when the pulmotor squad covered him with the crocheted throw that always lay folded at one end of the settee where they'd worked over him; not as they carried him out on a stretcher; not as he went into the ground; not as we sat *shiva* for him, a *minyan* drawn from Jews who lived in Cleveland, thirty miles away because there weren't enough Jewish families in Painesville at that time; not once during the year that I said *kaddish* for him every morning and every evening.

But—and if I repeat myself, permit it—I spent all day, *every* day for weeks, standing in our front yard, bouncing a tennis ball off the wall, catching it in my trapper's mitt, over and over, from sunup till it grew too dark to see the ball coming back to me. It was palinoia—the compulsive repetition of an action. (It was not till I was in my thirties, when I idly thought back on that time, that it dawned on me with chagrin and that special horror attendant on putting oneself in someone else's place, that *inside* the house at 89 Harmon Drive, my poor mother suffered what must have sounded like the equivalent of the Chinese water torture. Heartbroken, trying to make some sense of a world suddenly ended for her, the centerpost and light of her days taken from her, my mother was further driven to desperation by that metronomic bang-bang-bang reverberating in every room, endlessly, over and over without respite. And not once did she speak to me of it, not once did she ask me to stop that hellish repetition, nor did she allow any of the mourners come to offer condolence to speak to me about what I was doing. In retrospect, now long after she, too, is gone, I think I love her most for that kindness, which must have cost her dearly.)

And I became obsessed with baseball.

As a tiny kid, thin and small, participation in sports had been denied me. It was a different time then; the phys ed classes were called "gym" and the men who taught such classes had no grounding in child psychology. The tall kids were picked for basketball, the beefy kids were picked for baseball, and when we got up a sandlot game the captains sensibly picked even the girls for their sides before one unfortunate leader was left with me standing alone. But like all little boys in that time, I worshipped ballplayers . Bob Feller and Joe DiMaggio and Ewell "The Whip" Blackwell and Lou Boudreau and Harry "The Cat" Brecheen and Ted Williams and Satchel Paige and Johnny Groth of the Red Sox were my idols. But the Cleveland Indians and the New York Yankees were my teams.

The year before, the Indians had won the World Series. I knew every player on that team by heart, their stats, their flaws and strengths, their personal habits. And I would lie in bed and listen to night games all through that time after my father lay covered on the settee, and then was gone, never to be seen again, and what I knew was this: *it goes on*. Some things change, and some things change terribly, so unrecognizably, but *it goes on*. Please don't laugh but: like baseball, it's the only game in town; *and it goes on.*

I blocked everything, thought baseball, and did not cry.

Many, many years later, when I was a grownup as best I can be, and had already established myself as a writer, and was living a million miles in time and experience forgotten away from Painesville and our house at 89 Harmon Drive in which another family sat eating and talking, and the wooden face of that front yard wall had ceased to echo with the sound of a tennis ball, I was caught unaware by insight, blindsided by revelation. I sat one night reading an essay by William Faulkner. And in the middle of a page, in the heart of a paragraph, I came unsuspecting to these words:

> "No matter what it is a writer is writing about, if the writer is a
> man, he is writing about the search for his father."

And then I cried. More than twenty-five years later, all of it came back. Like rain, rain, go away, come again another day, it all came at once.

Those words were an epiphany for me. And when I went back and looked over the hundreds and hundreds of stories I'd written, I found that there were dozens and dozens in which the naked theme or the hidden subtext was me, trying to make contact with my dad. Trying to get the word through to him that I loved him more than a little kid could say, and that I'd learned how to be a decent human being from his example, and that I knew he'd be proud of what I'd grown up to be.

That, as with the fine man Kevin Costner portrays in *Field of Dreams*, my life had significantly ordered itself in aid of letting my father know that I regretted we had never played catch together. That whatever dreams I had dreamed and turned into reality, that they were *his* dreams, too; and that I was living not just my own life, but his that had been cut off too soon, as well. That, at the bottom of the ninth, all we have are the dreams, because the memories hurt too much.

And that, Larry, really and truly, is what *Field of Dreams* is all about.

I had to take a break. This stuff gets to me. But it occurs to me, now that the collected *Watching* columns have been published, and we're getting reviews as praising as *The New York Times* and as punishing as *Booklist*, that these are very peculiar film reviews. I suppose the one I've just written about *Field of Dreams*, a movie both meaningful and touching for almost everyone who's seen it, a fantasy in the purest sense, a film I want very much for you to go and see (if you haven't already, as it was released last June and these comments, bumped by the *Batman* review I wanted you to get while the film was still in the theaters, are now a bit dated), is the most peculiar of them all. "Idiosyncratic" is what the reviewers are most commonly calling these essays.

But more often than not, what a film is *about* has nothing much to do with how dense or full of holes may be the plot, nor how well it was acted, nor even how splendidly it was shot. More often than not film is *about* taking us beyond ourselves. That's what movies do best. For philosophical conundra, we have books. For purely esthetic response we have music and paintings. For the sheer pleasure of human movement we have sports and ballet.

Movies amalgamate all of that, and add a dimension, a unity so cathexian that they transcend the medium and manipulate us despite our best efforts to resist. Manipulate us even as we say to ourselves, "I'm being handled!"

Most of the time, with splatter films or Rambo/Rocky films, we are being chivvied and cozened in ways that aren't good for us, that diminish us, that make us see and think things not as fine and enriching as we might desire. Occasionally, as with films like **batteries not included* or *E.T. the Extra-Terrestrial* or *The Magnificent Seven*, we sense at a deeper level that this is a gentle, caring, even loving sort of manipulation. And we know it is for our own good. When mom says, "See, I took a spoonful of the medicine, and it doesn't taste bad; now it's your turn," we know we're being conned, but we don't resist…because it's for our own good. *Field of Dreams* does that.

And what it's *about* is that it *is* manipulating us. Not to weep crocodile tears at the *faux*-emotionalism of, say, *Love Story*, but to feel real, genuine, authentic compassion for, say, Gary Cooper's character in *They Came to Cordura*, or to understand the grudging but peculiarly sincere friendship between Rod Steiger's *bandido* and James Coburn's black Irish dynamiter in *Duck, You Sucker!*

You don't have to care a fig about baseball to be moved by *Field of Dreams*. Because what it does is to manipulate us in reliving that moment—that island of perfection—in our youth when we stood at twilight, smelling the freshly-cut grass, beside our mother or father, and they smiled down at us; and in that perfect moment all the joy of our childhood—no matter that the rest of childhood was a charnel house with drunken fathers and abusive mothers and horrendous schoolmates and the terrible powerlessness of the child—in that moment the joy of our childhood was subsumed. And it was perfect.

And we didn't know it.

We didn't know that one day it would all turn to shit.

Or maybe not even shit, but compromised, less than what we wanted it to be, average perhaps, mediocre perhaps, not quite enough. We didn't even *know* that we didn't know. We didn't even have any sense that there *was* shit. In that moment it was perfect. And we squandered it. The moment passed, and we didn't have a chance to savor it. Years flew past, and we thought back to that perfect moment, and we wanted it again, new, fresh, come once more to be properly treasured. But memory alone cannot do it for us.

And so, this movie. This *Field of Dreams* that manipulates us, for our own good, with gentle pull and cool palm against our cheek, with grace and love and now we begin to smell the grass and feel the evening breeze stir our hair, and now we are taken out of ourselves, back there when we didn't know...except we have our fondest wish...to be *there*, then, at that time, to be who we were then, at that time...and to know all we know *now*.

To tie up loose ends.

To say, at last, I love you and I've missed you since you left so unexpectedly, and oh how fine it feels to be standing here with you smiling at me.

Larry, what *Field of Dreams* is about, is taking you by the hand and leading you back for just a few hours to the perfect moment when nothing had begun to diminish you.

And I've heard there are people who come out of this film with a sneer on their lips, and corrugated remarks about what a manipulative movie it was, and I've got to tell you, kiddo, it just makes you want to go up to them and hug them, the poor things, and tell them everything will be okay.

And slip into their pocket a piece of paper with these words by Rimbaud: "Genius is the recovery of childhood at will."

ANCILLARY MATTER: Were it not for obsession, we would not have the Great Pyramid of Cheops, the Great Wall of China, the Great Awakening of the Protestant revival, the Great White way, and Dave Holland's great new book, FROM OUT OF THE PAST: A PICTORIAL HISTORY OF THE LONE RANGER. All the unthinking, casual denigration of obsession by enthusiasts in one arcane area of interest, fails to credit the treasures such singlemindedness of loving purpose has given us: the deciphering of the Dead Sea and Nag Hammadi scrolls, the preservation of the trove of American comic books, the opening of the Panama Canal, manned flight, fandom's archival bibliomania of the pulp writings of authors now dead and mostly forgotten...

And Dave Holland has been working for eight years on a holy obsession that collects in one elegant volume, everything you could possibly desire to know about the Masked Rider of the Plains.

In 444 oversized, beautifully designed pages, lavishly illustrated with more than a thousand black-and-white and color photos, Holland not only traces the origins (and auctorial controversy surrounding same), history, and mutations of the legend from the first broadcast of *The Lone Ranger* on Thursday, February 2nd, 1933 over WXYZ in Detroit to the present, but he deals exhaustively with all the sidebars: comic books, comic strips, novelizations, pulp magazines, Big Little Books, cereal premiums, movies, tv shows, *everything*! If, like the rest of the universe, you have adored The Lone Ranger since the first time you heard Brace Beemer cry, "Hi-yo Silver, awaaaay!" then you simply cannot allow yourself to pass up this incredible labor of love and historical investigation. (Available directly from The Holland House; 17142 Index Street; Granada Hills, California 91344. Price: $40.00 and worth every farthing.) This is the absolutely *perfect* gift: for your father on his birthday, for your best friend who has everything and flaunts it, for anybody you love or admire, to whom you've been wanting to say "thanks," but wanted to say it with something more remarkable than a greeting card. This is one of those artifacts you dreamed might one day come into existence, but you didn't hold out any real hope. It *is* real, at last, thanks to the love and obsession of Dave Holland; and it is, as we used to say in the days when we lay on our stomachs in front of the old Emerson, listening to the hoofbeats of the great horse, Silver...it is a *swell* book, a *nifty* book!

So be the first in your neighborhood...

39 In Which We Hum a Merry Tune While Waiting for New Horrors, New Horrors

Within a very few days of my sitting down to write this installment, as November draws toward Thanksgiving, your ever-faithful columnist will be seeing the Whitley Streiber-scripted, Philippe Mora-directed adaptation of Streiber's COMMUNION (the press release vouches that this is the "film based on the true story by Whitley Streiber" in which Mr. Streiber assures us that he was spirited away by aliens who stuck his head full of needles, for real, honest to goodness), starring Frances Sternhagen and Christopher Walken; and Rockne O'Bannon's *Fear*. (You all certainly remember Mr. O'Bannon, who wrote *Alien Nation*, on which I did rather a longish essay; and I promised that we'd take a long look at Mr. O'Bannon's virgin outing as scenarist-director. That look, in detail, nears.)

But that's within a few days, and deadline is fangfully upon me.

At the moment, like mariners becalmed in the Horse Latitudes, we have arrived at a point of no activity, and so I will take this opportunity to offer you what is commonly referred to as a "fill-in," a sort of marking time with which I can clean up some matters I think you'll find merrily enriching, intended to solve your gift-giving problems as the Channukah/Christmas season bays at your heels. Or better yet, suggestions for post-holiday wonders for which you can trade in the crap you received.

As I've noted in other installments, though this series of essays is principally concerned with motion pictures, I have taken it upon myself to extend the definition of "visual concern" to include ancillary matters that are usually beyond the scope of our resident book critics.

I can, however, suggest that you not miss Ron Shelton's new film *Blaze* (Touchstone), *A Dry White Season* (MGM-UA), *Glory* (Tri-Star), and *The Fabulous Baker Boys* (20th Century Fox) until I can get back to you with your usual fix of observations on films fantastical.

Among the 65-to-75,000 books in my home, there are a great many small press publications. Limited edition titles that were either too esoteric or too marginally profitable for the commercial houses to attempt. Over the years in fantasy and sf, the cutting edge of artistic endeavor in these (and allied) genres has been honed as often by the courageous (or obsessed) cottage industry aficionado as it has by the megalopolitan publishers. Donald M. Grant and his punctiliously loving editions of Howard's Conan stories, elegantly bound and in tray-cases. Bill Crawford of FPCI, who first published Cordwainer Smith's "Scanners Live in Vain" in *Fantasy Book* in 1950, bringing that most extraordinary talent to the attention of Fred Pohl, who reprinted the story in a mass market Permabooks anthology two years later. Had Crawford not plucked "Scanners" from a slush pile and showcased it, Pohl might not have been piqued with curiosity, might not have pierced the mystery of "Smith's" true identity, might not have solicited new work for *Galaxy*, and we certainly would not have been enriched by all the Cordwainer Smith classics that followed. Lloyd Eshbach and his fondly-remembered Fantasy Press, committed to the preservation of the best of "Doc" Smith, John Campbell, A.E. van Vogt, Jack Williamson, and so many others. Ever-youthful Lloyd, who published the very first book of symposium essays about modern sf, OF WORLDS BEYOND, and rescued from oblivion the marvelous 1919 dystopian novel THE HEADS OF CERBERUS by Francis Stevens under the short-lived Polaris Press imprint. Shasta and Gnome Press; Carcosa and Arkham House; Paul Ganley's quietly productive operation that most recently gave us a fine collection of Jessica Amanda Salmonson's stories; the breathless prolificity and stunning high quality of the Pulphouse Publishing axis; Ursus Imprints and the late Nemo Press; Kerosina and Morrigan in the U.K. (who else would bring into print so much splendid Keith Roberts material, or risk everything publishing the wonderfully loony ALLIGATOR ALLEY?); Scream/Press and Dark Harvest; Stu Schiff's Whispers Press that took the lead with horror fiction now emulated by every mainstream house; Borgo Press and Chris Drumm's booklets; the amazing Alex Berman and his ceaselessly collectible Phantasia editions; Underwood-Miller (who bring you HARLAN ELLISON'S WATCHING) and their collected Philip K. Dick set; Hadley and Mirage and Prime Press and the tiny Avalon—not the *other* Avalon—Cheap Street and

Footsteps Press...and hundreds of others that escaped my notice and the cigar box full of old memories I call a mind, for which omissions I plead exhaustion and limited space and the plethora of small operations that have come and gone through the years.

There isn't enough praise in the world to thank all these men and women: lovers of the fiction; fans in the noblest sense of that word fallen on infamous times; bibliophiles and historians; rescuers of the damned and overlooked; preservers of treasured incunabula from their teen reading; purveyors of lovely packages containing the writings of authors we would surely lose were it not for the underappreciated, possibly demented, labors of the limited edition and small press heroes.

And here, at hand, is surely the most beautiful limited edition in years...

The limited edition of Tim Powers's brilliant novel THE STRESS OF HER REGARD is the initial offering of a new small press called Charnel House, the obsession of a gentleman named Joe Stefko (who, apart from being—in the noblest way—an aficionado of the genre imaginative, is the drummer for The Turtles). The 544-page novel comes in two sumptuous Charnel House incarnations. The five hundred copy numbered edition goes for $125. There are twenty-six lettered copies, and they were produced for about $400 net. Don't try to find the latter edition, they're all gone; and if you can track a dealer who has one for sale, you'll discover s/he is asking between $600–800.

Why, then, do I commend at holiday time an item that is clearly not something you'll find in the racks at a Crown or Waldenbooks?

Because this is something to see, this Stefko-created book of books. The signed limitation sheet is made of African Maple, hand cut into veneer in Belgium. The text has been printed on seventy pound Mohawk Superfine. The endpapers are drawings by Mr. Powers, and there are a dozen vigorous Powers illustrations spaced throughout the body of the book. The numbered copies have been bound and slipcased in fourteen ounce, handstreaked denim (which was stone dyed by Mr. Stefko in his bathtub and at a local laundromat). The lettered copies have been handbound in full Morocco Oasis Niger leather.

This is a wonderful book to read, but it is also an object of bibliophilic reverence by someone who understands just how important and treasurable books can be. This isn't a gift to give to just anyone. It is for someone very very special.

And if you can obtain a copy, jump at the chance.

Try this address: Charnel House, PO Box 633, Lynbrook, New York 11563. Tell Mr. Stefko that Harlan sent you.

I'll make book that you'll thank me, the few of you who will happily sell your spouse or the family manse to snag one of these astonishingly memorable volumes.

Bruce Hamilton and Russ Cochran, the guiding intelligences behind a remarkable publishing *apparat* called Another Rainbow, have given us, over the years, definitive editions of cartoon treasures such as The Little Lulu Library, UNCLE SCROOGE IN COLOR, the Carl Barks Library (in nine exquisite volumes of Donald Duck art by "the Duck Man" of legend), and the complete EC comics series in handsome boxed sets. But now, they have outdone themselves, have bettered their best, have whipped a W!O!W! on us.

Another Rainbow has recently published the coffee table book no one can resist: MICKEY MOUSE IN COLOR. 250 giant pages (12½" x 16½") featuring eight complete, unedited daily and Sunday newspaper adventures of The Mouse by Floyd Gottfredson from the 1930s. In celebration of Mickey's 60th birthday only 3,100 copies of this special limited edition have been produced. (A smaller trade edition has been produced for Pantheon Books of New York, but only in this Brobdingnagian manifestation are the strips reproduced full-size as they appeared in daily and Sunday papers of the Thirties. And if you need further mark of the added-value attendant on the limited over the trade, Bruce and Russ point out in a prefatory note that the limited weighs in at nine pounds, the trade an anorexic two-and-a-half.)

You have never seen coruscating color of this brilliance, not even in the finest Swiss-printed art books. Quoting Bruce and Russ again: "…no expense was spared to re-create color—or to imbue art that was originally printed only in black and white with new color. Some sections of this limited edition were printed with an extra color or a 'hit' of varnish to achieve a rare effect. The black and white photos were run in duotone, to heighten contrast and to give the pictures a new dimension."

Even expecting the producers of a product to hype what they're hawking, let me assure you the foregoing is understatement.

If you are an animated movie freak, if you are a Mickey enthusiast, or if you simply understand the literary icon that The Mouse has become for the world, this is the gift (for yourself or a Significant Other) to end all gifts. But wait! There's *more*!

This most excellent edition is, apart from gorgeous just gorgeous, filled with additional marzipan and *rahat lokoum*: a bound-in parchment limitation sheet bearing the autographs of Barks—who passed away very recently—and Gottfredson, who died in 1986; an "in-depth look at 60 years of the Mouse"; an interview with Gottfredson by Disney Archivist David Smith; the text of a joint four-hour interview with the Duck Man and the Mouse Matisse; exhaustive and trivia-filled introductions and forewords; dozens of rare photos and cels; *and* (sound of sackbut, lyre, and dulcimer) bound into all copies of this deluxe edition is a 7-inch picture record, numbered to match each book, featuring a portion of the Gottfredson/Barks interview, in which they discuss their favorite stories. Which list of lagniappe only begins to summarize the special features.

The book is not, of course, cheap. It is two hundred and fifty bucks. That's $250, plus $20 postage for regular mail (from Another Rainbow/Gladstone; Box 2079; Prescott, Arizona 86302). And if you have that kind of money, worth every sou of the tariff. But here's the clinker in your snowdrift: there are less than two hundred of the numbered copies left. If what I have babbled about here lights your fire, I suggest you use the phone to order one before extinction. They take credit cards. Call (602) 776-1300 and beg for the opportunity to take out a second mortgage to obtain a copy of this extravagantly produced and absolutely whimsically wonderful publishing event.

It's your childhood dream realized.

You're going to *love* me for telling you about this one.

First, let me name-drop: Feliks Topolski, David Levine, Al Hirschfeld, Hank Hinton, Thomas Nast, Walt Kelly, Boris Artzybasheff, Ronald Searle, Pat Oliphant, Herblock, Edward Sorel. (Not to mention the deadly trio Mulatier, Rikord & Morchoisne.) If those names mean nothing to you, pass along to the next item. You are culturally deprived and the fine visual art of caricature is a vast echoing emptiness in your education.

But for those of you to whose eyes has come a twinkle at the mere mention of that pantheon, add the name Tullio Pericoli.

The book is a luscious 156-page trade paperback (61 pages in full color, bedsheet size at $9\,^7/_{16}$" x $11\,^{13}/_{16}$", selling for $24.50, from Prestel Art Books, distributed by te Neues Publishing, New York) and the title is WOODY, FREUD AND OTHERS.

It is a collection of savage, urbane, witty caricatures by a 53-year-old Italian whose interpretations of Orson Welles (a mountain with a face in its massif), Johann Sebastian Bach (two stools are required to support his fundament), Albert Einstein (freewheeling on a unicycle) and virtually every important literary figure of the past hundred years—Borges to Primo Levi, Proust to Pirandello, Baudelaire to Italo Calvino—will be fresh and fancy-filled for an American audience heretofore denied Percoli's perjinkities.

This is art of a disarmingly enjoyable fullness. It may seem slight to those who breathe heavily at the acres of rosy flesh in, say, Botticelli's *La Primavera*, but the bounty is in the afterstrike, the second-take, the lingering taste on the palate. Easy on the eyes, pretty to scan, and just as you begin to turn the page, the thorn draws blood. And you look back. Oh, sweet. But deadly. Like a Dorothy Parker *bon mot*, like an Astaire *jeté*, like an aperitif served by Lucrezia Borgia. Hemingway sitting roundshouldered and abstracted, sanguine in his reverie...as an iconographic Ch'ing period lion leaps at his back. Pier Paolo Pasolini, he who directed the sadistic, scatological, debauched *Salò, or the 120 Days of Sodom*, arguably the most depraved motion picture of all time, flesh the color of an asthmatic's piss, arms folded, staring straight at us as the blood-red rose he holds writhes with thorns. Umberto Eco, dwarfish votary, inscribing an illuminated manuscript...as a strangled cat hangs overhead.

Pericoli is not only a portraitist of the inner man (exactly: only one woman, Virginia Woolf, manages to crash Pericoli's old boy network), but he is a puckish fantasist whose denuding of these holy human artifacts seems almost wholly free of meanness. (His self-portrait casts him as Little Nemo in Slumberland.) Here is a sight-filled elegance to which the sophisticated intellect will return again and again, a first American publication of work that may one day be found somewhere between Daumier and Botero.

The passionate range of Christian art may be filled with fantastic tropes—angels, demons, resurrections and transcendancies—rich in the stuff of legend become literal; Amerindian art may inveigle with spider-women and manitou images, preserving in line and color the oral traditions of a people parted from their land; Vedantist sculpture and painting may resonate with the dark presences of Shiva, Kali, and the bodhi tree; but I challenge anyone to name an artistic aesthetic more drenched in magic than the Dreamtime of the Australian Aborigine.

What's that you say? A few fading cave paintings, a cairn of pebbles and sticks, snakes drawn in sand...how can we be expected to dine well on such thin broth?

You've been sitting down at the wrong banquet halls.

The feast you've denied yourself is to be found in a new volume from George Braziller Publishers. DREAMINGS: THE ART OF ABORIGINAL AUSTRALIA by Peter Sutton (272 pp., 150 color plates, 100 b&w, $65) is the "first comprehensive study...of the oldest continuous art tradition known."

In clear and exhaustive prose, Sutton traces The Dreaming, the itinerary of the Ancestral Beings' travels; the People Maker, the Ruling Mother, the Olgas, the Clever Man; the cagey bunyip; the visual handing-down of a society where secrecy is "not an absolute but a continuum."

Beautiful. Mysterious. But most of all, enthralling, in the sense that it takes possession of one's senses and wonderment. The Dreamtime is pervasive, enchanting in the way that road hypnosis during a thousand mile drive is enchanting: the point of perception narrows and passes through a membrane to another state entirely. All this, in the work of the Aboriginal artists.

Though I come late to it (its publication in 1985 slipped through my epistemophilial seine), a recommendation herewith: J.P. Telotte's excellent monograph on that master of cinematic suspense, Val Lewton. For all the *schlockmeisters* currently engaged in visualizing every last gobbet of gore produced by the likes of Jason Voorhees, Freddy Krueger, Michael Myers, and Norman Bates, here is yet another testimonial to the importance and artistry of subtlety and misdirection in filmic matters horrific: DREAMS OF DARKNESS: FANTASY AND THE FILMS OF VAL LEWTON (University of Illinois Press, $18.95). Lewton—legendary creative intelligence behind RKO's "horror unit" that produced B features of unparalleled excellence during the early 1940s, from the surreal chiller *Cat People* (1942) to *Bedlam* (1946)—demonstrated how films that shock and terrify can be crafted without insulting the intelligence of the audience, without recourse to the bloated special effects and cheap theatrics so totemized by today's artistically dessicated filmmakers. And though considerably drier than, say, the 1973 Joel Siegel study of Lewton, THE REALITY OF TERROR, which was distinguished by Siegel's actually hunting down primary sources and ferreting through the defunct RKO files for fascinating new minutiae, Telotte's academic approach dignifies the Lewton career in such manner that even the most lumpbrained slasher-horror devotee with confused or no criteria will derive desperately needed lessons in alternatives to the dripping blade, the kitten leaping out of darkness, the pulsing viscera.

Another tardy recommendation, nonetheless eminently giftable (did I make that up? is it grammatically loopy?) for my coming to it months after it has won major awards, is the Ursus Imprints edition of FIRST MAITZ: SELECTED WORKS BY DON MAITZ. You likely won't be able to find one of the 224-copy slipcased, signed collector's editions originally proffered at $45, but there are still lots of copies of the $25 trade edition. The printing is lip-smackingly luminescent, the design is clean and crisp, the running commentary by Maitz and the introduction by Gene Wolfe informative and easy on the idiomatics, but it is the scope and sheer *magic* of Don Maitz's artwork, inevitably, that makes this a book to cherish. I am not the first to say it: he is special.

Maitz has been around a relatively short time, little more than sixteen years as an illustrator as I write this. But while others have dominated the genre with their sweaty deltoids and flawless, soulless airbrush vacuities, Maitz has been quietly going about his business updating the Orientalists, painting in a way that is as far beyond his contemporaries as Michelangelo was beyond his. And if you think I invoke the master's name inappropriately—if there is a reservation where Maitz is concerned, it is only this: too often the material he is required to illustrate is beneath his highest abilities—all one need do is gaze with clear eyes on his oils, "The Road to Corlay" or "Flashman in the Great Game," as perfect a contemporary rendering of the lessons the Fauvists taught us as anything I can bring to mind.

Only sixteen years. Breathlessly, one contemplates what the next decade will permit Maitz to honor us with.

We live in days of movies and television. We are watching. Too often we forget that we were given eyesight so that we might use what men and women put on canvas to make our own stories. This, too, is watching. The dreams on the page are always there, unlike screen images. This has been a series of reminders, till the screen lights again. Keep watching.

40 In Which We Scrutinize the Sedulousness to Their Hippocratic Oath of Troglodytic, Blue, Alien Proctologists

My wife assures me she will leave me if I don't trash this movie.

Never has my marriage been on firmer ground. The film at hand is *Communion* (New Line Cinema), with a screenplay by the bestselling author Whitley Strieber, based on his bestselling book of the same title. Produced by the bestselling author Whitley Strieber in conjunction with Dan Allingham and the director, Philippe Mora, *Communion* stars three of my favorite thesps, Christopher Walken (portraying the bestselling author Whitley Strieber), Lindsay Crouse, and Frances Sternhagen.

You will notice I referred to the tome COMMUNION as "the bestselling book" and not as "the bestselling novel" or "the bestselling non-fiction work." To have employed the former categorization would have been to risk inflaming a substantial portion of the readership of COMMUNION, who have bought more than 2,300,000 copies of Mr. Strieber's book and who believe it is gospel, every word absolutely true, the real thing, and in no way a work of fiction. To have assigned to COMMUNION the latter designation would have been to incur the wrath of the uncounted *other* millions who have, or have not, read Mr. Strieber's literary offerings, who are convinced that the bestselling Mr. Strieber is, if not certifiably bugfuck, at minimum one of the most accomplished liars who ever stuck it to, and rotated it, and broke it off inside, the American Publishing Industry.

Because I am the product of sweet reason, a man steeped in fairness and even-handedness, I choose to sidestep the issue. I will refer to Mr. Strieber's bestselling book as "book" and leave the pamphleteering to the more passionate.

But before we get to the subtext of the issue at hand, let me render for you a detailed synopsis of this fillum. (And to those who justifiably decry the brutish practice of "spilling the beans" of a film's plot—a nasty bit of business practiced by far too many reviewers, a practice I have eschewed to the point where critics of WATCHING have accused me of "being vague about storyline"—let me assure you I'm not drifting into bad habits. At least not *this* bad habit. There is no great mystery revealed at the denouement of *Communion*; no shock surprise; no revelation that the serial killer is, indeed, Jeff Bridges come to murder Glenn Close; no ironic twist that shows Charlton Heston on his knees weeping at the ruined icon of the Statue of Liberty. If there is any mystery about *Communion* I submit it is how the film managed to get even the few laudatory comments it did.) So here's the story, front to back, *in toto*.

It is just before Halloween, 1985. Bestselling author Whitley Strieber is in the advanced stages of writer's block. To take his mind off his problem, he and his wife, Anne (Lindsay Crouse), and their seven-year-old, Andrew (Joel Carson), spend a weekend absenting themselves from the hurly-burly of Manhattan at Strieber's mountain cabin. Neither in the book nor in the movie are we told exactly where this situs of forthcoming bizarre events exists. In the book Mr. Strieber is careful to avoid disclosing this bit of information. We are told only that the cabin is in "a secluded corner of upstate New York."

The Striebers have asked a pair of close friends to share the bucolic weekend. But in the night, there are these...well, how to describe them...the studio pr handout refers to them as "nocturnal disturbances"...George Carlin would call it "weird shit"...the wind blows, the branches scrape the roof, mercury-vapor light blasts through windows, a roaring can be heard...it's all very vague and open to interpretation, all this hugger-mugger; but whatever it is, it is (in the words of the studio synopsis):

> "...so frightening that another couple, invited as guests, demand to leave early. While Whitley has no clear memory of what happened that October night, the unspoken fear turns this loving, vulnerable man into a sullen, hypersensitive shadow of his former self."

As far as I could tell, this loving, vulnerable man only became further surfeited with facial and conversational tics, as interpreted by Mr. Walken. I missed the sullen, hypersensitive shadow part. He just seemed to act a little weirder than he had from the outset. But I digress. Or perhaps I don't. Who knows? It's all in the interpretation, as who among us is not.

Anyhow, bestselling Whitley keeps getting more and more bizarro.

Loving and vulnerable becomes progressively more sullen and shadowedly hypersensitive until, during a trick-or-treat outing in their condo, he mistakes a little girl in costume for...well, it's all very vague and open to interpretation as to *what* he thinks she is. But he gets seriously uncool and gibbers at her quite a bit, screaming and hopping about, and otherwise letting us know that this loving, vulnerable man has begun to perceive a worm of psychosis in his psychic apple.

But undaunted by the disturbing turns his previously loving and vulnerable personality has taken (the technical, psychiatric terra professionals use is *freaky*), Whitley and his wife and son return to that "secluded corner of upstate New York" for the Christmas holiday. Not a smart move.

(Have you ever noticed that one of the staples of predictable cliché horror stories is that people we are asked to believe are sane and rational *always* rush back to the scene of some unspeakable nightmare? They can't wait to plunge headfirst into that abyss, lose their shoes dashing back into the Amityville house, ignore all warnings not to re-enter the poltergeist-ridden nursery, knock each other down getting back to the graveyard. I don't know about you, but I suggest that this trope be retired. Either that, or make it clear that these are protagonists who operate with diminished mental capacity.)

Anyhow, as expected, Whitley has another run-in with the ambiguously presented "nocturnal disturbances" on the night after Christmas. Had this taken place in England, it would have been Boxing Day. But I digress. Or perhaps I don't. (One does tend to feel cast adrift as the film progresses. We are left to our own devices to ascertain precisely what's going on. And you know how dangerous it can be to leave us to our own devices.)

Whitley begins either to a) have a series of bad dreams about alien visitors or b) is actually being beset by alien visitors. Or c) is acting-out the plot of his next book.

These extraterrestrials come in several shapes. The first are variants on the vaseline-smeared-lens vision of non-humans from *Close Encounters of the Third Kind.* You know: triangular heads, faintly metallic looking, slitty little eyes; the sort of kindergarten drawings baby tots make when they wanna show you the oogy-boogy monster. Then there are these gnomelike, blue trogs in monk's habits, who scuttle about like Munchkins on a break from Oz, trying to find the Cub Room at the MGM commissary. And I vaguely remember a third species, something hairy and bearlike, but I could be wrong. It was all so vague and open to personal interpretation, and let us not forget our own devices, still on the loose and confusing us. But it's the asexual slitty-eyed aliens, with their masklike faces, and the blue troglodytes who dominate Whitley's descent into paradoxical behavior. The mask aliens seem to be the big bosses and the Billy Barty-sized blue friars seem to work for them in a medical/technical capacity.

So Whitley bounces off the walls in the cabin, getting progressively more unhinged, until he caps his encounter by almost blowing away wife Anne with a shotgun. Understandably, this causes pique in Anne, and she tells bestselling hubby that he is putting a strain on their marriage by almost wasting her, by frightening neighbors, by alarming their son, and in general acting like a horror novelist who has been unable to write.

Incidentally...though most writers won't tip to this, what Whitley was undergoing is very much commonplace for us writers. As my wife said to me, the last time I leveled a Winchester 101 over/under 12-gauge at her, "I take it very much amiss that just because you're late with your script you have unleashed both barrels of that surrogate penis and reduced every item of clothing in my closet to rags fit only for dusting your many awards. Aim that thing elsewhere, Ellison, or I will feed it to you by way of an aperture that will avoid entirely your digestive tract." So I had no trouble identifying with Whitley's behavior in this part of the movie.

Nonetheless, Anne makes it clear to Whitley that he had best hie himself at once to a cranium cleaner who can give him a better handle on these "bizarre visions."

Whitley is shunted from his personal doctor to a psychiatrist (Frances Sternhagen, in a role so brief that one wonders why an actress of her great gifts bothered to get involved in such a project), to whom he imparts all his worst fears. Basically, what Whitley tells her is that these alien visitors have had their way with him, kidnapping him, taking him to their ship, and subjecting him to a medical examination that included sticking long, nasty needles into his brain, and giving him an anal probing with a device as thick around as a rhinoceros horn, a rectal rimjob that is to a sigmoidoscopy as the architecture of a Taco Bell is to one of Gaudi's towers.

And like the real-life bestselling Whitley, the cinematic Whitley keeps acting bewildered as to the *reality* of what's going on. He has managed to perfect the fine art of both eating and having his cake. He keeps saying, "Maybe I'm psychotic, maybe it's all a dream, maybe I'm going crazy," (to which most of us would answer, "That'd be my guess") but everyone keeps acting as if what he's gibbering about *might* be true—how can one sensibly cast doubt on a horror novelist's assertions that he's been *tuchis*-terrorized by pint-sized blue alien proctologists dressed for a roadshow revival of *St. Francis of Assisi*—and the shrink decides to put Whitley under hypnosis in order to break through his amnesia. (But I don't recall that anyone ever did an actual real-world anal examination to discover if Whitley's ass looked like ten miles of corduroy road, which would certainly have been the case if someone had shoved a length of stovepipe up there. But, perhaps I digress.)

Under the utterly scientific methods of this latter-day Franz Anton Mesmer, Whitley relives the ghastly encounter with the two (or possibly three) types of e.t.s, and remembers every icky moment of this unscheduled medical exam. The shrink sends him off to an encounter group for further "stabilizing" and he discovers that everyone in the cute little circle has had a similar encounter with marauding aliens. One gets the impression that these far voyagers are more common than the homeless, who also inconvenience us in our daily lives.

Those familiar with the common coin of UFOlogy will no doubt recall a 1975 made-for-tv epic titled *The UFO Incident* starring James Earl Jones and Estelle Parsons and Barnard Hughes, based on the "real-life experiences" of a New England couple named Barney and Betty Somethingorother, who went through exactly the same extragalactically-inspired *mishigoss* as Whitley reports, up to and including the amnesia, the unsettled behavior, the recourse to a shrink, the hypnosis, the total recall of alien invasions of privacy. This is either proof unarguable that we are little more than a 'burb for vacationing alien physicians who, presumably, don't spend their Wednesday afternoons golfing on Venus, or that Bill Shakespeare was correct when he told me last week that there are really only seventeen basic plots.

Moving right along. Whitley flees the encounter group with the certain conviction that these people are all bonkers, and that he didn't really get cornholed by Ben Caseys From Space, and that there must be some *other* explanation. "Then," as the studio synopsis tells us, "he discovers that Andrew has been having similar experiences, and he reaches a level of desperation that is literally beyond fear." Literally beyond fear is, I believe, about thirty miles this side of Cincinnati. And cleanliness is right next door to godliness, and godliness is next door to Woolworth's. But perhaps I digress.

So, for reasons not made terribly clear, Whitley decides to rush back into the Amityville house, er, that is, he goes back to that "secluded corner of upstate New York," to face himself...or the visitors. (Quoting again from the studio handout, for the existence of which I am eternally grateful, what with all the vagueness, ambiguity, and those goddam devises still running around loose.)

Up at the cabin Whitley has yet another encounter with the aliens; and in their inscrutable fashion they prove to him—and by extension to us—that they are real, that Whitley isn't just another guy two pickles and a sandwich shy of a picnic. "Reaching deep levels of inner strength" the studio synopsis tells us "he comes to an acceptance of them as an enigma and an unknown presence of great power in the world."

He goes home, now understanding that his cosmic mission is to write this bestselling book about his adventures, and late at night he sits down at the PC to begin work, having apparently broken through his block, but before he can write FADE IN, er, Chapter One, he sees a glow outside his apartment window. And as would be the first inclination by any one of us, he knows this is the visitors come again; and he and the wife and kid rush up onto the roof overlooking Manhattan, and (maybe, possibly) we see one of those masklike triangular faces in the stars. Or maybe we don't. At the screening I attended, a few people saw it, most didn't. Either way, there ain't no actual extraterrestrials up there on the roof. A lot of ductwork, some pigeon coops, a few pieces of lawn furniture, but no omnipotent e.t.s. Another big disappointment. Drat!

So Whitley rushes back down to the apartment and begins to write his bestseller. As he writes, the triangular mask face of an alien countenance drifts toward him. Christopher Walken looks up and, in the voice of a writer fresh from years of having been blocked, asks the visitor, "What do I call a book about you?" or words to that effect. I can't recall exactly. Kind of vague.

Fade out.

Now, as evenhandedly as I can put it, here is the subtext. Larry King has Whitley Strieber on his talk show more than once, and he speaks to him about the events I've just related as if he were talking to William Bennett about the war on drugs or to Christopher Walken about his latest movie role. Not once does anyone suggest that the bestselling, loving, vulnerable Mr. Strieber has winsomely stumbled on a sure-fire way to sell paralogia while showing us that his hands are clean. It could all be delusion, he keeps saying, while rendering the delusions concrete by means of motion picture.

Since we believe what we see on the screen, particularly when we're told it's "based on real events," Strieber has it both ways, and he is able to maintain a façade of calm reason in the face of a tall tale no one in his right mind would buy without hard evidence.

The film came and went in moments. Blessedly. But I've run into people who believe every frame of it, believe Strieber's books convey truth impeccably, and who—incidentally—

also swear their ex-spouse is having an affair with the Easter Bunny, that Elvis is working in an AM/PM Mini-Mart in Pascagoula, that Madonna can act, and that the U.S. Air Force has been keeping a crashed flying saucer under wraps since 1947. (Mr. Strieber's latest book, by the way, also deals with this dread secret.)

As regards showing us the ludicrous aliens in this film, I am put in mind of two quotations that should always remain uppermost in the minds of those making scary movies. The first, from Mallarmé: "To define is to kill. To suggest is to create." The second, from the late architect Robert Smithson: "Establish enigmas. Not explanations."

Unfortunately, these urgings do not apply to logical plotting or productive attempts to rid the human race of obscurantism and uneducated conclusions about the physical universe.

But perhaps I digress.

Only this as final, personal note: as one who recently underwent surgery for a horrendous case of strangulated, thrombosed hemorrhoids—an occupational hazard of writers common as threatening your wife with a shotgun—I can only tell you that the possibly homoerotic scenes of Mr. Strieber's thespic stand-in, Mr. Walken, getting his backside reamed by something the circumference of a Roto-Rooter hose and the salutary appearance of a jackhammer made me, how shall I put it, uncomfortable.

41 In Which an Extremely Nervous Fool with His Credentials Taped to His Forehead Tacks Trepidatiously between Scylla and Charybdis Knowing That Angels and Wise Men Would Fear Even to Dog-Paddle This Route

I am told there is an adage common among members of the 283rd United States Army Band that goes like this: "If you're going to make a mistake…blow loud."

Which is to say, with eyes wide and alert for Bouncing Betty mines, I am fearfully certain there ain't no way in this life that I'm going to pass through a review of *The Handmaid's Tale* (Cinecom) unscathed. No matter how sanely and sedulously I comment on this film adapted from Margaret Atwood's 1985 (in America, 1986) feminist/political #1 bestselling mainstream-sf novel, out there in Readerland lie in wait a slavering sortie of semiotic skirmishers, disingenuous bastards and crazy bitches, who will perforate me with esoteric and syntactically convoluted complaints about the political incorrectness of my shallow, revisionist, hopelessly sexist observations.

Knowing this, the best I can do is blow loud.

I begin by stating that I rather enjoyed this film. It is a motion picture I will not soon forget. Of the women to whom I've spoken about *The Handmaid's Tale*, most have had serious reservations. They tell me first that they hated it; and when they see my raised eyebrows they quickly amend the judgment to say they didn't actually *hate* it, but they didn't like it. And before I've been able to ask why, they back&fill again, and tell me that they don't really know if they *dislike* it, but they know they don't *like* it. And then they say perhaps it's the *subject matter* they don't like, but they approve of what the movie *says*. And then they sorta bite their lips and confess to being befuddled in some unarticulated way by this clearly serious-minded and important cinematic document.

Well, they're not alone out there on the ice floe.

The Handmaid's Tale comes bearing such a tonnage of subtext, sexual and sociological and religious and political energy, primary source impeccability, and heavyweight creative intellects…that it would give pause even to Hélène Cixous ("The Laugh of the Medusa"), Donna Harroway ("A Manifesto for Cyborgs"), Julia Kristeva, Luce Irigaray (THIS SEX WHICH IS NOT ONE), or Toril Moi (SEXUAL/TEXTUAL POLITICS: FEMINIST LITERARY THEORY). Imagine with what tremors a poor dork like me, surfeited with White Male Guilt, comes to the conversation. Just imagine.

In the climate that currently exists…

What climate, you ask? You want a context digression even before I talk about the film? Hey, I'm here to serve.

Then let me attempt a weather report using anecdotal materials that sum up the way the winds are blowing.

A highly regarded academic, a friend of mine, at a major American university (who begs me not to use his name for fear of reprisal), told me the following story:

He was one of five full professors in attendance at a "prospectus meeting," a procedure through which graduate students in English are put by the department, preparatory to the writing of their doctoral dissertations. Something like a blueprint session where the thrust and tone of the thesis is approved. The other four academics were women, strongly grounded in Feminist Theory. One of the grad students was seeking to do her paper on Feminist Utopias. Much of her source material came from science fiction stories.

My friend told me he had a chilling moment of Feminist/Masculinist epiphany when one of the professors idly, casually, offhandedly corrected the doctoral candidate by pointing out that in all of the fictional examples she intended to cite, men still formed a part of each society. "Of course," the Professor said, "in any *truly* Feminist Utopia, all of the men would have been exterminated."

That was anecdote the first. Just to get the wind up.

Before anecdote the second, permit me a moment of personal privilege.

I am fifty-five years old. By the time you read this in May, I'll be fifty-six. Rapid computation divulges the stat 1934 as my birthdate. That means I was born into, passed through, reached puberty, grew to manhood, and came to this sad pretense of intellectual maturity in decades of paternalistic, machismo-drenched, sexist attitudes. Though I was never a brutalizer of women (as a registered misanthrope I believe in savaging male and female alike with equal vigor), never a subverter of the feminist imperative, I was nonetheless and inescapably a child of my various times, and was as blissfully steeped in male chauvinist behavior as the best and brightest, not to mention the worst and brutish. No excuse, just explanation. Somewhere along about mid-Summer 1969—through the eloquent mechanism of Mary Reinholz kneeling on my chest and banging my head against the floor—I was brought to an alarming awareness of my inadequacies in re: the way I thought about, and treated, women. I won't say it was precisely an epiphany; more like a week-long headache that brought the imparted information to mind throbbingly, every time I drew a breath.

But I have always been a quick study; and it began to show in what I wrote, and how I altered my relations with women *and* men; and by 1973 when the National Organization for Women called for a boycott on those states that had not ratified the Equal Rights Amendment I made it a policy not to visit, and to refuse speaking engagements in, non-ratified states. (Except, of course, for lectures in defense of the ERA done at the request of, and in conjunction with, NOW.) In those days my speaking fee was close to five grand a night. *Many* such gigs were given a pass. To the extent that when I found myself inextricably committed to being Guest of Honor at the 1978 Worldcon in Phoenix, I performed my duties by traveling to Arizona in a specially leased Winnebago, bought no gas, no food, no nothing inside the state, and in 110° heat lived out of that damned camper. (For purists who may not remember the foofaraw this little caper caused, I didn't even put money in the three parking meters picketed at the curb outside the convention hotel where we beached the great whale. The vice-mayor of Phoenix—a woman—had the meters hooded as a gesture of support.) The NOW boycott of non-ratified states was honored until 24 June 1982 when the ERA went down to defeat.

And during those years I spent an actual 1,100 hours on the speaking platform urging adoption of the ERA. Eleven hundred hours actually *speaking*, which does not take into account the many thousands *more* hours spent in travel to those benighted venues, the hours flying home, the hours waiting in motels till it was time for the gig, the hours spent at greasy-spoon meals with members of the local NOW chapter planning press conference strategy, the hours spent doing call-in radio shows in receptive places like Salt Lake City, Shreveport, Greensboro, Tallahassee.

The point of waving these credentials: I have never been politically correct. I did whatever I did, because it made me feel good to do it. I did whatever I did because it was the correct behavior for me. But as a certified loose cannon, I was never knee-jerk about the Feminist Movement, which I consider one of the most pivotally important social awakenings of the century. I gave no longer shrift to idiotic females than I did to imbecile males. One does not judge a social movement by its worst, but rather, by its finest.

I did, and continue to do, the best I can with a consciousness raised by patient women of my acquaintance. That is to say, Ursula Le Guin doesn't seem more than mildly embarrassed to be in my company. And though I suspect Vonda McIntyre and Joanna Russ and Suzy McKee Charnas cluck their tongues about me in private, smiling sadly and saying, "Poor Harlan, he's such a schmuck…he tries so hard, the poor thing…but at least he's not Jesse Helms or Orrin Hatch," I think they think of me as trying valiantly to be on the side of the angels. Which is not to suggest that Alan Alda has to worry about me taking away the championship belt.

Nonetheless, I am a fifty-six-year-old American male, and sometimes I don't get it exactly right. Which brings us to anecdote the second.

Early in February of this year, I had occasion to write some laudatory words about Joanna Russ. In an essay I'd done for another couple of magazines in this genre. And I said this:

"If there has been a woman writer more passionate and outspoken about what concerns her in art and in society, who has been more forthcoming about putting those concerns in her work, I don't know who it might be." I thought that was okay.

One thing and another, and I sent that very long essay to both Vonda and Joanna, because I'd promised to send it five years earlier. And Vonda wrote me about the piece, and in the course of her letter she said, "Sweetie, I noticed a couple of minor typos…" and she corrected my spelling and went on, "The other is the bottom right-hand corner of page 8, which says, 'If there has been a woman writer more passionate…' It's clear from name, context, and the following pronoun that Joanna is a woman. 'Woman writer' is way too often used in the 'dog walking on its hind legs' sense. 'Woman lawyer.' 'Woman doctor.' 'Poetess.' Something that's sort of a writer, but not really, not quite. Sorry. It really is one of my fingernail-on-blackboard peeves. …Love to you and Susan."

I scratched my head. I've known Vonda forever, and value her not only as steadfast friend, but as a clear thinker. But I had *purposely* used that phrase to make the distinction between passionate and outspoken *male* writers, and their opposite female numbers. Why was this derogatory? So I called Vonda.

And I explained my calculated, purposeful reasoning in saying "woman writer."

Vonda tried to explain the subtext in more specific ways, but though I strained my pea-size brain, I still couldn't parse the subtle distinction. I wasn't *against* dropping the word "woman," but it seemed less specific if the word were deleted. I told Vonda I'd run it past Joanna, and since it was *about* Joanna, would abide by her choice. I was sure Joanna would say it didn't matter, or somesuch.

Well, Joanna agreed that Vonda had made a good call, and said if I could live with it, she'd prefer my excising "woman."

Should you encounter that essay—it's titled "Xenogenesis"—you will see that I dropped the word. Not merely because I wasn't nailed to it, and certainly not because I was worried about being politically correct, but because Vonda and Joanna are my friends and if they, in their more focused perceptions, were bothered by it...then t'hell with it. One does not trouble one's friends if they make it clear it gives them a twinge.

But I had my consciousness raised another increment with the knowledge that the current climate is such that you cannot win. That no matter how sturdy may be your credentials, they're yesterday's news and things have changed again when you weren't watching. That if you subscribe to the position of one or another Feminist Theorist, you will invoke the wrath of half a dozen others who read the portents differently.

That is to say, no matter how properly I analyze *The Handmaid's Tale*, whether as simply a movie, or as complexly as a social document, I ain't getting out of this jungle without getting my lumps.

And I suspect that will be the problem for *anyone*, male or female, who passes judgment on the film. *Variety*, for instance, gave it a mostly positive appraisal, but thought it was too pompous. High-minded might be a better term.

You see, *The Handmaid's Tale* is a fine film, a serious film, a demanding film, and an engrossing film; even an entertaining film. But it ain't nowhichway a loveable film.

It runs one hour and forty-nine minutes, and you probably won't sneak peeks at your wristwatch, but you *will* feel its boot on your neck. That happens with polemic.

It occurs to me, this far into the essay, that I haven't struck your awe with the roster of talents on their very best behavior in this $13,000,000 attempt to bring the Feminist Dialectic to Kansas, Louisiana, Orem, and Orange County. The film stars Robert Duvall in a deeply affecting performance as the Commander; Faye Dunaway as his ex-tv-evangelist wife Serena Joy, chillingly barren, emotionally as well as sexually; Natasha Richardson as Kate, the handmaid, far more memorable here than in her previous outing as Patty Hearst; Aidan Quinn as the Commander's chauffeur, Nick; and Elizabeth McGovern absolutely riveting, scene-stealingly so, as Moira, the lesbian who befriends Kate and winds up as a party girl for Gilead's corrupt, hypocritical top-level officials. The screenplay was directed cleanly and without tricks, if a trifle Teutonically, by Volker Schlöndorff, who brought Günther Grass's THE TIN DRUM to the screen in 1979 and won both a Cannes best film award and an Oscar for that disturbing allegory.

(It is, I think, no coincidence that *The Handmaid's Tale* similarly calls forth the adjective "disturbing," likewise the adjective "distressful." Schlöndorff is a visionary, and his selection of projects indicates a serious talent determined not to fritter itself. Following *The Tin Drum* he directed *The Lost Honor of Katharina Blum* from Heinrich Böll's novel, co-scripting with his wife, the actress/filmmaker Margarethe von Trotta in 1975; *Coup de Grace* in 1976, based on Marguerite Yourcenar's complex novel; the, well, *distressful* [if flawed] *Circle of Deceit*, filmed entirely in war-ravaged Beirut; and in 1983, *Swann in Love* starring Jeremy Irons and based on episodes from Proust's REMEMBRANCE OF THINGS PAST. It is often overlooked in the din of historiography attendant on Schlöndorff's status as one of the members of the Junger Deutscher Film movement that catapulted to fame Werner Herzog, Rainer Werner Fassbinder, and Wim Wenders, among others, that prior to 1965, Schlöndorff worked with Louis Malle, the magnificent Alain Resnais—he was assistant director on *Last Year at Marienbad*—and Jean-Pierre Melville. Even his first film, in 1966, *Young Torless*, shared the International Critics Prize at Cannes. Perhaps you saw the film he directed for cable of Arthur Miller's *Death of a Salesman* in 1985, starring Dustin Hoffman, Kate Reid, Charles Durning, and John Malkovich. This is a major, world-class director with his eye cocked to posterity; not at all the sort of man one would approach to helm, say, *Police Academy 12.5: Mooks on Motorcycles*.) It is his first American feature film.

The screenplay was adapted from Atwood's novel (and she aptly refers to him as "magnificent") by no less than Harold Pinter.

Want to talk about credentials? Want to talk about tonnage of creative intellects validating seriousness of purpose? This is the most high-falutin' gathering of quickdraw pistoleros since the disastrous 1981 remake of James M. Cain's *The Postman Always Rings Twice* assembled David Mamet, Bob Rafelson, Jack Nicholson, Jessica Lange, and John Colicos for a cinematic catastrophe paralleled in history only by the extinction of the saurians, the eruption of Miyi-Yama in 1793, and the decimation of the Amazon rain forests.

I am happy to report that *The Handmaid's Tale*, for all its gravity, is anything but a disaster. It is a coin that adheres to the Gold Standard, as opposed to the half-tin, half-cardboard slug most often tendered by the American cinema.

Set in the near-future, it postulates a United States *roman à clef* called Gilead that has succumbed to right-wing, racist religious Fundamentalism, to a decline in the Caucasian birthrate, and to a rise in infertility due to chemical pollution and radiation. It is a world based firmly, insanely, and specifically on Genesis 30:1–13—the story of Jacob, in which the patriarch must inseminate his wives' handmaids to produce heirs. This is the handmaid's tale; the fate that befalls Kate (generically renamed Offred) when her aborted attempt to flee Gilead across the Canadian border results in the slaughter of her husband and the loss of her daughter; the progression of events that takes her from the training center where fertile women are bullied, beaten, and brainwashed into their roles as brood mares for the ruling male *apparat* whose wives can no longer deliver.

Margaret Atwood continues to contend that this is not science fiction. "Despite its futuristic setting..." she has written, "it is not science fiction, if by that you mean Martians, teleportation, or life on Venus. Nor is it a travelogue of the future. It's the story of one woman under this regime...firmly based on human nature and fact."

This of course is the standard party line of all parvenus who come to the genre for their source-material, unashamedly anxious to pilfer the coffers, but unwilling to accept the label. I can understand that. I've been trying to get people to understand that I'm not a "science fiction writer" for twenty-five years. Wearing that badge of infamy means career suicide, ghettoization, dismissal by "serious" critics, and lowered literary expectations. But that's another story of gored oxen, for another time.

The point being, it's a science fiction movie, no matter how much corrective orthopedic surgery you employ to get rid of the webbed feet. And if there is a stick-up-the-ass Late George Apley *serioso* rectitude that suffuses the movie, it comes straight down the pike from Ms. Atwood.

Yet I urge you to resist the negative aura you will certainly encounter in reviews by men and women as intimidated by the underlying dialectic as I am. It is a fascinating film. It just ain't loveable. If you need Bette Midler as Stella Dallas, or Stallone as Rocky, then you'll fidget for an hour and forty-nine minutes. But if you are one of those individuals as rare in this world as intelligible heavy metal lyrics or compassion in a splatterpunk novel, one of those individuals who continues to seek out motion pictures that convey *ideas*, no matter how distressful, then I push at you firmly to seek out *The Handmaid's Tale*.

As for getting the Feminist Theory subtext right in this analysis, let me take the craven's way out by advising you that I watched and now choose to view this movie as being more about the tenebrous threat of right-wing Fundamentalist power in America today than I do about Marxist Feminist Semiotic Autopsy.

This may be the only review you'll encounter taking that position; and if so, it can be chalked up to the fact that in very short order as the film progressed, I came to care about Kate and Moira and even the Commander a little. It was that Faulknerian imperative I've quoted so often to you, that the only things worth writing about, worth the agony and sweat, are "the problems of the human heart in conflict with itself which alone make good writing…"

And if I can't counterbalance your reluctance to go see a movie that is *about something serious* with the GeraldOprah titillation that there is a message here for every obedient, quilting, dependant wife and every blockheaded keep-'em-barefoot-and-pregnant husband, then let me do it in traditional *National Enquirer* style by telling you that this film contains a sex scene or two that will make your flesh crawl and your eyeballs go strobismic. As I said earlier, I'm only here to serve.

Readers of this column have, in recent months, responded to my advisements of off-beat books of visual interest with all the uniformity of opinion to be found among the Saturday morning crowds at an abortion clinic. The level of passion in these letters is, likewise, reasonable and charitable.

That is to say, several of you have made me out to be some sort of Renaissance Man for demonstrating a scope of interest in that which is visually exciting beyond cinema; several others have, well, blown their tops at my "wasting space" recommending books on Aboriginal art, The Lone Ranger, high-ticket limited editions, Mickey Mouse, and other ancillary subjects. Both camps have got me wrong. The concept is *watching*. In my arrogance I persist in believing that too often those who dote on sf/fantasy neglect the non-cinematic treasures that will inform a more sophisticated, more sedulous set of criteria for what is given to us on the silver screen.

Apart from merely recommending or denouncing films, these little outings will (I hope) continue to serve to broaden the cultural view. And that's why I take a few paragraphs to bring to your attention, for instance, something as seemingly far afield as the new Abbeville Press volume THE ECCENTRIC TEAPOT by Garth Clark (120 pp., 119 illustrations in color, $29.95).

Teapots? Has he taken total leave of his senses? What possible connection can there be between *teapots*, fer pete's sake, and movies? Imagine my pleasure at your asking!

When the final shot of a film fades to black, and the credits begin to roll, and you get up and put on your coat, thereby blocking the screen for everyone in the rows behind you, what you fail to notice are the names of men and women designated Production Designer, Art Director, Set Decorator, Property Master, and Props. As you shove your way to the aisle, turn your back on those rolling credits, and trudge up the ramp toward a waiting pizza or the bailout of your children from the sitter, you are leaving behind recognition of the guy who searched through a hundred jumble shoppes, flea markets, and rural antique boutiques to find that bubinga wood walking stick with the carved ivory wolverine head the mad scientist used to club to death his hunchbacked assistant; the woman who located the 1923 model L.C. Smith office standard typewriter with the broken "k" that provided the clue to the trail of who wrote the ransom note; the set decorator who called Paris for an overnight express shipment of that rare Susse *fréres* patinated bronze lamp with the etched blue glass globe in which the desperate diabolist trapped the demon.

Every fork, easy chair, art deco sconce, and orange juice squeezer in a movie was consciously selected by an unsung intelligence to meld with the overall ambience of a scene, an era, a social milieu…to win your trust.

Historical accuracy keeps you in a state of willing suspension of disbelief. Let a child in 1945 pick up an issue of *Spider-Man* from 1972, and suddenly your eye begins to look for inaccuracies. Selecting the proper comic book for that scene is as important in its way as having put the kid in corduroy knickers with a Kellogg's Pep comic character button on his t-shirt.

Films that work have a sense of place and time.

Books that inform our breadth of knowledge by forcing us to look at the ordinary in an extraordinary way, by gathering samples of that which we take for granted and giving them meaning by their accretion, are books that serve us invaluably as reversicons, those back-formation dictionaries that list definitions as entries.

THE ECCENTRIC TEAPOT is such a one.

Tracing the development of that most mundane of table items from the Ming dynasty through Wedgwood's 18th century creamware (one example of which predates, with its motif emulating the fossil shapes in limestone strata, a plethora of contemporary sculptors trumpeted as "innovative") to the rambunctious American George Ohr's early 20th century "clay babies" right up to Anthony Bennett's *Dinosaurs Pointing* (1981) forces us to readjust not only our perceptions of everyday utensils, but to expand our definition of what is "Art."

(Consider the pair of Bennett teapots in the color plate on page 68: *faux*-humanoid ornithopods, something like pudgy caricatures of Stegoceras, their boneheads sporting graceful crests; they are reared up on hind legs, their five-fingered hands clutching outstanding penile members that form the spouts. Now, if *that* doesn't provide tabletalk at teatime, you're doing Earl Grey and bikkies with the wrong crowd!)

THE ECCENTRIC TEAPOT is a work of fantasy of the highest order. Not merely because the subjects chosen to be rendered as teapots are wild and phantasmagorical, but because it shows us that extrapolation is a universal game played more adroitly by some few, much more freely than by most.

And as surely as a fascination with Egyptian cartouches leads the inquiring eye and questioning mind to Aztec and Inca iconography, so does THE ECCENTRIC TEAPOT lure us to a second Abbeville Press title, THE MAD POTTER OF BILOXI: THE ART & LIFE OF GEORGE E. OHR, whose name I dropped a mere three paragraphs ago.[2]

I cannot recommend this astonishing retrospective strongly enough. If we accept as more urgently true for the genre of fantastic literature than for any other, this admonishment by Ambrose Bierce in THE DEVIL'S DICTIONARY (1906)—"...the first three essentials of the literary art are imagination, imagination, and imagination"—then no reader or writer of this form can afford to be ignorant of the work of the man who published this advertisement for himself in 1901:

<blockquote>
REV. GEORGE E. OHR
begs to introduce himself
to the Philistines as
POTTER TO THE PUSH
also

Originator of the Bug-House Renaissance in Life, Letters and Art. Mr. Ohr, like Setebos, makes things out of Mud—and never duplicates. Correspondence solicited. Address, BILOXI, MISS.
</blockquote>

---

[2](By Garth Clark, Robert A. Ellison, Jr.—no relation—and Eugene Hecht; photography by John White; 192 pp.; 140 photos in color; $65.00.)

☞ P.S. Mr. Ohr wishes to explain that the prefix Rev. to his name does not signify that he is a preacher. It only means that he is worthy of Reverence, because he does his work as well as he can, and Minds his own Business.

George Ohr was a craftsman-poet, an artist so tragically ahead of his time that during his life (1857–1918) he was rudely taunted by critics, when they weren't summarily dismissing him or pervertedly ignoring him. He died in obscurity. And it was not until 1968, when an antiques dealer from New Jersey, traveling through Biloxi, having heard of the Ohr Boys' Auto Repair Shop, and hoping to find a classic car, chanced to discover a collection of more than 7,000 breathtakingly original pots "of unparalleled virtuosity and imagination crammed into barrels in the family attic. ...While his thin-walled, paper-light pots were labeled grotesque in his day, they can now be seen as masterpieces of delicacy and restraint, and stunning explorations of the plasticity of clay."

Imagination. We speak of it in terms of fantastic literature as if anyone who works in the medium has been touched by the macrocosmic wand. But, in truth, much of what passes for the Sea Serpent Greater than Nations is merely device to fool the senses. It is performance, flummery, derivative posturing. When we are confronted with pure originality, the perfect dreaming, we can tell the difference. Because, like the stopped time in which truly great events are transpiring, as opposed to the mere lub-dub of a moment's caught breath when we are subjected to the will-o'-the-wisps of staged p.r. urgencies, nothing moves:

No sound, no distraction; we are gripped and held; and in a truly humbling congress with the infinite, we perceive how much further above us than we'd ever imagined lie the vaults of the heavens, how shackled has been our ability to conceive the Great Dream.

Look at any scene in a science fiction or fantasy film in which the protagonists use a pitcher, throw a vase, or remark on the futuristic design of a bowl. Then look at any page of this book, and understand just how far short of imagination has fallen the "futuristic design" of those set decorations. George E. Ohr styled himself an eccentric, but if he was that antic creation, it was only to sustain himself surrounded by people who were more mud than his masterworks.

Like Vonnegut's Billy Pilgrim, the mad potter of Biloxi was "cut loose in time" and if, here's the belated happy ending of the tragedy, his genius did not speak to the straitened proles of his day, its voice rings loud and clear to any one of us "moderns" now prepared to hear. Find this book. It is a lost continent vivid with color and form and soul, risen at last from barrels stored in an attic for half a century.

In its way, this book is as necessary for the strengthening of the eye of the dreamer as a hundred Spielberg *piñatas*.

42 In Which It Waddles like a Duck, Sheds Water like a Duck, and Goes Steady with Ducks, but Turns Out to Be a Tortoise

"When we were little," the Mock Turtle went on at last, more calmly, though still sobbing a little now and then, "we went to school in the sea. The master was an old Turtle—we used to call him Tortoise—"

"Why did you call him Tortoise, if he wasn't one?" Alice asked.

"We called him Tortoise because he taught us," said the Mock Turtle angrily. "Really you are very dull!"

Money, as all of you know (and if you don't, you should), is the least permanent measure of artistic worth the human race has ever devised. Money is usually what employers throw at you, to get you to involve yourself with frivolous or even downright indign projects. Saul Bellow put it this way: "Writers are not necessarily corrupted by money. They are distracted—diverted to other avenues."

Once, long ago when I was a little kid, my father and I were walking down Main Street in Painesville, Ohio, and we passed an appliance store that was selling a then-popular, but inferiorly made television set. There was a line entering the front door; it stretched partway down the block. Those sets were flying out of the store. Now, less than a year earlier, my father had opened his own jewelry store in Painesville, and he also sold small appliances, like tv sets. (This was in the late forties and tv was quite new; and it was a product that guaranteed big sales; everybody wanted one.) My dad had been offered the exclusive franchise in the area for that brand of tv set, and he had turned it down. The sets were cheesy, and my dad didn't care to hawk such goods to his neighbors. But this other store had gone for it, and now I could see they'd made a smart decision. Smart, because the street was filled with people double-parked so they could get in there and plonk down their cash. (It was also a time before credit cards.) So, as we were crossing the street to proceed on our way, not wanting to have to elbow our way through the crowd, I said to my father, "Maybe you shoulda sold those televisions, he looks like he's makin' lots of money."

(We called them "televisions" in those ancient times, the phrase *teevee* had not yet come into common use.)

And my good old pop, who wasn't much of a philosopher, but could turn a cute phrase when he had to, my dear dad looked down at me without a smile and said, very seriously, "He's going to miss seeing the blue skies a lot; but he'll find some pennies."

I hadn't the vaguest idea what he meant by that (we didn't know from Zen sayings in Painesville). So I asked him what he meant by that, and *then* he smiled. "See if you can figure it out," he told me. And we went and had T-bone steaks at Jerry & Bert's. And much later, the light dawned, and I worked it out in my head, and I asked him if I was right, and he kissed me.

What he was saying, of course, was that the man who owned the store that was selling tv sets that would soon break, and would make the purchasers unhappy, was going to have to walk around town unable to look people in the eye, and he might find some spare change dropped by passersby, but he would have lost everyone's trust.

That was my first really worthwhile lesson in understanding that money is a cheap way to gauge success or ultimate value. Making money is easy. Far easier than demonstrating courage, or being loyal to those who don't reciprocate in kind, or resisting sleaze temptations. Thereafter, I added to that lesson until I had reached a stage of enlightenment where I knew instantly, when I first heard it, that the excuse given for doing lousy but dollar-heavy work, "He's laughing all the way to the bank," was thoroughly ethically corrupt.

I suppose I've gulled myself occasionally, as have we all, into taking on a job that was beneath me, because it promised big bucks; but I like to think that, for good or ill careerwise, I've always done what I thought was artistically *and* ethically correct. For instance (and I cast no judgment on those who've done otherwise), I find it no trouble at all to reject blandishments to write stories for those "sharecropper books" based on other writers' concepts or previously published works. There's a lot of money to be made there, but I'd miss a lot of blue sky and wind up only with dropped pennies.

Believing this, I take enormous reassurance from the every once in a while success of some writer or artist or explorer or corporation that eschews the fast bankroll and its accompanying trashy job, but rather sticks with some pet project or whacky idea...and succeeds right through the roof.

Which brings me to *Teenage Mutant Ninja Turtles* (New Line Cinema) which, as of the middle of May, had made not only $109,585,273.77 and millions of kids goofily happy, having cost a reputed mere 12 million to make, but had borne out the anti-American viewpoint expressed above.

You see, there were these two young guys barely out of their teens, name of Kevin Eastman and Peter Laird, from Sharon, Connecticut, and they...

But wait; I get ahead of myself.

Because it's not a review of this film that's important. The story is a charmingly silly, latter-day Aesop's fable about a quartet of teenage mutant ninja turtles, just as the title says, and about whom you've already heard a great deal (perhaps *too* much, if you have little kids around the manse). That they are omnipresent, literally in your breakfast cereal, is not really important, either: because soon enough the fad will burn itself down to a charming, silly, warmly nostalgic ember and continue to make money for a great many people—but nowhichway the kind of megabucks it's minting currently—and *money* as the yardstick of intrinsic merit will become unimportant, too. Even for the ones who admire those who laugh all the way to the banks.

What *is* important, in my view, is *TMNT* as a manifestation of human endeavor. (Oh, no, is he going to do one of *those* riffs?! Lawd spare me!)

Yet hold, I say. I do pace before mine own self.

Here's where your faithful columnist's diverse knowledge of many literary subcultures redounds to your benefit. Because, to understand at the highest level the wonder, nay the grandeur, of *TMNT* and their creators, and their success, you must let me take you gently by the hand and lead you back through the mist of particulate matter that is Time...

It begins with the legendary Stan Lee of Marvel Comics. And the year is 1964, the month is April. And Stan Lee has created (and Bill Everett has drawn, and Sam Rosen has lettered) the first issue of a new comic book for Olympia Publications (which was what Marvel was called before it officially became Marvel Comics) called *Daredevil, The Man Without Fear!*

It was a comic that told the story of young Matt Murdock, a teenager who, returning one day from studying at the library, sees a blind man crossing a street, unaware that he is about to be run down by a truck. On page 9 of that first issue of *Daredevil* we see that the big red truck hurtling toward the old man bears the legend

AJAX ATOMIC LABS
RADIO-ACTIVE MATERIALS
DANGER

"Without a moment's hesitation...his supple muscles responding to the emergency with the speed of thought...Matt Murdock hurtles toward the scene of impending disaster..."

He won't have a chance...unless I can reach him in time!

"The swift-moving teenager hurls the unsuspecting blind man out of the truck's path...but he himself is not so fortunate..."

Ohhh...

And in the next panel we can see the top of the Ajax truck in the background; and in the foreground a crowd of lookie-loos, and a cop, staring down at something on the street, something we cannot see; and they are saying:

"He saved that man's life!"

"Most heroic act I've ever seen!"

"Don't just *stand* there! Someone call an *ambulance*!"

And (pay close attention):

"But a cyclinder fell from the truck...it struck his face!! Is...is it something *radioactive*??"

Well, Matt recovers, though he's blind; and he goes on to become Daredevil, this incredible crimefighter who, though he's blind—which the underworld does not suspect, of course—has developed heightened sensory powers because he was conked in the head by a canister of "something *radioactive*!"

And that's where we take leave of Stan Lee and his creation. But right there, in panel four of page 9 of that now-valuable comic book, we begin the trail of wonder and grandeur that has allowed Eastman and Laird to purchase the entire state of Connecticut, while buying Maine and Rhode Island for their mothers.

(And I'll thank you not to ask how a cylinder of unspecified radioactive material being improbably schlepped through the middle of a city during rush hour in a vehicle that looks like a moving van could have bounced out of said sealed vehicle and caromed *forward* in defiance of the laws of gravity, as well as action/reaction, and hit a kid in *front* of the vehicle, and cause him not only to go blind but to develop a "radar sense." This was written in a more innocent time and Stan Lee will have to explain it all, no doubt, before the Pearly Gates.)

We move forward in Time. It is 1975, and my pal Len Wein, the well-known Jewish comic book writer (and currently *macher*-in-chief at Disney Comics), is working for Marvel. He revivifies a superhero group that Lee had originated years before, but that Marvel had put on hiatus: *The Uncanny X-Men*. (A name that always pissed me off, seeing as how one of the X-*Men* in the original team was Jean Grey, Marvel Girl, who subsequently became Phoenix; and at various times the cadre has included such females as Rogue, Psylocke, Storm, Dazzler, and Shadowcat.)

He does such a great job of reinventing The X-Men that, after he's moved on to another company, Chris Claremont comes to the project and makes The X-Men the top selling comic in America, spinning off such mutant teams as Excalibur, X-Factor, New Mutants, Alpha Flight, Power Pack, X-Terminators, and a plethora of mini-series and single-character magazines that virtually crowd everything else off the stands. The craze for teenage mutant superjocks is so hysterical that by the summer of 1983 Wolverine and Nightcrawler are so successful that they make Superman and Batman look like a pair of old farts.

And in that summer, having left his mark on *Daredevil* over at Marvel, Frank Miller moves over to another comic company and creates a groundbreaking mini-series titled *Ronin*, which combines science fiction with the wildly exotic world of ninjas, samurai warriors, martial arts, ritual violence, and Japanese culture. It is too offbeat and intellectual to be the popular moneymaking success Miller will later bring forth when he conceptualizes Batman as over-the-hill in *The Dark Knight Returns* (which leads directly to the tone and look of the *Batman* movie); but *Ronin* is clearly operating at such an elevated level of craft and erudition that it becomes the talk of the industry.

It strikes a spark that such previous forays into martial arts comics as *Master of Kung Fu* or *Richard Dragon* had been unable to generate. It throws wide the door for other Eastern-influenced comics, *manga*, and outright imitations.

Miller's ninja assassin work on *Daredevil*, and *Ronin*, have made him the hottest artist/writer in the game, and anything he touches becomes collectable. He is suddenly the success icon for all struggling comics wannabes, the envy of most comics professionals sweating their butts off in the work-for-hire talent graveyard, and the sour grapes target for self-styled analysts of the medium who equate popular success with sellout, regardless of the facts. But at whatever intensity, what Miller has done, and the way he's done it, becomes mythic.

Among those lusting for acceptance are Kevin B. Eastman and Peter A. Laird. As a parody, they devise a silly plot that melds the teenage mutant superhero craze with the passion for Miller-influenced samurai stories, and for chuckles they plant the in-group joke of using the radioactive cylinder that had blinded Matt Murdock and created Daredevil more than twenty years earlier.

What if—they suggested, puckishly—that radioactive canister bonked Matt in the head, kept going, rolled into the gutter, fell into the sewer system, and contaminated four baby turtles someone had flushed? What if those turtles became (stupidest idea ever conceived, no one'll ever go for it, don't be ridic—) Teenage Mutant Ninja Turtles?!?

They took the idea to then-editor of Marvel Comics, Jim Shooter, and they floated it toward him. With the sort of incisive judgment-making ability, insight, foresight, and just pudding-plain human kindliness that marked Shooter's tenure as Marvel's gray eminence, he rejected it, and them, with the now-legendary dictum, "Too amateurish."

This canny demonstration of business acumen is now almost universally considered to be right up there at the tippy-top for bold executive thinking with that of the guy at M&M candy who refused to let Spielberg use them things what melt in your mouth and not your hand as an element in *E.T. the Extra-Terrestrial*, thereby forcing the filmmaker to substitute Reese's Pieces.

And in April of 1984, determined to ignore invitations from the mainstream comics companies to hire on as beanfield hands doing scutwork on corporate-owned properties, Eastman and Laird formed Mirage Studios and self-published the first issue of *Teenage Mutant Ninja Turtles*, a black and white comic with a two-color cover and a puny press run of 3,000 copies. The second printing was in June: 6,000 copies. And the third was in February of 1985: 35,000 copies. To date, that first issue has been reprinted at least six times, with sales in the hundreds of thousands, if not more than a million. It was the phenomenon that, in the words of industry-authorities Don and Maggie Thompson, "fueled the blaze of interest in independent comics."

It has been six years since Eastman and Laird had their little in-joke, Mirage Studios has licensed *TMNT* to everyone in the known universe, through Surge Licensing, Inc.; in September a 1.3 million dollar "Live Arena Show" will visit every major city in America backed by major sponsors; thirteen half-hours of the new *TMNT* Saturday morning animated series will air on CBS; and the live-action motion picture has been #1 at the box office for seven weeks.

If you go to one of the many direct-sales comics shops in your area, and you want to buy a copy of that first issue of the comic, you will pay in excess of $160.

And if you don't think that Eastman and Laird's creation is a singular wonder, *sui generis* in terms of public acceptance, then consider these two incidentals: first, according to *The New York Times*, merchandising of *Batman* is more than $500 million, but merchandising of *TMNT* has exceeded $650 million. And second, in the wake of the instant success of *TMNT*, a rash of imitations broke out on the body of the comics:

Adolescent Radioactive Black Belt Hamsters; *Cold Blooded Chameleon Commandos* ("featuring genetic mutation at its best"); *Mutant Ninja Mutants*; Don Simpson's *The Uncategorizable X-Thems*; *Pre-Teen Dirty-Gene Kung-Fu Kangaroos*; and an item originally announced by "The House of Ideas," Marvel Comics, as *Adult Thermonuclear Samurai Elephants*. Coming only a tad late to the picnic, Marvel at least had the acumen to kill the comic just as all the others were failing dismally. It appeared in September of last year as a one-shot: *Power Pachyderms*.

The only survivor, having created and filled its own category, was *TMNT*. Leading to the five-part *TMNT* animated cartoon mini-series done for syndication in 1987 by Murakami Wolf Swenson, Inc. As written brilliantly by David Wise and Patti Howeth (who wrote all five parts between April and June of that year, for a mere $45,000) the series served as pilot for the syndicated series, for which Wise has written more than thirty episodes.

The animated series, and the deluge of licensed products from quartz digital watches and skateboards, lunch boxes and canned pasta for Chef Boy-Ar-Dee, children's swimwear and wallpaper borders, to greeting cards and Nintendo videogame cartridges, and the millions upon millions that have been raked in by Burger King promotions…did not pass unnoticed by Golden Harvest, the Hong Kong-based film company helmed by Run Run Shaw and best known for its kung-fu moneymakers, notably those that brought Bruce Lee to international prominence.

And so it came to pass that an in-joke about a lost canister of radioactive material from a comic book more than a quarter of a century old, a desire to pay homage to (and cash in on) the innovative work of yet another comic book visionary, an insulting and peremptory dismissal of anxious young amateurs by an arrogant business executive, and the awesome stick-to-it-iveness of two feisty kids, has reached its most successful road marker to date with the arrival of a PG-rated, 93-minute running time full-length live-action translation of the dopiest idea for a film since *Howard the Duck*.

And its success in terms of that cheapest commodity, money, would not mean a thing had this movie turned out as soddenly as *Howard*. But the demented clarity of the Eastman and Laird original idea has been captured so expeditiously; and the movie is so damnably pleasant; and the tone is so dreamily reminiscent of the kind of stuff Jay Ward did with Rocky and Bullwinkle and Tom Slick and George of the Jungle and Mr.

Peabody and Dudley Do-Right; and the mix of juvenilia with adult-pleasing references is so surefooted; that *Teenage Mutant Ninja Turtles* turns out to be one of the surprise treasures of a season of sf/fantasy films most notable for their idiocy and amateurishness.

After *Howard*, we had no right to expect something this scintillant. The duck came out of the production waters as sticky and lugubrious as something left in the wake of the *Exxon Valdez*. It was a disaster of teeth-grinding awfulness.

Why does *TMNT* work, where *Howard the Duck* didn't?

They're both ideas for films that any production exec capable of human speech should have laughed out of his/her office. They're both translation-dangerous, considering that what works in a comic book most often doesn't work up there in live action. They're both dependent on a degree of audience disbelief-suspension that demands utter confidence and clear thinking on the part of the creative team. They're both very expensive to mount properly.

But *Howard* was universally despised, an unregenerate failure, embarrassing even the talented creator of the quacker, Steve Gerber; and *Turtles* has charmed damned nearly everyone. (Except the usual snarling, rabid pack of Fundamentalist mad dogs who continue to demand the "god-given" right to beat and sodomize their children, yet try to throw everyone off their bloody trail by pointing to the make-believe cut-ups of terrapins and shrieking, "Violence! Violence! We counted seven hundred and fifty-two individual acts of…Vie-oh-lennns!") It even rated three out of four stars from *USA Today* with this sally at making the movie critic-proof:

"Of course, those who insist on acting their age instead of their shoe size might not appreciate four adolescent terrapins who camp out in a sewer, chow down on massive doses of pizza and pal around with a giant rodent who talks in fortune-cookie proverbs. Go rent a Bergman film and let us kids enjoy these reptilian warriors."

(Not meaning to be stuffy about it, but the reviewer from *USA Today* really ought to learn the difference between reptilian and amphibian.)

Why should this be, that one quacks and the other causes quakes? Well, the Todd Langen-Bobby Herbeck screenplay is apple-smart, and sweet, and goodhearted—a real pippin—and there is an unabashed insouience to it, like kids at recess on a vast playground… a smartass hipness absolutely devoid of embarrassment…that allows us to cut loose, to feel free, to let go and be nothing but silly along with the charming and adroit animatronic characters created by the late Jim Henson's Creature Shop. The production is top of the line, and you cannot locate anything cheesy, no matter how beadily-eyed you scrutinize any corner of any single frame. Steve Barron has directed as seriously and defiantly, without artistic excess or cultural cringe, as if he were shooting *Gandhi* or *Glory*. The actors all take their parts with verve and bemused dedication (and none will ever have to delete this credit from their *vitae* out of chagrin); and the two major human characters—Judith Hoag as the newscaster April O'Neil, Elias Koteas as the macho vigilante Casey Jones (whose free-for-all battle with Raphael in Central Park is a ring-tailed doozy)—are splendid, holding their own and better, in no way upstaged by four martial arts savants in full turtle regalia. Add that one to the warning about never playing opposite children or dogs.

Or it could be that the film is full of the most wonderful puns...and you *know* how I hate puns. Or that the Henson Muppet of the *sensei*, Splinter, is simply amazing; capable of a range of facial expressions that soon divest your attention of the impossibility that what we're seeing is a talking rat. Or that there are conscious attempts on the part of the makers to pique your fondest memories: when we see the kid-corrupting environment that the evil Foot Clan has shaped for its little street thugs, we are surely and smartly put in mind of the Pleasure Island sequences in *Pinocchio*; when we see dear good Splinter wired up to chain-link, we are gently put in mind—with no *frisson* of blasphemy—of the Crucifixion. The only *unreal* thing in the film is that the heroes find a parking space without difficulty in the streets of New York.

From time to time you ask me to tell you how such and such a film came to exist, what was the process that made them make *this* one and not *that* one, why this one works and that one sucks. In the progress of *TMNT* from comic book idea based on affectionate parody, through its separate existence as a mind-croggling moneymaking machine in the world of product licensing, to its adoption based on greed for the small screen, to its reception as a commodity that could support a feature-length motion picture, it has not been altered. It is the same simple, goofy concept that Eastman and Laird cobbled up out of innocent affection for comics.

They have been blessed. Everyone has been rendered a child in the face of the turtles' personalities. Everyone, from production executives to film distributors to exhibitors to audience to critics.

It is, I submit, the purity of the innocence of childhood that flows through this film. A purity that none of the Spielberg films, with the exception of *E.T.*, can touch.

And it demonstrates that though it can pick up all the pennies off all the sidewalks of the world, it is the illogical determination of its creators to have their whack at the plate, knowing that there is scant possibility they'll be making any laughing trips to the bank, that has been the power behind *TMNT*'s success.

These sliders and snappers can look anyone in the eye, and grin. We call them Tortoise, because they taught us.

43 In Which We Lament, "There Goes the Neighborhood!"

Well, hell, you know me: the kind of pain in the ass who gets invited to someone's house for dinner only once. Doesn't like the main course because it's too rare, refuses to eat the vegetables with some dopey *bon mot* like, "That's why I grew up and became an adult…so I wouldn't have to eat the green stuff." Gets into a genuinely mean argument with one of the other dinner guests about his politics. Reminds the teenage daughter of the host about some embarrassing thing she did when she was ten or eleven. Dominates the conversation and makes everyone long for do-it-yourself home crucifixion kits. A real rain cloud kinda guy. The sort you can always count on to rust the Jell-O.

So there I am at this elegant party that Stan Lee of Marvel Productions threw, back in December of 1987, and his and Joan's home up in the Hollywood Hills was jammed to the walls with the hoi and the polloi, and at one point I'm introduced to these two young guys named Ed Neumeier and Michael Miner, and Stan or somebody says, "These are the guys who wrote *RoboCop*. Didn't you just write a piece on *RoboCop*?"

Well, they knew damned *well* I'd just written a review of *RoboCop*, and I'd worked it over like a slab of beef jerky, because forty-something minutes into the damned flick, I'd had it up to here with the idiot violence and the low animal steam heat of the audience and the after-the-fact addition of "socially relevant satire" and I'd said, in effect, this is mean widdle kids pulling the wings off butterflies and setting fire to pussycats and nailing spaniels to ironing boards, and frankly, Scarlett, this is like a pavane for perverts…so lemme outta here!

And, well, hell, you know me: the kind of pain in the ass who, when he's asked by guests at a party, what did you think of our incredibly successful, extremely popular, critically drooled-over movie that has made us two smartasses real hot tickets in this town, answers as charmingly as a cactus spine in your tongue, "I think they ought to nuke you two until you glow."

Well, not exactly. I didn't *exactly* say that. But Stan and Joan haven't extended a dinner invitation since 1987, so I am driven, lashed if you will, toward the conclusion that I acted in a somewhat less than gilt-edged fashion.

I cannot remember precisely what I *did* say to them, but for those of you tragically bereft of a copy of HARLAN ELLISON'S WATCHING (Underwood-Miller, 514 + xxxvii pp., $29.95) a volume of antic cinematic wisdom paralleled for sheer urgency and pertinence only by the Magna Carta and the more ribald sections of the Nag Hammadi scriptures—a book absolutely guaranteed not only to lift your spirits, unclog your pores, breathe new vigor into your ethical substructure, and get you laid regularly...but it also removes rust, bird doodoo, and rain-spotting from your car, front bumper to trunk lid, a showroom shine, in just twenty minutes...where the hell was I...oh, right: for those of you sans the book or back issues containing my review, here is what I said of the original *RoboCop* movie in this column:

"*RoboCop* (Orion), despite its popularity, is as vicious a piece of wetwork as anything I've encountered in recent memory. Devoid of even the faintest scintilla of compassion or commonsense, it is as low as the foreheads of those members of the screening audience who cheered and laughed at each escalated scene of violence. It is a film about, and intended for, no less than brutes. It is a film that struck me as being made by, and for, savages and ghouls. Written by Edward Neumeier and Michael Miner, and directed by the Dutchman Paul Verhoeven, this is a template for everything rabid and drooling in our culture. That it has been touted—after the fact—as being a 'satirical' film, a 'funny' film, is either ass-covering or a genuine representation of the filmmakers' ethically myopic view of what they've spawned. If the former, it's despicable hypocrisy; if the latter, that's just flat scary." That's what I said in print, and an approximation of my remarks at the party.

Went down smooth, as you might imagine; and I've got to hand it to Neumeier and Miner—they gritted their teeth and didn't invite me to step out onto the patio for a little *alfresco* snack of fat lip sandwich.

Subsequent viewings of the film on videocassette and cable provided me with a more complete picture of the picture—to the point where I was drenched, immersed, saturated in it. I wanted to discover if I'd "*over*reacted" by walking out of the film at the point where Neumeier-Miner-Verhoeven paraphrased the assassinations of San Francisco mayor George Moscone and supervisor Harvey Milk (27 November 1978) as a mordantly "amusing" trope to enable a bit of Robo's highly visual violence.

(Sidebar: that absolutely wonderful, self-serving, sort of doublespeak gibberish, *overreaction*. Whenever the reckless behavior of the self-justifiers calls down on their heads more opprobrium than they bargained for, they indict the accusers with the devastating comeback, "You *over*reacted!" Those who try to manipulate the audience do so cynically, but they never seem to understand that the aroused mob knows no boundaries of behavior; the mob may very well get *only* as excited as the manipulators wished, providing the cheap-thrill-hungry media with momentary red meat and twitchy ganglia—a few tsk-tsks of outrage from special interest groups, a bit of transitory minority outrage, another diatribe by that sterling arbiter of artistic worth, Rev. Donald Wildmon and his American Family Association in Tupelo, Mississippi—or it may get as aroused as a teddy-boy contingent at a Brit soccer match and trash a theater or write a review that trashes the film. Then comes the affronted bleat of, "You *over*reacted!" meaning: we didn't gauge just how gross we got, and instead of milking you for some publicity that would push our little strip of depraved fiction to greater boxoffice receipts, we actually pissed you off, and you're calling us on it, and we are into medium-high dudgeon in an attempt to cover our idiocy and our asses.

(As with the constantly used and wholly incorrect construct "side-effects" when talking about medicine [all reactions to a specific drug are *effects*: some may be unexpected or undesirable, but using such specific terms contributes to our suspicion that some members of the AMA may not always know what the hell they're doing, so they dissemble with that *side*-effects bushwah], the manipulators put the weight of rationality on the critical observer who reacted more negatively than served the original duplicitous purpose of the outrageous material. In fact, and simply, one can only *react*. If the intensity of one's reaction contains more heat than the self-serving creator of the work desired, that's too goddam bad, but it ain't overreaction.)

The original *RoboCop* is easier to take on the small screen, and in the relative safety of your own home. Removed from the beast lair environment into which a multiplex theater is transformed when one of these killing-spree scenarios has its way with an audience of teen trogs and their adult apologists, scaled down in size and sensurround ambience, the cleverness of the Neumeier-Miner splatterpunk overstatement frequently asserts itself; and Verhoeven has a steely eye for ultra-violence (as we can see in *Total Recall*, the most recent film he has directed, but a film I will not be reviewing, don't ask) that *in situ* rivets one's fascination.

So, from down the line, I report back that yes, the original *RoboCop* film has some stuff, and it is likely that my *reaction*—not over, under, or wherever, but simply *re*—was only in part due to the actual movie. Nonetheless, I found my perception of the film as a coldblooded exercise in cynical exploitation of violence undiminished.

And so, when I was told by my friend Frank Miller, along about summer two years ago, that he had been signed by our mutual theatrical agent, to script *RoboCop 2* (Orion), I received the intelligence with a mixture of delight and trepidation.

Delight. Because Frank Miller (whom I praised in another context in the previous installment of *Watching*) is a powerful and original writer; he is a sharp observer of contemporary society; he demonstrates both a fascination and a revulsion for sociopathic behavior that makes for fresh insights; he has a singular design and visual sense; and I have long felt he is one of those rare individuals whose life and work have the potential for being societally significant. And yes, for those of you who seem to object to my "name-dropping" as something Freud might want to examine, he is a close friend. He and his wife, the talented artist Lynn Varley, are very dear to me and Susan; and I tell you this upfront so there will be no secret agenda that can be used to discredit the opinions expressed here about the film Frank has written. Because...

Trepidation. When Frank got the assignment to script *RoboCop 2*, (after a Neumeier-Miner treatment for the sequel had been rejected by Orion), I knew that some day I'd have to review the film, and what if I raved about it? He's my pal, so I must be ass-kissing, right? There are actually corrupt spirits out there who attribute such motives to others. And what if I deplore the film? Will I lose the trust and friendship of a man and an artist I admire at both levels? Budrys wrote a column last year on just this topic: the difficulty of reviewing your friends honestly, and the perils it entails.

So it came to pass that Frank and Lynn invited us to a prerelease screening of *RoboCop 2*, and we sat side-by-side (with Dustin Hoffman half a dozen seats away) (which really *is* name-dropping, but c'mon gimme a break, we're talking Dustin *Hoff*man here!) and I watched the one hour and 58 minutes that lay at the end of two years of Frank Miller's labors.

And it may be that I won't be invited back to dinner.

Alex Murphy (Peter Weller) was "top of his class at the Police Academy, devout Irish-Catholic family man, imbued with a fierce sense of duty." He was murdered by thugs in the first film. The locale and time of both movies is Detroit, "near future." Urban violence is pandemic and at a level of intensity that makes what Batman faced in Gotham City seem like the cranky behavior of babies in a sandbox. It's so bad that the city has franchised its peacekeeping needs to the giant cartel Omni Consumer Products, and OCP gathers up what's left of Officer Alex Murphy and implants his brain and neural network in an ultra-hi-tech assault armor body, thus producing not a robot, but a cyborg (so why wasn't he called CyborCop?). And though they believe they've programmed the poor sonofabitch to think of himself only as "RoboCop, Crime Prevention Unit, O.C.P." he continues to flash back on the identity of Alex Murphy and Murphy's wife and Murphy's son.

The first film dealt primarily with establishing the vicious future society of Detroit, and of RoboCop's merciless revenge on the gang of amoral punks who slaughtered him.

RoboCop 2 runs the same raw meat through the grinder again. This time Detroit is besieged by a messianic monster named Cain (Tom Noonan, who will be remembered as the serial killer in the Michael Mann film *Manhunter*, adapted from Thomas Harris's novel, RED DRAGON). Cain and his cult of leather-stud street trash push a cheap and freefall blow your brains melt your eyeballs dementia furioso drug called *nuke*. And the Detroit cops can't really hobble this psychopathic savior because OCP has cut their salaries by forty per cent, has canceled their pensions, and won't even enter into binding arbitration. So the cops are on strike. And we swiftly learn that it's intentional, this disarming of the police apparatus. Because the city owes OCP thirty-seven million dollars, it can't pay, and OCP doesn't *expect* them to pay; because if Detroit defaults, then OCP forecloses on all city assets. In short, OCP manages a raid on the city itself, a gargantuan hostile takeover, and the corporation takes the city private. Then loots it as they would an unproductive grommet factory or woolen mill.

These are the two major themes of the movie. Around and through this scenario wind the subplots of RoboCop being superseded in effectiveness by RoboCop 2, a larger and meaner version of the already too-triggerquick original; the corporate ladder climbing of an OCP bitch-goddess scientist named Dr. Faxx; Murphy driving his wife-of-a-former-life crazy by hanging around in his metal suit, sneaking peeks at her and son Jimmy, to the point that she is suing OCP because Alex isn't really dead, he's just a "prisoner" in that metal suit; the discovery that to make a bigger, better cyborg unit they have to get the brain of a real pervotwistodevofreako; and attempts by the mayor of Detroit to raise the 37 million that will bail the city out of deep OCP water. Some of these subplots work, some of them haven't held a job in recorded memory.

There are two primary set-pieces of unending cornucopial violence—the raid on the *nuke* processing plant and the solo attack on Cain in the old River Rouge sludge plant by Robo, who gets "stripped" and the parts unceremoniously dumped on the sidewalk as his fellow cops trudge the picket line. But these are just the two *main* panoramic chunks of slaughter. There are at least a dozen other, smaller, scenes of innocents, cops, killers, thugs, hookers, children, *latina* factory workers, and assorted bit-players being savaged and butchered. Within the first five minutes a man is electrocuted by a Magna Volt security system in a car he's trying to steal, his still-smoking body dumped into the parking lot; an old lady wheeling a shopping cart full of tin cans is sideswiped by a car and then she's robbed as she lies in the gutter; the purse-snatcher gets his eye put out by a couple of bimbos in razor-spike heels who resnatch the purse; a gun shop is blown open by a gang of toughs who shoot the defenseless owner; and a half dozen or so creeps get their chests exploded via Robo's Ronson-thin equalizer. Each death is accompanied by the sound of a shank roast being pummeled with a maul, juicy gobbets of stringy innards and Heinz thick blood doing a Jackson Pollock on the scenery, and stuntmen being yanked into the air ostensibly by the impact of an explosive round. It is the sort of movie you watch with smarting eyes and your fingers in your ears. If you're a parent, however, you can take your twisted offspring with you, and they can feed you the popcorn, while you protect your eardrums. It won't bother them, of course: they're trained and acclimated to listen to thundercrash at the decibel level of Lita Ford, Aerosmith, and Motley Crue; and as for mayhem, well, that'd be mother's milk to them.

No, I'm not going to object to *RoboCop 2* on the grounds that it contains a gratuitous body-count somewhere just shy of a hundred. No objection because, at last, the saturation point of what was begun with *Bonnie and Clyde* and *The Wild Bunch* in '67 and '69 has been reached. *RoboCop 2*'s bloodbath is, a third of the way through the flick...boring. Those aren't human beings getting as perforated as passersby in a Fearless Fosdick strip; they aren't anydumbthing but space-fillers and time-killers. They are just inarticulate shorthand. Commas. Stutters in the plot. The script notes from Director to Stunt Coordinator: give me eleven faceless *vato locos* in this scene, rig them with squibs, we'll blow 'em away in one take.

But it isn't just the stunt extras and day-players who are roundfiled. Patricia Charbonneau, exquisite in *Desert Hearts*, has a few dozen lines, none of which mean anything, and her part never pays off; Nancy Allen, who was the humanizing element in the original film, but who hasn't been allowed to work to the elegant standard she set in *Dressed to Kill* or *The Philadelphia Experiment*, is criminally subjugated to a rambling series of action scenes posing as a storyline, and deafening fusillades of gunfire; Dan O'Herlihy, who can out-thesp ninety per cent of the actors working today, even when he's rigged up in anthropoid lizard makeup, as he was in *The Last Starfighter*, is relegated to a few grimacing walk-ons in which he has been directed to play the head of OCP as if he were a demented Lex Luthor; and a black actor named Willard Pugh is condemned to play Mayor Kuzak, the mayor of Detroit, if you will, as an hysterical, twiddlebrained, prancing queen. (Apart from the utter ludicrousness of the characterization, this is a representation of a black mayor of a major American city that should infuriate blacks and gays alike. It is revolting in its racism, homophobia, and shrillness. Shameful!)

And finally what we have in this pointless sequel is yet another *Death Wish* clone, tricked up with some sf extrapolation of inner city crime and degradation, no more startling at this advanced stage of the genre than *Streets of Fire* or *Terminator* or *Escape from New York*. It is murkily directed by Irvin Kershner, who has yet to fulfill the promise he showed at the helm of *The Luck of Ginger Coffey* in 1964. And Frank Miller has had his baptism by fire.

Miller, if I am any judge of screenwriting smarts, has it in him to become a major resource for the American cinema. He needed this credit to get into the game, just to pony up the necessary ante to obtain some clout. But he's seen what they do to a script—such as dropping the brief beat of a scene in which the metal-clad Robo goes to the cemetery to say goodbye at Alex Murphy's grave—a scene excised for time-considerations—but a heart beat sacrificed to the glut of butchery scenes because the makers of this film knew it was the nasty boys in the potential audience who had to be fixed again and again to feed their slice'n'dice jones. And he's gotten some mean lessons in the business, up to and including having another writer ride his coattails to an onscreen credit. He may not care to spend much of his creative life in a pond this polluted; but if he does, *RoboCop 2* will have been a toughening experience.

As for the meaning of this latest entry in the Gunfire Makes for Good Government logbook, it has no more meaning than that to be found in a quotation from Cicero:

"If we are forced, at every hour, to watch or listen to horrible events, this constant stream of ghastly impressions will deprive even the most delicate among us of all respect for humanity."

Film is a community. Of creators and aficionados. Product like *RoboCop 2*, transparently intended for the debased and lip-licking, only serves to turn the neighborhood into a run-down, seedy, impoverished nightmare of the homeless, the heartless, and the talentless.

The sort of place to which one doesn't even *want* to be invited for dinner.

44 In Which the Good Ship Coattail-Ride Sinks, Abandoning Hundreds in Treacherous Waters

Prognostication is not my trade. Nostradamus was a bad free-verse poet, about as accurate as gimpy frauds like astrologers Sidney Omar, Jeane Dixon, Joyce Jillson, and Nancy Reagan's own Joan Quigley. Every year the Bay Area Skeptics compile a survey of the specific predictions of "psychics" and every year those who, in January, claimed for themselves "the gift of prophecy" are shown once again to be no better at piercing the veil than the rest of us. Of the top ten news stories of 1989–90—including the tearing down of the Berlin Wall, the collapse of Communism, the capture of Noriega, the Pete Rose and Marion Berry scandals, the failure of the Hubble Space Telescope in May, the release of Nelson Mandela, the debacle of the savings & loan system, and Iraq's invasion of Kuwait leading us to the brink of a major war—not one of these bullshit soothsayers hit with a single prediction. They missed with *anything* of consequence. And as for the San Francisco World Series earthquake, those who have claimed they "saw" it coming have been logged-in as making the predictions *after* it happened, as did you and I. (Not to mention that one of the standard "glimpses" these clowns make *every* year is that a major temblor will hit the Bay Area. The big prophecy they all subscribed to, that it was supposed to happen in 1986, was just one more in the long unrealized string of such warnings. But *not one of them* predicted it for 1989, presumably because they'd been burned so many times before, they figured they'd just omit it from the traditional "you will meet a dark stranger" and "you will go on a long journey" nonsense on the reliability level with fortune cookies.)

Reasonable and logical extrapolation of current trends, as practiced by keen-eyed observers like John Naismith or Roberto Vacca is about as close as any rational person would expect us to be able to plot the future. And just the development of something as underrated as the microchip or The Pill or the fax machine or AIDS can throw even *those* educated guesses into a cocked hat. Imagine what the breakthrough of fusion power will do.

No, as C.S. Lewis put it in THE SCREWTAPE LETTERS, "The future is something which everyone reaches at the rate of sixty minutes an hour, whatever he does, whoever he is." So I try to keep my trap shut on such long-term guesswork.

The one time I ventured a prediction that we would *never* have a nuclear holocaust, a theory I came to after long and sedulous analysis of history and human nature and current events, and mentioned it *en passant* on a radio show I was hosting each week, I was greeted by sufficient opprobrium that I vowed such forecasts would no longer emerge from my face, no matter how compelling the auguries.

Having sworn off public auspication, I will now demonstrate that I can't maintain a resolution any better than the rest of you, by presenting a seditious and heretical theory predicting the utter vanishment of the horror genre within two years.

As a founding member of Horror Writers of America, who has won two of the handsome Bram Stoker awards for work in the genre (one of them for the book that collects these film essays), who currently sits on HWA's Board of Trustees, I'm sure this theory will endear me to not only the membership at large, but enshrine me forever in the affections of all the paperback publishers currently shoveling out as many possessed mansion and demon child novels as they can locate. Caution to the winds.

Let me start with the word *horror*.

Look at it once more. HORR-OR!

(There is this word, which word I cannot now remember, that is the proper term I'm seeking. It's a word like *epizeuxis*, a noun that means emphatic verbal repetition; but it's a different word. And that word is the proper nomenclature for repeating something until it loses its meaning and sounds like gibberish. Like, f'rinstance, take the word *gibberish*. Start to say it, and keep at it till it is just a mouthful of glossolalia, which also isn't the word I'm hunting for.)

Horror.

HOR-ROR!

(I've noticed a linguistic tendency toward concretized thinking where certain groups are concerned. Take the words "science fiction" for instance. They no more reflect what is being written than "Food, Folks, and Fun" as Madison Avenue doublespeak for McDonald's reflects the muck one can purchase 'neath them Golden Arches. But there it is, that outmoded, inaccurate, hincty phrase, "science fiction," stamped onto everything from Edgar Rice Burroughs and Tolkien at one end, to Vonnegut and Stephen King at the other. It's epizeuxis to the point of glossolalia. But heaven forfend anyone suggest a better literary designation might serve individual writers better. The words "science fiction" are as sacred a cow as the shape of the Hugo, an icon long overdue for reshaping.)

Oh, the HAWR-OR of it all!

A word that has been foisted off on an entire cadre of disparate talents, for the convenience of marketing. Just the way they decided "science fiction" or (dare he speak the name) "sci-fi" has been rubber-stamped, accurate or not. But just think about that word: *horror*.

It ain't terror. And it ain't suspense. And it ain't psychological thriller. And it ain't macabre. And it ain't even weird stuff. It is *horror*. Now, if you look in your dictionary—as those who permit the word to be used on their books clearly do not—you will find that *horror* is followed by such words as dreadful, abominable, extremely unpleasant, deplorable, disgusting, terrible, awful, appalling, hideous, grim, ghastly, revolting, repulsive, dire, and repellent.

In short, everything that any normal, sane human being *doesn't* want in his or her life.

For some time now, I've been *nuhdzing* Horror Writers of America to come up with a new way of identifying itself. With very little success. They seem to be as wedded to the word *horror* as forty years of demeaning press has wedded *science fiction* to a genre that deserves better.

I wonder if they would be as set in their ways if they were synonymously known as Extremely Unpleasant Writers of America. Or Hideous Writers of America. Or Ghastly, Revolting, Repulsive, and Repellent Writers of America.

It wouldn't matter, I suppose, if it weren't already written in the stars that about two years down the pike, there won't *be* any horror genre for them to be Writers of. America or otherwise.

And if it isn't a message all that clear in the firmament, it has certainly been a *mene mene tekel* in the boxoffice stats for 1990. I'll get to that in a moment, but let me round out the implications, as I see them, for the genre in print.

I think it is obvious that there is a major shakeout on its way. The signs and portents are all there, if one cares to look. Half a dozen of the most popular writers in the second tier of successful "horror" writers have been told by their publishers that they don't want any more of that stuff. They've been told that if they want to see their forthcoming efforts accepted, they had better start moving away from "horror" into thriller or suspense or psychological terror. But no more of that icky crap with the oozing blood and the brain-eating zombie, neck-gnawing vampire, nameless evil from the fetid swamp, ancient curse in the possessed mansion hokey-pokey. Most of the major paperback houses have already cut their lists, or repackaged titles originally intended as horror entries so they look like something else. (Yes, I know that Dell seems to be flying in the face of this trend with a Jeanne Cavelos-edited horror line, and I can't explain that; but John Silbersack, over at NAL, has smartly opted for a "weird" or "dark fantasy" aspect to his forthcoming series. We'll see which of the two is around, in 1992.)

My instincts tell me that never before has a category of literature cannibalized itself so quickly. But then, I never thought there was much meat on this beast to begin with. All of the major themes had been handled *ad infinitum* before the horror boom ever started. Stoker and Walpole and Poe and Lovecraft and Blackwood and Mary Shelley and Shirley Jackson and even Henry James had gone at the form, and done it as well as anyone might wish. And they were only the tip of the best work available in the genre. Davis Grubb and Clark Ashton Smith and William Seabrook and Hodgson and Bierce and M.R. James and Le Fanu and Machen and Wm. Sloane and the best of us all, Fritz Leiber, had been tilling that field for a hundred years. There was little enough to work with, even for them; from the golem to smoke ghost. But what possibilities existed were explored.

Doesn't anyone ever ask why, prior to 1974, there was no deep and wide stream of American horror writing? There was never enough fecundity in the form to support a large roster of individual talents. There was the occasional Kafka or Matheson, and they found new ways of doing the demon and the witch and the creature with no face. But there were only a couple of dozen McGuffins in the genre, right from the start.

Then along came Stephen King.

Sui generis. Whether it was that the form had been waiting for him, or he had been born to be the next significant worker of those ancient materials...he was the new Poe, the latest Lovecraft, the direct lineal descendant of Polidori. With CARRIE he revivified the category, and made it his own.

And he had long coattails. And the kind of money he made with what he did was too great a lure to ignore. And the venal and the imitative licked their chops. And they rushed in behind him to create a market that didn't exist, to feed an audience that wasn't hungry, to dig in like fleas on a basset hound.

There never *was* a blossoming for "horror." There was only Stephen King, and everyone else.

Now, that is not to say that there weren't golden moments. SONG OF KALI comes to mind at once. But even there, considering Dan Simmons as a writer, as an individual intellect, one can clearly see that SONG OF KALI is hardly a "horror" novel. It is a novel that floats on an undercurrent of horror, of *horrific* possibilities; but it is in the traditional mode of mainstream Western Literature. It does not rely on the coarse thumpings and clotted structures of what has come to be known as the "horror" genre.

There was a rush, and the newsstands and bookstores suddenly were overrun with ham-handed amateurs, all gnawing at the meatless bones. Bucks were made, bad books were written, good writers deserted their own voices to speak in forked tongues.

And good writers were led astray by greedy publishers, by editors who should have had more spine to resist; and bad writers were dragooned to fill those publishing slots. Until they had wrung the threadbare cloth dry. And still they kept dumping their wearisome rehashes on the market. Until the audience that had never existed to begin with, turned away. Turned back to the suspense novel, the thriller, the mysteries, and the psychological dramas.

That was yesterday. And this morning, if one climbed to the top of the tower, and gazed out at the horizon, one could see the shakedown coming.

When it hits full force, all those who existed merely because Stephen King dominated the landscape will find themselves homeless. Dean Koontz will remain, and Joe Lansdale; Rick McCammon and John Saul; Lisa Tuttle and Dan Simmons (if he chooses to write in that vein); Bloch, as always, and Ramsey Campbell, probably. Half a dozen others, who will retool in time, and who will survive. And all the rest will drown. They won't desert the ship...the ocean will dry up.

It's coming in on the wind. You can sense it. And if the Horror Writers of America have the sense to blow off that ridiculous infatuation with the *word* "horror," they will quick as a bunny get themselves a more universal and capacious moniker. Don't ask me what that ought to be. I'm not clever enough to figure out something market-worthy and prestigious; I'm only clever enough to have perceived the problem.

A problem that was inevitable, but perhaps need not have progressed so rapidly to a terminal condition. There might have been a few extra years in the carcass, had not the need to cannibalize the form gotten so out of hand.

When a literary form begins to run out of ideas, the last stop before the abyss is the escalation of the elements, the coarsening of the themes, the amateur's belief that simply to shock is enough. And so, if we begin with the discreet shadowing of the scene as the vampire bends to the throat of the victim...and we move a little closer into the light with each succeeding vampire story...then we come, at last, to the crude writing that describes in detail every spurt of blood, every diseased puncture hole, every last bit of bodily functions minutiae, abhorrent perversion, disgusting child molestation, exploding heads: morsels for rodents, overstated and purple-prosed phobias. In short, the salting of the land.

And that is where the "horror" genre has come to a death rattle. I choose not to name the names, because some who perform in this manner are friends of mine; but you know who they are. They say they are only writing thus to "awaken" us, to "bring us in touch with our nerve-ends." What a load of horse shit.

We *live* in times that are rife with horror. One cannot open a newspaper without confronting a monstrosity greater than the one met the day before. One cannot listen to the news first thing in the morning without being lashed by the terrors that possessed the night streets through which we slept.

No one needs to be shaken by the shoulders to feel the terror of the age. If you're unfortunate enough to live in a city of almost any size, you exist with fear morning and night. Drive-by shootings that waste two year old kids. Joggers brained till they're comatose so some clowns can steal their Adidas. Rapacious developers and their cronies in city government who tear down the past and blight the landscape for a cheap buck. Illiteracy and alienation. Random rudeness and capricious street madness. All around you are the warning signs that if you look at someone wrong, or you happen to be at the wrong stoplight, or you pass the wrong alleyway...that you may come up short of luck, and next day's news notes you as a statistic. So you stay alert. In the cities we call it "street smarts" but what it is, simply, is being in touch with the terror. And if you're unfortunate enough to live in a small town, or the countryside, the terrors you face are the petty censors and the White Supremacists, the bigots and the bullies; the dumping of industrial waste in the night, and the encroachment of the cheapest aspects of mass marketing on a bucolic way of life. The Klan and the fundamentalists, racist cops and righteous citizens who know what you should read and what movies the single theater in town should play.

And the inept writers who escalate violence and loving detail of autopsies tell us how they serve the commonweal...by bringing us to an awareness of the dark side of human nature. They obfuscate with that sad, sorry song about how they need to shock us to awareness.

In medicine, they only use shock treatment when the patient is insane, cataleptic, or dead. Just as the horror genre is dead. Or insane. Or cataleptic.

The end of the road lies just ahead. The ship is sinking. The train is pulling out of the station. The fuel tank is empty and we're flying on one engine. (The nice thing about ridiculing the awful, is that one can mix metaphors like veggies in a blender, and no matter how purple you get...you're pale blue by comparison with the crap that's actually being published.)

The foregoing has been an alert for any writers who have the taste for survival that it takes to stay in the game. Beware the Ides of March. Selah.

The foregoing is the scenario for the genre as it appears in the print medium. The buttressing proofs deal with what's been going on in film this past year. The same story is told, but more clearly.

Consider the top ten boxoffice films of 1990 (beginning with the 1989 Christmas season) as clocked by *The Hollywood Reporter* in August, in descending order of gross to date:

Pretty Woman	164,142,466 in 19 weeks of release.
Teenage Mutant Ninja Turtles	131,693,386 in 18 weeks.
The Hunt for Red October	119,973,212 in 22 weeks.
Back to the Future, Part II	116,425,676 in 15 weeks.
Total Recall	112,709,460 in 9 weeks.
Driving Miss Daisy	106,517,604 in 33 weeks.
Dick Tracy	101,117,485 in 7 weeks.
Die Hard 2	95,625,666 in 4 weeks.
The War of the Roses	86,048,662 in 28 weeks.
The Little Mermaid	84,335,373 in 31 weeks.

Check the list. There are, if one stretches the category, four films of a fantastic nature, excluding *Dick Tracy*. One is an animated Disney fantasy; one is a live-action version of a fantasy cartoon series; and two are more or less science fiction.

Not one horror film in the batch.

During the week of August 5–11, there was not one lone single solitary horror film in the top *fifty* boxoffice winners. *Ghost* and *Ghost Dad* and *Arachnophobia* (about which more in a moment) were about as close as anything came to being spawn of that genre.

Now, granted that any year in which the best "serious" film is *Driving Miss Daisy*, in which snooze-inducing sequels glut the available screens, in which as sloppy a piece of work as *Presumed Innocent* (a cheat of a film if ever there was one) draws slavering praise is not a year to be enshrined in the Parthenon of Great Art, even so, one is required to ask, "Where are all the horror films?"

And answer there comes none.

The fad is ended. The stove has gone out. The camel has had his last drink. The embolism has reached the heart. The metaphors have run amuck. And of horror films there come none.

Nothing even that close to horror has been seen in a year.

The summer was a burn ward filled with ambulatory corpses. Even granting that Hollywood films during the vacation season, the school is out season, come to us from some demented Never-Never Land, produced by lost boys who don't wanna gwow up, even so, *this* summer had worse dregs than usual. And the two closest things to a proper horror film were *Arachnophobia* (Hollywood Pictures/Amblin Entertainment) and *Darkman* (Universal).

The former can be dispensed with quickly. Unless one is totally unhinged when a Tegenaria, the common House Spider, runs across the kitchen floor, one will find this movie a predictable bore. At one hour and forty-three minutes of spiders springing out of every niche and cupboard, the gag gets mighty stale, mighty fast. Because that's all there is to it. Spiders jump out and occasionally bite someone, who twitches a while, then croaks wearing a hideous rictus. The tv spots kept showing John Goodman (Roseanne Barr's hubby on the sitcom) as a pest control guy, looking pretty funny. Well, that was the totality of his contribution to this film. He could have been excised without notice, without damaging the "plot." Goodman was a loss-leader, shoehorned into this standard ooga-booga to con an audience that wouldn't otherwise pay any attention. As for the direction, though Frank Marshall has a spectacular track record as producer (*Raiders of the Lost Ark*, *Who Framed Roger Rabbit*, and the first *Poltergeist*, among many others), he should stick to second unit work. This is as creaky a directorial debut as anything I've seen in a decade of wretched no-talent directors, all of whom get a possessory credit before the title.

There is virtually nothing else to say about this clinker. In the '50s it would have been done on a shoestring by somebody like Babe Unger or Sam Katzman, and it would have immediately sunk to its proper level at rural drive-ins, to become one of those gawdawful cult icons one sees lauded in *Fangoria* or one of its clones.

If there is any genuine horror passim this production, it is in the amount of money that was thrown at it, to no avail.

As for the latter, *Darkman* is the triumph of form over substance. It is *Phantom of the Opera* impregnated with pure Bronson *Death Wish* violence. Sam Raimi's direction of a five-credited writer screenplay is all snap crackle and pop, with the latest SF/X razzle-dazzle. But the story is howlingly stupid...

...f'rinstance: the McGuffin in this one is a memo that links a rapacious developer with payoffs to city officials. I suppose back in 1940 that would have worked; but we live in the real world these days; and when we see felons like Michael Milken and Ollie North and Imelda Marcos and the S&L sharks doing eight months in a slam where their biggest worry is that the Jacuzzi water ain't too tepid...if they do any time at all... well, such a memo seems pretty pale as the impetus for mass murders, blowing up laboratories, and initiating a vendetta.

But even *more* imbecile is the manner in which that memo keeps turning up. The bad guy loses it at the beginning of the film (though we're not told how), and even though the killers cannot possibly know that the woman who copped the memo left it at the lab of her paramour, Dr. Peyton Westlake, they impossibly show up there, burst in with assault rifles (instead of waiting till he went out and quietly searching the place), beat the crap out of the Doc, set fire to the place for no good reason, and make more noise than a Mötley Crüe concert. And later, when the memo has been restored to the possession of the bad guy, does he just burn the goddam thing (and why didn't he do it in the first place?) so he'll be safe? Ah no, he *leaves it on his otherwise empty desk* so that attorney Julie Hastings—the one person he has spent the entire movie trying to wrest the memo away from—spots it...and swipes it *again*!

Look: *Darkman* is so slam-bang that you have no inclination to think much about it, as it's happening. But after all the lights and bomb-blasts have dimmed, and you think about it, this is another one of those cacophonous no-brainers intended as the first of a series of money-making, cynically-slanted fish-wrappings intended by Universal (once the house of horror with Frankenstein, the Wolf Man, the Mummy, Dracula, and the

Creature from the Black Lagoon) to get back into the grue and guts business. It's an amusing bucket of blood and brains, I guess; and it will make its nut; but if this is the closest to a true horror film that Hollywood can give us, then I rest my case as to the demise of the form.

(And just a word about the violence level in this season's films. 16 dead in *Dick Tracy*; 12 slaughtered in *Another 48 Hrs.*; 28 or 30, as best I can calculate, in *Darkman*; 62 in *Total Recall*; you lose count near fifty in *RoboCop 2*; not to mention losing everyone on a 747 plus assorted bad guys and non-speaking cops in *Die Hard II*; and so on, and so on. Keep it up, you guys; just keep it up. And continue to wonder at the increase in random street violence. I'm *sure* there's no connection.)

As for *Martians Go Home!* (Taurus), Fredric Brown is no doubt whirling like a gyroscope in his grave. Avoid this one at all costs.

If you can catch the John Varley-scripted *Millennium* (Gladden Entertainment) on cable, do so. It got such a badrap last year when it was released briefly and then deep-sixed, that any wary filmgoer would naturally run a mile to miss it. But it isn't the turkey we were led to believe. It's hardly a perfect gem; but there is a wealth of inventiveness in it, and it is clear to see where other hands than Varley's stirred the pot. Hell, even as flawed as it is, it has more heart and merit than *Dick Tracy*, *Gremlins 2*, *Arachnophobia*, and *Darkman* lumped together. You done good, Herb; don't let them tell you otherwise.

And as long as I'm mentioning it, just to satisfy your curiosity, *Dick Tracy* (Touchstone) was okay. No more than that, in my view. I admired Dustin Hoffman's Mumbles; I was impressed by the seven-basic-colors look of the film as captured by Production Designer Richard Sylbert, Art Director Harold Michelson, and Cinematographer Vittorio Storaro; and I managed to stay awake to the end.

But I suppose if we hadn't seen *Batman* last year, this would have been a knockout. The problem is…we did…so it ain't. Not from my seat, it wasn't. Everything from the egomania of Warren Beatty needing to jettison the Chester Gould art in lieu of second-rate cartooning that uses his puss instead of Tracy's classic square jaw, to the Danny Elfman score seemed to me just okay. So-so. Middlin'. No big deal.

I do think, however, that it was cheesy of Touchstone to panic in expectation that the Code censors would object to the see-through clothes Madonna wore, and rotoscope shadows onto her so no one in Utah would be offended by her nipples and the cleft of her ass.

And speaking of Danny Elfman, who created the score for *Darkman*—as well as *Beetlejuice*, *Batman*, and *Tracy*—he's just about worn out his welcome. What was fresh and intriguing as background for *Beetlejuice*, and darkly compelling and heroic for *Batman*, has become, with his *Dick Tracy* and *Darkman* soundtracks, a predictable calculus of finite differences. Apparently—and I hope I'm not condemning Elfman too quickly, because his theme for *The Simpsons* is just ducky—this guy seems to have run out of his caesuras and cadenzas. What he has to say, he's said at least twice too many times already. He's the overused composer of choice this season, and he's working, which is always nice for any artist, even one I've enjoyed since he did the crazy score for his brother's flick *Forbidden Zone* (featuring the Mystic Knights of the Oingo Boingo) back in 1980; but these are meters and figures that have grown rapidly contemptible through familiarity. The most memorable legacies of *Dick Tracy*, in fact, may not be the film itself, nor its planned sequel(s), but the ancillary soundtrack albums, excluding the forgettable Elfman epodes.

If you haven't yet cupped your auricles and membrana tympani around Madonna's *I'm Breathless* (Sire/Warner Bros. Records 1-26209) and *Dick Tracy* (Sire/WB 26236-2), a collection of Andy Paley's 1930s style songs from the movie, performed by certified killers LaVern Baker, Al Jarreau, Darlene Love, k.d. lang and Take 6, Brenda Lee, Patti Austin, and the Killer himself, Jerry Lee Lewis, consider your summer misspent. Even MTV can't resist lang's "Ridin' the Rails"; and Ms. Baker belting the gutbucket double-entendres of "Slow Rollin' Mama" reminds us that it ain't a matter of censorship that consigns 2 Live Crew to musical oblivion, it's the paucity of their talent, their crassness and obviousness, onaccounta Ms. Baker is a hundred times steamier than the rap-rats, but not even a mook like Jesse Helms would dare to suggest that it's anything but Art, High Art!

And though I haven't heretofore been a big booster of Madonna, because denied all the amplification and razzmatazz she's got a little voice that a whisper from Ella or Billie or Bessie would blow away, but I've got to say that her way with the slick Stephen Sondheim compositions on *I'm Breathless* would set a tuffstone Easter Island statue to scatting. In the blaze of these two sets, the repetitious Elfman elevator music stands deep in a darkness that oozes over to *Darkman*. If anyone out there knows Mr. Elfman, and values the not-inconsiderable talent he clearly possesses, you might pass along these caveats and whisper a couple of names to him: John Barry and John Williams, film composers who burst blindingly, overexposed themselves, marked time in place, and burned out, the former almost forgotten, the latter Boston popped. Then speak these names louder: Alfred Newman, Nino Rota, Ennio Morricone, Bernard Hermann, Claude Bolling, Miklos Rozsa.

Do the litany strike a familiar note?

ANCILLARY MATTERS: The University of Nebraska Press (901 N. 17th, Lincoln, Nebraska 68588) has published THE STRANGE CASE OF DR. JEKYLL & MR. HYDE, illustrated by the incredible, the breathtaking, the astonishing Barry Moser, with a foreword by Joyce Carol Oates. It's the version based on the original 1886 edition, and the dozen wood engravings by Moser will knock you out. It's only fifteen bucks, and you *must* own it!

The damnedest part about this "film critic" crapola is the frequency with which readers of the column (or the book) feel the need to come up to me and say, "I enjoy your columns…I don't always agree with everything you have to say…but I like reading them…even when I don't agree with everything you have to say."

Now where the hell did they (or you) ever get the demented idea that I need everyone to agree with everything I have to say in these little outings? Hell, *I* don't even agree with everything I have to say in these columns!

You show me someone who agrees with *everything* I have to say, with every lunatic theory or opinion I exude, with every weird position I take (sometimes just to piss you off), and I'll show *you* someone who made re-entry at too steep an angle.

As I said in the introduction to the original volume, first edition (HARLAN ELLISON'S WATCHING, 1989), everyone has a hatful of opinions about movies, no less fervently held than their absolute certainties about religion, politics, proper behavior, and the sexual proclivities of celebrities whom they've never met, but about whom they've read in supermarket tabloids. When I express my admiration for David Lynch's version of Frank Herbert's DUNE, or my loathing of the twisted view of history in *Mississippi Burning*, I often have nose-to-nose confrontations with filmgoers who act as if I've attacked their deepest religious beliefs.

Opinions. That's all I offer, that's all I tread upon. And when someone comes up to me at a lecture, or a book-signing, and runs that ramadoola about not agreeing with everything I have to say, the best I can do is to interpret it as an attempt on the part of the speaker to prove his/her independence as buttress against their misperception that I demand slavish agreement on all points. And I am bewildered; because I seek no such thing.

This agreement thing extends to my relationships with other observers of the world of cinema. As you've read in these pages, over the years, I fancy the way of thinking of Pauline Kael and Jeffrey Lyons and David Denby and Molly Haskell…most of the time. You see, I enjoy their criticism…but I don't agree with everything they have to say…but I like reading them…even when I don't agree with everything they have to say. But if I encounter them, as I occasionally do, we never have to run that ramadoola because *it's a given*. We deal in opinions (or as Voltaire put it: "My trade is to say what I think") and so we understand that half the time we'll be at loggerheads over a specific chunk of film, even though we'll be *simpatico* as to general criteria for good or bad. I wish readers of these columns would grasp same, and refrain from telling me how independent they are.

Now if you want to read some *other* critic with whom I find myself agreeing a *lot* of the time, try a perceptive essayist name of Kathi Maio. She appears mostly in a publication called *Sojourner* (after Sojourner Truth, one of my personal idols), and she has a collection of her reviews/criticism currently available, name of FEMINIST IN THE DARK. (The Crossing Press; Freedom, California 95019; 239 pp.; $7.95 in paper, with a cloth edition available, but I don't know at what cost.)

Ms. Maio has a sharp eye, and a keen sense of rightdoing, as well as wrongdoing, when it comes to what Hollywood (and Otherwhere) gives us to mull over. She has altered my viewpoint more than a couple of times, and changed my heart several more oftentimes than that. She is so smart, and so clever in the ways she uses that smartness in her writing, that you will never again be able to look at *Dirty Dancing* or *Jewel of the Nile* or *Fatal Attraction* without her ingenuous voice whispering in your ear that not only isn't the emperor wearing any clothes, but that his wee-wee ain't all that spectacular, either.

And if the word "feminist" in the title of her book gets you nervous, I can allay your twitchiness only to this degree: she isn't a stuffy semiotic bore, she is a real honest-to-peaches *writer*, with wit and bemusement and passion. And I hope you will seek her out, because there aren't many film commentators as good as Maio and me around, and you'd better be nice to us or we'll abandon you to Siskel and Ebert, and *then* where'll you be?

45 In Which *Tempus* Fidgets, *Fugits*, and Inevitably Omnia Revelats

Like idle hands, my unattended mind is The Devil's Plaything.

Turn my back for three seconds, to check the ingredients in a Gourmet Pride, examine the pocket lint caught under my fingernail, shun a Bud commercial during the World Series...and I begin with the bizarre suppositions:

All we've ever found are fossilized remains, so how do we know dinosaur skins were that Lake Erie gray or Fort Benning olive-green we always see in the paintings? We've never found any preserved epidermis, no frozen Polacanthus with its tarp intact. And there are lizards around today, descendants of the saurians, with iridescent hides, with the chameleon ability to change color, with protective pigmentations in a host of decorator hues...so how do we know that Montanoceratops wasn't maybe paisley? Here comes a sixty-nine foot long Alamosaurus in a fetching coruscation of rainbow shades with pastel fuchsia, carnation pink, and sky blue predominating. Sure, Baryonyx is a pain in the ass, always running around chewing out the throat of some unsuspecting Massospondylus, spraying graffiti all over the Morrison Formation, bringing down Early Cretaceous, Late Triassic, whatever, property values, but wouldja just give a look at that nifty plaid overcoat he's wearing! Who's to know? I think about stuff like that.

Or how about this: the exquisite Chinese novelist and philologist Lin Yutang (1885–1976) opined, "What is patriotism but the love of the food one ate as a child?" That insight always knocked me out; and so I began extrapolating on it. Could not one postulate that *religion* might also, likewise, be nothing more than a love of the food one ate as a child? And if that were so, then perhaps all the trouble Moses had with the children of Israel after they fled Egypt had less to do with the worship of golden calves than it did with fast food. That is to say, here they are schlepping around in the desert, Moses having chosen (not too wisely) to go east into the wilderness of Sinai instead of heading north, following the coast, taking the shortest-distance-between-two-points route into Canaan; and here are the 12 Tribes, cranky and exhausted, and already pretty nervous about following this guy maybe to the ends of the earth who is "slow of speech, and of a slow tongue," which maybe meant he was a stammerer, but also could mean he lisped, and following a guy who sounds like Porky Pig or a drag queen into the desert has got them major twitchy; and they're heavily traumatized already, having barely survived lousy labor relations building the pyramids, on which gig they would get the crap kicked outta them if they asked for a gourdful of water; and this Pharaoh, Ramses II (though some say it was Memeptah), was such an uptight putz that he got God and Moses cheesed off at him, so they called down this icky concatenation of plagues including frogs, flies, turning the river to blood so all the fish went belly-up, something called *murrain* (which I looked up and it means all the cattle and other livestock started to puke, and they came down with anthrax and hoof-and-mouth and Texas fever, and like that, also sweating blood), and hail, and locusts, and blotting out the sun, and eventually because Pharaoh was such a slow learner God called in this hit man, the Angel of Death, and he knocked off all the first-born of Egypt, which was worse than *Friday the Thirteenth, Part VI*—and the 12 Tribes had to sit through all *that*; not to mention following this guy through a body of water that opened up to let them pass and then came flooding back in to wipe out the entire standing army of Ramses II (or possibly Memeptah); so by the time they find themselves schlepping around in the desert, not too terrific a location, for three months…their nerves are, not to put too fine a point on it, most severely frayed. And they get to Mt. Horeb (some say it was Mount Seir), and all they've been eating for the last ninety days is this manna. Now, manna is okay once in a while, as a side-dish in place of potatoes or Mrs. Cubbison's stuffing, but day after day for three bloody *months*! Come *on*! I mean, you know how sick you get of turkey leftovers after Thanksgiving, for just under a week? Picture how sweet-tempered *you'd* be if you had to go footing it through some miserable desert with nothing to scarf down but turkey giblets. So they get to Horeb, and some of the shop stewards of the 12 Tribes come to see Moses, and they lay it right on the line. "Look, Mo," one of them says, "let me be frank with you. We're up to here with the manna, you know what I'm saying? We don't mean to bitch about it, what I mean it was strictly swell of Yahweh to drop the manna on us—even if we had one helluva time getting all the sand and grit out of it—but c'mon already, we've had manna sandwiches and manna *soufflé*, manna soup and manna pudding topped with creamed manna, chipped manna on toast, rack of manna, sunnyside-up manna on matzoh, manna *purée* and those cute little manna croquettes—and to be absolutely candid about it, Moses sweetie...IF WE EAT ONE MORE FUCKIN' MEAL OF MANNA WE'RE ALL GOING TO SLASH OUR WRISTS!!! So Moses says okay, okay, don't bust my chops (to which one of the shop stewards murmurs, "I'd go through frogs and flies and *murrain* for a nice chop"), and he tells them to cool it till he goes up on the mountain and has this sit-down with the Lord, and as soon as he gets back they'll detour toward Canaan and find the first clean roadside diner, and everybody can sheep out (because to *pig* out would be *trayf*). So Moses takes off, and the 12 Tribes wait around for forty days and forty nights— eating nothing but fried manna, stewed manna, manna ragout, cold poached manna on a bed of shredded manna, manna *crêpes*, manna fingers with grit topping, broiled manna, and those nasty little manna croquettes—and somebody in his right mind says, "Let's look on the bright side: maybe Moses was eaten by a bear, and let's get the hell outta here and find a nice Howard Johnson's or at worst a Burger King, and t'hell with this wandering in the Sinai shtick!" And everybody says something in unison like *Works for me*, and they get Moses's brother, Aaron, to make up this golden calf to kind of raise their spirits preparatory to moving out, and all of a sudden here comes Moses, after forty bleeding days and nights, and he's schlepping these stone tablets and he starts screaming at them that one of the Commandments is that they're not supposed to make any graven idols because it'll get Yahweh really pissed off, and they all yell back at him, "Hey, schmuck, how were *we* supposed to know that was one of the rules? You're just bringing them down now! What're we, supposed to be telepathic!?!" But Moses keeps *geshrying* at them, and they tell him to get stuffed, all they wanted was a nice piece gefilte fish or a piece flanken, and God hears all this and directs that half the Tribes should murder the other half, not to mention that for punishment they've got to wander in this stupid desert for another forty *years*! Geez, talk about a tough grader! I think about stuff like that.

    I wonder who Ben Gay was; and was there ever an Absorbine, Sr.

    I muse about weird stuff like: if DNA contains all the memory of the original organism, is capable of transmitting genetic information, then isn't it possible that the molecule could also transmit racial memory, and if that's so, then maybe the persistence of belief in reincarnation is nothing more than our DNA giving us the genetic *déjà vu* of "past lives" experienced by the RNA and other nucleic acids. I think about stuff like that.

    And I had this peculiar, but I think logical, surmise: since Neanderthals had no understanding of "time"—that is to say, no possibility of comprehending the concept of "the future"—when Pleistocene Patty seduced Sly the Slope-Browed into hauling her ashes, or Harry Hominid committed date-rape on Aliciapithecus, did they make the connection between the, uh, er, connection *now*, and the birth of Java Junior nine months down the line?

Without a sense of being part of a chronological flow, how did Cro-Magnons understand that a fiery itch in their loins *today* could result in another mouth to feed about a year from today? And who was the first to figure it out? Sure as hell wasn't Jesse Helms, despite the resemblance to *Dendropithecus*.

Which random woolgathering brings me, widdershins and clanking, to my cinematic subject, to wit, the value of the *Back to the Future* trilogy. I think about stuff like that.

Back in the January 1986 installment of this column, I had more than a few things to say about *Back to the Future*; none of them likely to be ellipsed and quoted on the one-sheets. At the time I wrote installment 14—with subsequent opprobrious references to the film in essays on other topics—sort of a paradigm for all that had become "trivial as a Twinkie" in sf movies—I was unaware that two sequels were in the planning stages. Nor was I aware of how smartly I would turn on my heel, now, four years later, in my opinion of the work.

It's not so much that my opinion of the first film was "wrong" or even wrongheaded. My judgment of that single film, standing alone, is stet. But taken as one-third of a cinematic triptych, well, not judging the first *Back to the Future* as part of the whole, *in situ*, would be like passing an esthetic judgment on Bosch's *The Adoration of the Magi* having seen only the right-hand panel.

That is to say, upon reflection and viewing of *Back to the Future II* and *Back to the Future III* (Universal/Amblin) the whole is definitely greater than the sum of the parts.

The contrived shenanigans of Michael J. Fox's "Marty McFly" and Christopher Lloyd's "Dr. Emmett Brown" and Thomas F. Wilson's "Biff Tannen" are not the impetus for this reevaluation—which plot folderol still seems to me hardly a patch on the human and philosophical questions raised by *Peggy Sue Got Married*, the time-travel film that was contemporaneous with the first *Back to the Future*—but their tripartite hugger-mugger assumes a greater significance, and an unexpected possibility of richer purpose than the first film implied, taken on sum.

The second film was almost universally panned as incomplete, unable to stand on its own without the buttressing foreword and afterword. Naturally, being out of synch with the rest of the universe, I admired *Part II* the most. Probably because it was the most inventive, and consequently the least accessible to the general viewing audience (and fer damned sure harder to understand for the general run of film critics whose bleary confusion was hysterically evident).

Part I was a slaphappy teen movie with a standard timetwist. *Part III* is equally goony in an obstinately lovable, Keystone Kop, rubberfaced manner. (And one day soon remind me to give you some thoughts on movies that fall all over themselves trying to make you love them.) The paradox problems raised in *Part II* pay off as Marty goes slipstreaming back to 1885, the Old West of John Ford and Anthony Mann, riding his faithful cayuse, the 1985 DeLorean. He rescues Doc Brown from a preordained demise, he defies the wobbly internal logic of time travel set up in *Parts I* and *II*, and finally comes home in time (and space) to an acceptable status quo, *avec* steam engine.

Nothing in the first and third segments of this trilogy will strain your mind much. Which is likely why they were so outrageously praised.

But *Part II*, in which Marty and Doc Brown have to set things aright in the year 2015, after setting up a kind of chronosynclastic infindibulum in 1955, is twisty, turny, and terrifically tangy. It is also sf/fantasy of a considerably higher order than we usually get in theatrical features.

After viewing *Part I* four years ago, I didn't expect much from a sequel that I presumed had been ordered up as strictly a moneymaking endeavor. And when I learned that *II* and *III* were to be shot together, well, I fear my cynical nature slipped a drop or two of hemlock into my expectations. But *Part II*, which I admire considerably when melded with its sidekicks, may possibly be an icon that will serve the commonweal. A postulation that may be as ineffective as emetic, as was the hemlock of my cynicism. But what the hell.

The nihilism of the '80s, which with only a trembling of wariness at the sight of Charles Keating in chains and Michael Milken in the dock seems to be living on into the '90s, is a far cry from the much-derided sense of social conscience that fueled the reforms of the '60s and '70s. I've belabored this elsewhere, so I won't reiterate, save to suggest that neither an Ollie North nor an Ivan Boesky would have been tolerated in those days of social upheaval.

But Reagan and Nixon and Bush have had their way with the *vox populi* and me-firstism has been the order of the times for far too long.

So I'm grasping at straws when I suggest that *possibly* a trio of popular flicks, the *Back to the Future* totality, might serve to pique the intellect of the pithecanthropoid who, having had sex nine months earlier, might experience that leap of extrapolation and connect it with the birth of the baby today.

Because *I*, *II*, and *III*—but primarily the unjustly maligned *II*—deal with the subject of responsibility. Not just to the loved ones, but to the world as a whole, to posterity, to the generations yet unborn. These films traffic in cause and effect, a concept earlier times in this country dealt with regularly. A concept that seems nonexistent in the world today.

If you suggest to the rapacious mini-mall developer that leveling the woods and rendering much of that acreage as concrete parking lot will surely raise the mean temperature of the area, s/he will stare at you as if your eyes droop on stalks. S/he will then talk about "progress" and "jobs" and how selfish you must be to want to thwart honest enterprise.

If you brace a kid three blocks from a McDonald's, who has just pitched his milk shake cup and french fries container into the street, and you point out that litter is not only unsightly, but has to be cleaned up by others, that it is probably nonbiodegradable, and that s/he ought to think of others, s/he will flip you off, snort derisively, log you in as an uptight looney definitely uncool, and go on her/his merry way.

And if you go down to Brazil and tell some poor *mestizo* getting a measly hundred *cruzeiros* a day to clearcut the rain forest, so it can be planted in grain to feed beeves that will then be converted into precisely those McDonald's goodies whose wrappers find their way into city streets in Akron and Anchorage and Amityville, he will tell you that his three babies up in the *favella* need milk, that his wife has rickets, that this is the first steady employment, however exhausting and minimally rewarded, he's been able to get since last *Fevereiro*. And how do you fight that, looking into his weary face?

So we live in the moment, having been brainwashed for decades like the Me Decade to believe that it is not what we *think*, but what we *feel*, that is worthy of attention. We live on the edge of the instant, with no regard (and seemingly no understanding) for what comes next, and how every breath and gesture and movement is linkage with the future.

We do not seem to understand that if we fuck today, we will give birth nine months from now.

But here is this trilogy of lightweight, happy-go-lucky films with a lovable mad scientist, an oh-so-hip role-model for kids, and a standard issue schoolyard bully (brilliantly assayed by Thomas Wilson, whose performances seem richer and deeper with each viewing), and the films *demonstrate* that every action has a resultant price that must be paid. If not today, then next week, or next year. The films say: Caution! Think about it now, while you have the chance.

That's no small message in these parlous times.

Responsibility.

An abstract concept when Mom and Dad speak to the kids; a nebulosity when teachers program it into their lessons; a vagueness having no immediate worth when people do what they do. (Which is why I've never believed for an instant that the death penalty deters *anyone* from acting like a thug.)

But here come these three funny, action-filled movies...

All three of which are available for straight-through viewing on videocassette, all in one long evening. And there is just this tiniest tinkle of a salvation bell in my head, that says if cinema is *truly* as influential as Hollywood would have us believe, then for once maybe the message hasn't been that women are fodder, that vigilantism is the only answer to street crime, that villains need not necessarily be Dr. No or Manuel Noriega...that the villains may be us only and simply because we didn't think about tomorrow.

And that's some terrific supposition, even if it's crazy as an optimist in front of a Dachau oven. But it's stranger things than that to which we can pay homage in the erratic progress of our species from Paramecium to pollution.

Yeah, even a cynic thinks about stuff like that.

46 In Which We Bend So Far Over Backwards to Be Unbiased That You Can See the Nose Hairs Quiver with Righteousness

Every now and then, even these days, I'll find myself of an odd evening in company with friends who just want to hang out around the house; maybe we've had dinner; maybe they've come in from out of town and they're too bushed to make a night of it, out and around Hollywood. And we find ourselves up in my big office, sitting around in the gloaming, perhaps one low-wattage light shaping shadows, and someone will say, "Put on something interesting," by which she or he means: hey, mister music buff, play something from that great repository of lps up beside your desk, something we don't know. By which he or she means: *étonne-moi*.

And every now and then, even these days, I'll smile with a secret pleasure—because it's a pleasure returned to me after a great many seasons of having been denied me—and I'll say, "Oh, okay...listen to this. See if you can tell me who's singing on this album."

Then I go to that bin of record albums within arm's reach of my typewriter, where I keep the couple hundred albums that no amount of time or fashion has managed to render hincty for me—a pair of Jack Teagarden sides on which he does Willard Robison blues; Big Miller's first set for Columbia; half a dozen David Grisman lps, a few with Grappelli; The Crusaders with B.B. King and the Royal Philharmonic recorded live at Royal Festival Hall in London in 1981; Stevie Ray Vaughan; Blind Blake; Bob Dorough and Jackie Paris and The Tango Project and Mike Nesmith's *From a Radio Engine to the Photon Wing*; lots of Django, Gerry Mulligan, Dr. John's *City Lights*, and Van Dyke Parks; Otis and Lenny Welch and Alan Price and the only album, I think, that was ever recorded by this astonishing young woman named Judy Roderick; and Aretha's first album and that heartbreaking Chet Baker with strings set—and with great affection and expectation I slip onto the turntable an album I've played so many times it's soft as glove leather with groove erosion, and I crank the gain to about 5 (which is maybe a fourth of the way around, but enough to let the Quad electrostatic screens pick up everything), and in the slippery darkness there comes this ecstatic, mesmerizing jazz voice doing tricks with Duke Ellington's and Juan Tizol's "Caravan" that sends the tectonic plates of your heart sliding and gliding. It's a Teo Macero arrangement with Hal McKusick on clarinet and alto sax, Nick Travis on trumpet, and a cadre of some of the finest jazzmen of the mid-fifties...but it's that unbelievable voice that paralyzes everybody in the room.

You've never heard anything like it.

And when the track is ended, I move the tone arm to "Cabin in the Sky" and then "Angel Eyes" and finally I let them hear this guy perform the absolutely most beautiful version of Duke's "Prelude to a Kiss" orchestrated by John Lewis of the MJQ when he was at the peak of his talent...and I let it slide into silence...and everyone sits in darkness having been caressed and indulged and taken away from there for a few minutes...and finally, after a while, even these days, someone will murmur, "Jeezus gawd who the hell was *that*!?!" And I smile gently in the shadows and I say, "Johnny Mathis."

And they can't believe it, because all they know of Johnny Mathis is the commercial crap he's recorded for the past three decades or so; all the oleaginous makeout music they used to get them in the mood; and what I've just taken off the turntable is a jazz voice so sinuous, so subtle and supple, backed by arrangements so smart and so hip they are timeless, that they think I'm yanking their chains. And they come and pick up the worn, frayed album sleeve, and there he is:

Mathis when he was nineteen years old, fresh out of San Francisco, recorded on Columbia by George Avakian, with a set of songs arranged and conducted by the likes of Gil Evans and John Lewis and Teo and Manny Albam and Bob Prince, most of which are names my visitors don't know were traffic-stoppers before Dee Dee Ramone was out of swaddling.

It was Mathis's first album. He'd been singing around San Francisco; he'd done some college gigs; and they'd found him bigtime at Ann's 440 Club up above the old Barbary Coast line; and they'd schlepped him to New York; and nestled him like a diamond in this recording session setting of the best, the very best in the world. And he done jazz. Not that pop schmaltz that dripped ooze off the albums so you had to wear workgloves or the platter'd slip out of your hands, that lachrymose trick-up payroll music that made him a star and a millionaire and a voice I didn't want to hear.

But every once in a time, even these days, I repeat what I used to do in those first days of his arrival, and I astound a whole new bunch of listeners the way I did then, as if it were thirty years ago again. It's a pleasure denied me for a long time. And I'm struck by this subhuman very-human failing most of us share, which is that when we've discovered some writer or singer or piquant little restaurant, and nobody else ever heard of it (or them), we revel in it (or them), and we laud them (or it) to the skies, and we feel like a *pezzonovante* because we've shared this unknown treasure.

And then everyone else discovers the singer, or the writer, or tells their uptown friends and the restaurant is jammed and the prices climb and you can't get a seat without you gotta wait a week for some tightassed maitre d' to deign to notice you and they're doing numbers with arugula and radicchio, and then one afternoon some halfwit sufi-faced systems analyst in a J. Press suit confides in you that he's reading *your* writer and have you ever heard of this guy; or he's been listening to this really hot new CD on his beamer's surround-a-scape and have you ever heard this guy; or he can't wait to take you to dinner at this oh so chic and ultimately inward little café off the beaten track where simply *everybody* is eating and have you heard of this treasure...and the next thing you know you've buried a paving stone in the gink's brainpan and they're dragging you off for trial, and even in the joint there are cons telling you how you ought to get with such and such a writer or singer or (when you get sprung) swell nifty little restaurant.

And the treasure has been stolen from you, because now *everyone* knows about it and, like a lover who comes to see his paramour and has to take a number, you despise and revile that which you adored when it was yours and yours alone.

You hear yourself running down the artist, trying to puff yourself up by saying how this new book is just commercial tripe and that's why the writer is suddenly, for the first time, on the bestseller list, and the new book isn't a shadow of what the writer created when s/he lived in poverty. And you're saying s/he has "sold out" because you're a jilted lover. And unless you wrench yourself up like a man on a gibbet, and slam yourself mentally and face the fact that you're being irrational...well, you're being a righteous poop; and unfair; and unworthy.

I went to see the world premiere of *The Rocketeer* (Disney Pictures) the other night. I've been waiting maybe five years for it.

The creator of The Rocketeer is a swell guy named Dave Stevens. He is about as gentle and decent a young man as you'd ever want to meet. Looks a whole lot like the actor they've got playing Cliff Secord, The Rocketeer. That's because when Dave drew the first installments of the comic for the long-defunct *Pacific Presents* back in 1982–84, he drew himself.

I've known Dave a long time. When the first five chapters of The Rocketeer continuity were pulled together for the splendid Graphitti Designs graphic novel, the thirty dollar signed limited edition, in 1985, with that remarkable cameo illustration of Doug Wildey as Peevy, Dave as Cliff Secord, and Betty Page as curvaceous Betty, Cliff's girl friend, adorning the cover, it was I whom Dave asked to write the introduction.

The point is: I *love* Dave Stevens's Rocketeer.

I love his artwork, over which he labors like a beanfield hand, bitching endlessly that the litho plant put too much red in the skin-tones when they printed it. I love the story-line with its absolute 1938 authenticity, because Dave is a maniac for perfection of background. I love the playful references to Doc Savage and his associates, who turn up in the story so unexpectedly that Stevens never calls them by name and you sit there wondering *is that who I think it is*? I love the fact that, like Eastman and Laird of Turtles fame, here is this talented kid who worked his butt off, and unlike most hard workers who slave away for an in-group audience and never make a dime, Dave has hit it big and may have a chance at the big score. I love it that this major film company spared no expense in bringing his creation to life and Dave is riding the crest of the wave and everyone is proclaiming him the flavor of the month! I love it all.

Which makes me the single most untrustworthy critic of the film you will encounter this summer season. How the hell can I be relied on to tell you the straight of this film, without I'm either goofy prejudiced in its favor because of all the baggage I'm hauling, or bitter rotten shitfaced cynical about it because now *everybody* is eating there and I can't get a seat?

Hell, I wouldn't trust me as far as I could throw the entire staff of *Entertainment Tonight*, left-handed.

Nonetheless, it falls to me to report on *The Rocketeer*, because it is certainly going to be the big fantasy film of the season; and let me tell you I've worried this matter some serious time before I selected the m.o. I will now forthwith describe.

I will state baldly and shamelessly that I enjoyed the hell out of this movie. If you have no negative feelings about being a dirty-faced seven-year-old kid at a Saturday afternoon matinee, then you cannot save yourself from falling headfirst into this flick and swimming right along with Cliff and Peev and swarthy Eddie Valentine and nefarious Neville Sinclair and pneumatic Jenny Blake (who is chickenshit Disney's substitute for Betty) and all the rest of Dave Stevens's characters in a knockdown special effects and slamdunk adventure extravaganza that will fricasee your eyeballs with action and derring-do very much like that you enjoyed when your heart was younger and your taste was too good to be refined.

And having said that, I will now point out every error I could spot in the movie.

I think I'm doing the right thing here. This has not been an easy path to select. But Dave Stevens will understand.

One ground-rule. *The Rocketeer*, a graphic novel, was written and drawn by Dave Stevens. *The Rocketeer*, a motion picture, was written for the screen by Danny Bilson and Paul De Meo from a story by both of them with William Dear. In fairness, they have been true down the line to Dave's original. And where they have deviated, their choices have been inspired. (For instance, the excellent substitution of Howard Hughes for Doc Savage, which makes for some of the sharpest moments of the replotting.) But as I must admit that I have found Bilson and De Meo's work on the tv version of *The Flash* moribund and pallid, so do I attribute the flaws in the film at least 50% to their contributions.

In short, I'm discussing here a movie and not a graphic novel. I'm nitpicking at a committee-product, not the singular conception of the original creator.

The basic flaw of the film is in the characterization of the hero, Cliff Secord. In the graphic novel Dave made Cliff more than endearing. He was charming. He was naive, but steady; headstrong, but not a doofus. In the film Bill Campbell has been given a character who is not only foolish and foolhardy, he's imprudent, idiotic, sappy, and often plain stupid. It makes for a hollow core to the adventure. Let me give you a major f'rinstance. (This is a Bilson-De Meo departure from the canon.)

At the beginning of the story, Cliff and his mechanic, inventor pal Peevy have been working for three years on readying the GeeBee racer for the National Air Show. They have sunk every cent they possess into it. Cliff takes the plane up for a test flight. Meanwhile, Eddie Valentine's pistoleros—who have swiped the Cirrus X-3, an experimental strap-on rocket pack designed by Hughes—are being high-speed chased by the FBI in the vicinity. Secord flies directly over them. He can see that the fleeing car has a guy in the open rumble seat who is spraying the chasing vehicle with a Thompson submachine gun. He can see that the pursuing vehicle has a guy leaning out the window firing a pistol at the fleeing car. He can see this, and we can see that he sees it. Now any rational person, hero or otherwise, having sunk three years and everything he and his friends possess in the plane he's flying, would have done a barrel roll and gotten the hell out of there. But (and this may be in the inept direction of Joe Johnston, a former artist, designer, and Artistic Director for Lucasfilm's Industrial Light and Magic, whose only previous directorial credit is *Honey, I Shrunk the Kids*, which ain't exactly *The Magnificent Ambersons*) Cliff flies low over them, for no particular reason we can discern. He "buzzes" them, in effect, though that's probably the last thing Johnston and the scenarists wanted us to think.

So Secord gets his plane shot up by the goon in the fleeing roadster, the plane crashes, burns, explodes into dead dreams; everything is lost. It thus makes the imbecile protagonist, whom we're to perceive as being of heroic stature, a simpleton, a reckless jerk who has bumpishly put in harm's way the single most important object in his (and his friend's) life. Everything that follows is as a result of his stupid curiosity, his doofus irresponsibility.

But wait, as they say on the Ginsu commercials, there's more!

Not too much later, the thugs of Eddie Valentine (played to the hilt by Paul Sorvino, whose appearances were much too brief), looking for Secord, come to the Bulldog Café, where all the airfield chaps hang out. They grab Secord's best friend, his closest buddy, the staunch and admirable Peevy (an antic and, but for one inapt line, charming performance by Alan Arkin). They drag him over to the short order griddle and they start to press his face down onto the red-hot metal. Tell us who and where Secord is! (Cliff is sitting right there.) Peevy won't talk. No one else talks, either. Including Secord, who is sitting *right there*! He makes a move to pick up a ketchup bottle, but one of the mobsters holds a gun on him. And Peevy's face gets closer and closer. Secord says nothing. No one says anything.

At the last instant, one of the goons sees a clue written on the wall beside the telephone. It is utterly gratuitous and happenstance, the kind of last-instant save that makes one groan. But the lameness of the plotting—a clear example of the basic weaknesses of Bilson and De Meo's abilities—the kind of inability to plot well enough that would preclude writing yourself into that corner, but not the sort of thing these guys were taught in "film school" (in this case both got their degrees in Theater Arts at Cal State San Bernardino)—isn't the quibble here. The awfulness of their lame plotting is that it makes Secord seem not just a miserable liverguts coward, but willing to sacrifice his best friend rather than risk his own ass. There's his mentor, the sweet and gentle Peevy, about to get his face seared on a greasy grille unless he finks on Secord, and he won't spill the beans…but Secord doesn't make a move!

These two pivotal moments, plus the endlessly childish and essentially dopey behavior of Secord, makes for a sense of impropriety that such a lox should be gifted with the rocket pack and the secret identity of The Rocketeer, the traditional "magical appurtenances" of this sort of legend. The young knight must never be given the cloak of invisibility, the winged horse, and the enchanted sword unless he is worthy. One does not put the golden greaves and mystical helm on a plowboy who is a craven.

And if the homage to Rondo Hatton, the villain of one of my favorite films, 1946's *House of Horrors*, is wonderful; if the dead-ringerism of the nightclub's clarinet-playing bandleader to Artie Shaw is terrific; if the Billy Strayhorn opening to Duke Ellington's "In a Sentimental Mood" is spectacularly well-placed; if Hughes and his Spruce Goose are a hoot; if the tongue-in-cheek destruction of the last four letters of the HOLLYWOODLAND sign is a must-see filmic moment...these joys are unbalanced by such silly (and avoidable) gaffes as these:

• Secord, posing as a waiter, sets a soup bowl containing a note that is written in ink in front of Jenny as she dines with the villain Neville Sinclair at the South Seas Club. The note says: Meet me by the big fish *now*! She sees it, is startled, looks up, recognizes Cliff, and he pours soup over the note to conceal it. Later, Sinclair (Timothy Dalton) spies the floating paper when Jenny has left the table, fishes it out, and reads it, thus tipping to her charade in leaving, and thus alerted to Secord's presence at the Club. Except... in 1938 there was no such thing as a ballpoint pen, no such thing as fountain pen ink that wouldn't run, no way that note could have been read. It would have turned to a smear. (No, I've checked it out, gentle arguists; it wasn't written in pencil. It was in ink.)

• Early on, someone (either Cliff to Peevy or Peevy to Cliff, I believe) looks at the Cirrus X-3 and asks what it is. The other answers, "A rocket pack, like in the comic books." No way. In 1938 there were only a few comic books in existence, and none of them featured people using rocket packs. What he *meant* to say—but Bilson and De Meo are too young to know—was "just like in the comic *strips*" because the reference is to Buck Rogers, who *was* the model for such rocketman concepts.

• With the possible exception (I'm told) of one busboy, nowhere in this film is there a black face. Now it may be that Disney wished to recreate the feel of 1938 Los Angeles, but since the original founder of Los Angeles (after the Mexicans) was a black man, I feel certain no one's sense of authenticity would have been jarred had there been *some* indication, however minuscule, of the traditional racial diversity of LA's population. I'm not talking Political Correctness here, or even tokenism...I'm talking simply The Way It Was, Is, Always Will Be, here in the City of Variegated-Hued Angels!

• Two points about Jennifer Connelly, the young woman who plays Jenny. One may seem churlish, the other has to do with costuming. On the former point, I risk the sort of opprobrium that critic John Simon drew when he correctly pointed out that Liza Minnelli looks like a plucked chicken, when I say that Ms. Connolly has the hugest teeth in the civilized world, a set of choppers that Bucky Beaver would envy; and every time she skinned back her lips and unsheathed those ivories, it was as if she were advertising Pepsodent. Now I realize that since several less-than-veiled references were made to the size of Ms. Connolly's breasts, we were supposed to fixate on her cleavage; but her secondary sex characteristics were put in the shade by the dazzling effulgence of her blazing bicuspids. Were it one of director Johnston's fortes to handle actors well, he might have noted that when Ms. Connolly did the tooth thing all the background was lost in the glare, and we might have been spared that aspect of her otherwise pleasing manner.

As to the costuming error, it is one we are *meant* to notice, for meretricious intent. I mentioned that our attention is regularly drawn to Ms. Connolly's chest. Well, they have her in a tight sweater at one stage, and we can see the outline of nipples. In a modern drama or comedy, no big deal. But in 1938 not only were women still following the fashion of flatness, as represented by such stars as Myrna Loy (who is mentioned), to the extent that they often bound their breasts to appear trimmer, but a "nice girl" like Jenny—and we are endlessly reminded that she *is* a nice girl, no matter how venally she wishes to be a movie star—would *never* have worn a bra that permitted the outline of her nipples to protrude. Remember that when Marilyn Vance-Straker gets her Oscar nomination for Best Costume Design next year.

• The unbelievable hokiness of having a hundred Nazi commandos in ninja outfits suddenly jump out of the bushes at the Griffith Observatory. Not even a premiere evening audience, totally going for the ambience and grandiose exaggeration of the pulp-magazine plot, not even they could restrain a groan of disbelief. If you're going to rely on the willing suspension of disbelief of an audience to con them with this kind of florid storyline and pictorial, you'd better make damned sure you don't cross the line into ridiculousness, which is where Bilson and De Meo and Johnston went sashaying with the Nazi attack squadron.

The astute reader will now take the patented cortical-thalamic pause of A.E. van Vogt and say, "*These* are your damning negatives? These are the flaws? What a picayune pain in the ass you are, Ellison!" And with the exceptions of the rotten character plotting I mentioned at the outset, you're right. This is piddling stuff. But I said I was an untrustworthy observer on this one, because of vested interests. I've tried to be evenhanded, scrupulous to a fault, beyond fair into ultra-fair...but I wouldn't accept for a moment my opinions on this snazzy film. I would doubt the praise, the brickbats, all of it.

If I were you, I'd just go see for myself, and to hell with Ellison's bifurcated balderdash.

And if you want the undiluted stuff, go out and buy the gorgeous graphic novel as done by Dave Stevens. (There are Disney-generated versions, and they're fine, too; but they aren't Stevens. And if you want to see the magic that ensorceled Disney into buying The Rocketeer concept in the first place, it is the Dave Stevens version that burns brightest.) The introduction to the book ain't too dusty, neither.

ANCILLARY MATTERS: All together now, in the voice of the late Heather O'Rourke in *Poltergeist II*: "He's baaaack!"

Yes, I know I've missed column deadline after deadline. But as I told you a few years ago, I've got this crummy illness called Chronic Fatigue Syndrome and, well, sometimes it's worse than others. But I *want* to get back on schedule, and I did promise to be more attentive to schedules, so if you'll be patient, and if you'll take this installment as the beginning of a rededication to regularity, what we might call the Ex-Lax Imperative, I do not think your forbearance will be misplaced.

There have been, as you may have noticed, some big changes around here since last I visited with you. The Noble Fermans have given over the editorial reins to large degree to a person named Rusch. When, late last year, I was approached by my theretofore employers, with the advisement that they were seeking some wretched figurehead personage to accept the rotten remarks and threats of cancellation of subscription if they didn't dump me forthwith, when they confessed that having worked with me for what-is-it something like seven years, and were sick to tears of it all, and needed some peace and quiet in their twilight years, I guffawed at their lack of tenacity, knew I'd at last beaten them into submission, and lived in fear of what mountebank they'd slip in as titular whipping-post. When they selected Ms. Rusch, I was asked for a statement that could be used in a press release. I accommodated twice over. I sent *two* press releases. To my knowledge, neither was used. But I get paid by the word, and I'll be damned if I'll let them go to waste. And besides, I think you ought to know where I stand on this Rusch appointment. So here are the two versions of my position on our new editor:

VERSION A

When advised of Ms. Rusch's selection as the new *F&SF* trail-boss, Film Editor Harlan Ellison remarked, "Thank heaven! We were all wondering when Ferman would pack it in. Covering up for his, well, increasingly embarrassing memory-lapses and incontinence was becoming a burden. Not to take anything away from him—he has been a splendid editor since early in the Jurassic—the man has been slipping of late. Hell, he even considered publishing Piers Anthony and Jack Chalker. That was when his long-suffering wife, Audrey, and the rest of us who slave for a pittance on the magazine knew he had to be put out to pasture. It'll be good to have someone who can be bribed again at the helm of *F&SF*. What did you say this guy's name was? Chris Rowsh? Have no idea who he is, but he's got to be more on the ball than Ferman."

VERSION B

When advised of Ms. Rusch's selection as the new *F&SF* editor, the magazine's film critic, Harlan Ellison, said, "This is sensational good news! Kris Rusch combines respect for the traditions of the genre and the magazine with a fresh and uncluttered view of what it takes to keep *F&SF au courant* as we enter a new decade and a new century. Ed Ferman's choice of a talented *woman* demonstrates once again his taste and sagacity. She will certainly be a worthy successor to the chair so prestigiously occupied by Boucher, McComas, Mills, Davidson and, brilliantly, by Ed Ferman. A new day dawns, and I, for one, could not be more pleased."

Next, is the matter of Kathi Maio. If you recall, some months ago I sang the praises of a film critic named Maio, whose perceptions and pluckiness as a filmwatcher I commended to your attention. Well, Ferman and Rusch noted my enthusiasm, and as it seemed I might never again meet a deadline, they wisely decided to adopt a policy of encouraging Ms. Maio to join our happy little band. Her first appearance follows this column.

Let me be candid about this:

I think she's smarter than I am, more insightful than I am; and a damn sight more polite than I am. Which does not mean that she can't kick ass when she chooses. I am a 100% Maio fan, and in the event I screw up and miss a deadline, you can count on an even better dose of film criticism than mine by Ms. Maio's appearances here. That doesn't mean I'm packing it in. By no means. I can still write a line or two, and I have no plans to go away. But there is a need for regularity here, and I cannot think of *anyone* better for the job than Kathi Maio.

Further, let me tell you right now, though she and I have never met, I am by way of considering myself her pal, and if any of you smartasses give her a hard time, you're gonna have to go through me to get to her. There is nothing paternalistic about it; consider it more Athos to her Porthos. But as I am regularly knocked out by her insights, I would take it as a mark of proper upbringing on your part to give her a chance to get comfy here before you start busting her chops the way you do mine.

Like, for instance, R. Metzl of Rock Hill, South Carolina (among half a dozen others) who picked up on my asides last installment, in which I asked who the hell Ben Gay was, and if there had ever been an Absorbine, Sr.: "I'm sure you know this, and were only playing for comedy, but...

"Yes, there *was* a Ben Gay. He was Dr. Benguet and his formula has been popular for many years.

"Absorbine, Sr.? Yeah, also a long time product. It's for horses. I hope this helps."

Now I could dissemble and pretend I knew that. But I didn't. I just thought it was some funny shit. But I thank the lot of you who jumped on my ignorance and set me to rights. Imagine my gratitude.

Which also goes out to Rick Thocker (I *think* that's the spelling; jeez, Rick, what lousy printing you have) of Russen, Kansas (I *think* it's Russen; jeez, Rick, what lousy printing you have), who sends the following advisement:

"I could not help but write to you concerning your March column on the *Back to the Future* movies.

"You wrote Marty's car is a 1985 DeLorean. As owner of such a car, I feel it is my duty to correct you as to the year of manufacture.

"DeLorean automobiles were built from late in 1981 to early 1983, making a 1985 model impossible."

Yeah, well, you print badly, and you made three grammatical errors that I didn't register here, and anyone who could afford a DeLorean is a smartass anyhow.

It feels good to be back among you. Welcome Kris, welcome Kathi, hi Ed and Audrey, and next time I'm going to do a simply breathtaking piece about *Edward Scissorhands* and a less breathtaking piece about the animated *Lensman* feature, and I've got a whole slew of wonderful visual-type books to recommend.

You simply didn't know when you were well off.

47 In Which Artful Vamping Saves the Publisher $94.98

Years ago, in this space, I promised to do a long essay on the work and vision of David Cronenberg who seemed to me then, as he seems to me now, the preeminently original directorial intelligence of the past decade. I have not forgotten that promise, though I haven't even *begun* to assemble the stock of inside data, interviews, analyses, and brilliant insights I'll need to do an astaire on you. Last time, or perhaps the time before that, I made another promise: a detailed piece on *Edward Scissorhands*, late last year's extraordinary allegorical fantasy from scenarist Caroline Thompson, director Tim Burton, and production designer Bo Welch, with the superlative efforts of thesps Johnny Depp, Winona Ryder, Dianne Wiest, Alan Arkin, et al.

I may have been wrong about the Laker's ability to withstand the carpet-bombing of Air Jordan, but I am burned into the face of the Rock of Eternity with my certainty that *Edward Scissorhands* is not just a fantasy classic, but a *cinematic* classic that will become a cultural staple along with *The Wizard of Oz, Fantasia, King Kong, Pinocchio*, and perhaps a handful more that compel and command us by some *recherché* legerdemain, by some lapidary skill that the Muse imparts to one lost soul of our hapless number only when the moon turns blue, by some implausible concatenation of personal loneliness, peer-group ostracism, and other-directed need to prove one's worthiness through special dreaming.

In short, I believe *Edward Scissorhands*, and its director Tim Burton, to be unnatural wonders; and I lust to ramble on about them at sesquipedalian length. Ergo, the promise.

There is but one roadblock to our ramble down that road:

It's been almost a year since I saw *Edward Scissorhands*, and the voluminous notes I took at the time, written in a *lingua franca* of mine own devising, have become (over the months of exhaustion and inability to do much work) pure gibberish.

So I have to view the film again. And yet again. And (with exquisite joy) perhaps half a dozen times more. I do not think the chore will do other than enervate me, but it *is* the m.o. I employ for painting frescoes this ornate, two coats, matte finish, five year guarantee on parts & labor.

There is but one flaw in that otherwise excellent plan.

The cost of most videocassettes is between twenty and thirty dollars, usually less if you hit one of those shifty outlets where knockoffs of commercial tapes can be purchased. (There is a flourishing market in bootleg tapes, as you no doubt know. Recently, the excellent sf novelist Allen Steele was gracious enough to send me a pair of pirate tapes of *A Boy and His Dog* selling for $9.99 each; he found them in St. Louis video shops. One such emporium was a Suncoast in Crestwood Plaza, the other a Musicland in the St. Louis Galleria. These bogus tapes, in crummy-looking packages, bore such ersatz company names as "New Pacific Pictures" and "Front Row Video." Turns out these are blinds for a pirate videotape factory that has been successfully sued for similar previous infringements. It is their method to set up a labyrinth of diversionary addresses and mail-drops, corporate shells and time-wasting dog-legs that discourage most claimants from pursuing legal remedy. But once in a while someone is sufficiently determined, and when they get caught they are forced to pay up...after which, they change their name, change their location to yet another industrial park used for making connections with the video shops that knowingly sell these illegal items, and go right back into business with some new moniker on the packages.

(This is a multi-million dollar scam and, while it may seem nifty to be able to buy *A Boy and His Dog*—or some other excellent film—for a mere $9.99 as opposed to, well, we'll get to that in a moment, what you're getting is a markedly inferior second- or third- or even later-generation duplicate off an already existing prerecorded piece of merchandise. Not to mention that no one who sweated bullets to *make* that film gets a cent from the sale.

(And were it not for guys like Allen Steele—author of such swell novels as ORBITAL DECAY, CLARKE COUNTY, SPACE, and the recently released LUNAR DESCENT—books so fine that *Booklist* wrote of Steele: "Ingenious...an author with the potential to revitalize the Heinlein tradition!"—and don't say I don't know how to repay a favor—if it weren't for hawkshaws like Allen Steele—whatta guy!—poor slobs like your faithful columnist would never even *know* they were being mulcted out of the tiny royalties flowing [or rather, trickling, seeping, dribbling] from work done with the foolish expectation of establishing some sort of annuity against the coming of senility.)

But *Edward Scissorhands* does not sell for twenty or thirty bucks. *Edward Scissorhands*, all one hour and forty minutes of it, is available only on a CBS videocassette for $94.98, a sum I find I cannot, in good conscience, expend in your behalf as long as my poor wife and I are forced to continue plucking, boiling, and eating the tiny birds that knock themselves senseless against the mirrored windows of our modest hovel.

It is common knowledge, of course, that I am paid munificent sums for weaving these word-pictures at fairly regular intervals. Those who have dined with the Missus and me on golden breast of guinea hen and Lachryma Christi, here in the south wing of Chateau Grandeur, off plates of topaz, with pure silver utensils, as the full-time-employed strolling minstrels wander the Great Hall of Gourmandaise, as the distant voices of my *goyishe* serfs can be faintly heard singing their charming native tunes ("Sugar, Sugar" in the original Archies version, "Mellow Yellow," "Stayin' Alive," and "Welcome to the Jungle") as they labor happily in my shekel coffers, shoveling money from one bin to another…any such who have seen how The Li'l Woman and I live, here on the glass mountaintop, can easily attest that, yes, the management of this journal stints not in rewarding its faithful columnists.

It is *because* of this largesse, and because I have padded my expense account with the House of Ferman (soon to leave for rulership of the planet Arrakis) that I could not, in fairness, expect good old Ed to shell out the staggering sum of $94.98 merely to afford me the convenience of watching a film sixty-three times. ("Why don't you just rent it for a couple of days?" good old Ed suggested, when I broached the subject.)

Therefore, I have chosen to postpone the long essay on *Edward Scissorhands* for an installment or two, until the tape comes down to a price that does not suck the air from the lungs; and in its place I give you a charming congeries of oddments and tag-ends, unanswered comments and idle conjecture, bits and pieces and recommendations that have been piling up here for at least a year, in some cases longer, thereby making the data hideously outdated and utterly useless.

Hoping you are the same, I remain vampingly yourn…

Late last year, in installment 44, I went on at considerable length passing to my readers my perception of the "horror market" as one that would very quickly vanish as a viable (word used in its proper sense) workplace for writers of fantasy. I did *not*, ever, at any time, suggest that the form of fiction we know as "the horror story" would vanish. I pointed out that there would *always* be a Bram Stoker or Mary Shelley or Dan Simmons or Suzy McKee Charnas who could invest the old bones with new life, but that as a viable (word used *im*properly) category which B. Dalton or Crown Books could ghettoize on one wall between the mysteries and the science fiction, that "horror's" days were numbered. I did the column not only to apprise an alert and intelligent constituency of what I took to be a major trend in film and book publishing, but also to warn as many writers as I could of what I saw to be a very real and hurtling danger to their survival.

A goodly number of writers both known and unknown to me a that time, from both the world of novelists and the realms of screenwriting, called or wrote or personally thanked me for the warning, said they were acting accordingly.

Unexpectedly, though, a counter-revolutionary sentiment was expressed on those idiot computer bulletin boards, in small press journals, and in industry newspapers, that I was full of crap and oh let's just smile tolerantly because Ellison is at it again! A few small-time agents actually wrote rebuttal articles pointing out that gee, hadn't *they* just sold two novels to this or that paperback house for three or four or five grand just that week? Ms. Lori Perkins was arch and more than a tot condescending in *Mystery Scene*, advising everyone (and her clients in particular) not to panic, that the sky was not falling, and though Ellison was occasionally charming, he was, as usual, full of crap. I didn't view that as particularly responsible or astute behavior on the part of someone pledged to serving the survival of those who had put their careers in her hands, but it wasn't my problem, folks, and I held my silence.

It is now almost a year after installment 44, and today I learned that Lou Aronica at Bantam has killed the Bantam horror line. Not one or two books, but the entire line. Rick McCammon (in *Publishers Weekly* for August 2nd) gave an interview in which he advised that he would no longer be writing books that could be tagged "horror." His reasons were as complex as his work is excellent, and much of his decision had to do with not being typecast, but the exit line was nonetheless that "horror" wasn't a place he wished to be any longer. An artist friend of mine in New York (who has asked that I not use her name) called a while back to tell me that she had had three cover paintings for horror novels returned to her, from two different houses, with instructions that she should revise them to look more like psychological suspense novels. The publishers were repositioning books in which they had faith, trying to distance those titles from a genre identification they felt was now nugatory. Warner Bros., Tri-Star, Morgan Creek, and Paramount axed a total of fourteen horror or horror-oriented projects from their "in preparation" schedules, though not a lot of stock can be put in something like that, because three-quarters of *everything* that gets flacked at the beginning of the production season winds up as little more than hot air. Even so...

I think (of *course* I do) what I wrote was on the money. I didn't say anything in response to the Ellison's-fulla-crap essays because, as I say, it wasn't my problem. But a year has gone and went, and the facts *seem* to bear out the warning; and so Ms. Perkins's perky poo-poo'ing notwithstanding, I restate my perceptions on this matter as a final gardyloo to writers whose survival seems as important to me as I hope it is to them and those who take 10% off them.

Ted Geisel, known to everyone as Dr. Seuss, died on the night of Tuesday 24–Wednesday 25 September, age 87. AND TO THINK THAT I SAW IT ON MULBERRY STREET and THE 500 HATS OF BARTHOLOMEW CUBBINS were the second and third books I read, as a child roaming the public library in Painesville, Ohio in 1940. His gifts and legacies to the world of fantasy writing, and fantasy films, and fantasy thinking, are incalculable. (What's that? You say you've never even seen *The 5000 Fingers of Dr. T*, a gloriously Seussian 1953 film written by himself? How sad for you.) When I turned on the radio for the news as I made my morning coffee, at 5:30 in the dark of the day, and heard he was gone, I found myself weeping like that kid in the Painesville public library. It is possible some of you found yourselves similarly, unexpectedly, doing the same. And when, later that day, I had occasion to call Bob Silverberg upstate, and reviled the World Fantasy Awards and their like for never having noticed Seuss, Bob put me very much in my place by saying, "He had bestsellers. His name was known to everyone in America and most of the rest of the world. He was loved and his books will live on. Do you think he really missed anything by not being noticed by Those People?"

As usual, Silverberg was sensible and correct. So why do I feel that the award-glutted, award-loopy world of fantasy fans and pros should be ashamed of itself?

By way of Guilty Pleasures, I have come to a secret joy in viewing the last few *Nightmare on Elm Street* flicks, as well as Chris Matheson and Ed Solomon's *Bill & Ted* movies.

If I have denigrated the former and ignored the latter in previous columns, I want to come clean now. With the current release of *Freddy's Dead: the Final Nightmare* (New Line) and *Bill & Ted Go to Hell* (which will forever be the title by which I refer to this movie, its original designation, before Orion Pictures developed water on the knees and timidity on the *cojones* and, I suppose fearing that the Rev. Donald Wildmon and his illiterate army of gargoyles who have no lives beyond beating the bible and writing ungrammatically distraught letters to sponsors would rise in wrath, retitled this amusing little fable *Bill & Ted's Bogus Journey*), it is possible for you, too, to play catch-up.

The Freddy Films, as *Film Comment* will no doubt one day validate the cycle, have become more interesting as they went along. This is in defiance of all natural law for movies. The dopey flicks usually get dopier and dopier, until they implode. But the smart cookies at New Line have, one after another, hired clever writers for these shockers; and with this last number I am put more in mind of something Luis Buñuel or Man Ray or Salvador Dali or Fernando Arrabal would dream up than what we usually associate with four-wall exploitation. The last four *Nightmare* scripts have been small masterpieces of surrealism, filled with grisly wit, exciting juxtapositions of contemporary references with historic fear tropes, and rich subtexts that one can enjoy in echo, without feeling artsy-craftsy about the perceptions. Somehow, and don't ask me to explain it in such a snippet of comment, the *Nightmare* films down the line have managed to escape the meanspirited feel of the power-drill-in-the-brainpan *oeuvre*, and have accrued the goodwill of those who still dote on the best of the old Universal or Hammer scare films.

As for Bill & Ted, well, when I saw the first of the (sure to be a longer) series, I shook my head and dismissed it as a paean to the institutionalized stupidity of a debased audience devoted to Nikes, mall-speak, and anti-intellectualism. Well, maybe that's so, but every time *Bill & Ted's Excellent Adventure* showed up on cable—and it showed up a *lot*—I found myself rewatching it, and giggling. And that, folks, is my moviegoer's bullshit detector: I cannot watch *Mountains of the Moon* again, or sit one more time through the boredom of *A Cry in the Dark*, but Bill & Ted suck me in like the Sargasso every time I see Keanu Reeves and Alex Winter sowing havoc through time and space.

I guess what I'm saying is that if pure pleasure is the criterion for a film's worth... these two dudes are doomed to Posterity's Pucker.

It is a tiny book—merely 5¼" x 6"—and it contains only 80 pages, but if any of you are telling me the truth when you drop me a line to say thanks for recommending this or that item, then I ask you to trust me yet again, and to seek out as assiduously as you can, a blessed event called SKYSHADES (A Panache Press Book from Clarkson Potter Publishers, New York; $17.50).

This is a book of sixty small oil paintings by an artist-fantasist named Fanny Brennan. When I say *small* I mean in comparative size to, say, Botticelli's *La Primavera* that takes up more than seventy square feet of wall in the Uffizi in Florence, not in breadth of imagination. The largest of the sixty—and they appear as painted in their full size—is maybe 3"x4", the smallest looks to be about the size of a U.S. commemorative stamp with a thyroid condition. But one shows a dune-filled horizon as background to a pair of calipers measuring a bubble in the foreground; and another shows a rocky spire pierced by a pencil; and in others (as noted art critic Calvin Tomkins says in his foreword) "clouds escape from sacks on an empty beach, and landscapes peel away at the corner to show different landscapes underneath; where gravity takes time off and the normal scale of things is askew...and trickery is not in the painting but in the mind—hers and yours."

Repeatedly in this column I have suggested that watching films and reveling in unusual art books are allied pleasures, the one buttressing the other, and both serving to give you new eyes for seeing new things. If this is so, then you will treasure SKYSHADES. Because within its pocket-sized universe Fanny Brennan has provided postcards of a series of surreal worlds that will return to you the vision of childhood. As were grass and sky and ocean, fresh and new and wondrous, the first time you recognized them, filled with whimsy and inviting infinite mystery...thus reinstated are clouds and forests and islands through the tiny, glorious masterpainting of Ms. Brennan, who will put you in mind of Magritte and de Chirico and Ernst and Dali, come again more delicate and cheerful and exquisitely memorable.

You may have to order this one specially from a good bookseller—it came out last year, in a small printing—but don't go to your final sleep never having been thrown into the sky like a baby, laughing and gurgling with pleasure, by Fanny Brennan's tiny, sure, paintbrush-blessed hands.

ANCILLARY MATTERS: From the mail bag I've plucked a few items requiring short shrift. Incidentally, something weird has been happening to the lot of you. Formerly, I received as many letters telling me to drink Lysol as I did benighted plaudits from certifiably demented enthusiasts who cooed over my every word. Then I guess I got cranky about it, and I complained that I was being abused; and whammitybang the mean letters stopped, for the most part, and now I get these pronunciamentos from everywhichwhere that some of you cannot hope to live out your lives, there in the asylums, unless I keep writing this column. Only joy you know, you say. Brilliance uncontained, you say. Call the ward attendant, I've wet myself, you say.

Well, I'm duly grateful for all the good wishes and kind thoughts, but to tell you the truth it's like those Cagney movies where Jimmy starts out as a street thug, feisty and mean and filled with piss'n'vinegar...and then he gets religion or something, and turns into a good guy. Fascinating at the start, but boring as hell by the denouement. We always like the bitches and bastards best. The villains are always more intriguing than the sanctimonious breakfast-cereal-eating heroes. Mencken said he most enjoyed writing and reading about unusual people, and that meant he read mostly about rotten sonsofbitches. I'm not asking for opprobrium, I'm just saying that something weird has happened to you folks, and I'm getting worried that I'm not doing my job when you're not screeching at me.

Which brings me to Shirley Wander, John McCready, Amanda Summers (who likes Kathi Maio's stuff, too), David E. Penney, Carla Schoenstein, and Herb Gh— (I couldn't make out your signature): thank you. Thank you every single one.

Mike Firth sorta corrected me as follows: "It is indeed unfortunate that in your Oct/Nov column you chose Myrna Loy as the example in your comments about breasts showing through clothing, since at one confused point in my sexual wanderings I was surprised and pleased to discover that several of the outfits that Myrna wore in the *Thin Man* series of films allowed her nipples to appear visibly behind the cloth.

"Since I do not watch endless old movies and didn't live through the era, I can't effectively point to other examples; but the gal in the *Thin Man* movies wasn't a complete slut, even if she did enjoy drinking, and manage to be rich."

Mr. Firth, a resident of Dallas, certainly means well by passing along this intelligence; but I confess to being totally at sea in commenting. Save to make this observation: of *all* the words one might apply to the character of Nora Charles, wife of 'tec Nick Charles, mother of Asta, as splendiferously played by the elegant Myrna Loy, the absolutely very final *last* word I would have considered would be "slut," complete or partial or heretofore. Maybe I'm missing Firth's forth. Or something.

And as for the several readers who jumped all over Rick Thocker of Russen, Kansas for correcting me on the year of model of the DeLorean in *Back to the Future*, youse guys just leave Rick alone. First of all, I was wrong and he was right. Second, he was only having fun and meant no bad cess. And third of all, geez gang, lighten up, willya!?!

And on that note of civil defense, let me point out only this: the nastiest, ugliest, most vomitous jokes about Pee-wee Herman and Jeffrey Dahmer and Rodney King that are told to me…are always told to me by cops. Cop humor is so brutal, it does give one pause about Daryl Gates, if I can make the connection. See ya in the funnies.

48 In Which the Wee Child's Icons are Demeaned

Okay; so you're in the wrong, and you know it. You made a right turn from the left lane at the last corner, and you cut the guy off, and you're embarrassed as hell because you *know* what a feep you've been, and now you spot the destroyer coming around the corner behind you, swelling like a tumor in your rearview mirror, and you think, *Oh boy*, not because you're as much afraid as you are chagrined at having been just the kind of careless, out-to-lunch asshole as *you've* given the finger to.

About a hundred times in the past six years, right?

So this maddened vehicularist pulls up alongside you, and his power window skims down, and he's screaming imprecations and blasphemies against you and yo Mama till these two big pulsing cords bulge out either side of his neck like the pillars between which Samson stood in the Temple of Dagon, eyeless in Gaza, and the motorist fuming along beside you has this demented face all over him that says if he got the chance he'd rain down an entire Philistine temple on *your* head, you dimwitted chunk of semi-human excrement behind a steering wheel, which you shouldn't oughtta be!

Now it looks as if maybe he's going to keep at this thing till one or both of you swerve up and over and enter a Taco Bell not through the drive-in port, but maybe the front window, so in the name of terror and sanity, you pull over or slow down, and you start tugging your forelock in guileless consternation. We're talking major league shriving here. You admit to stupid, you cop to thoughtless, you plead brain-dead, you vouchsafe radical DNA damage all the way back to the Mesolithic, including that embarrassing contretemps involving your ancestor Hoockmuh of the Clactonians which resulted in your being minus a lobe or two of brain, and thus you are truly and genuinely contrite about having cut him off. You drool quite a bit. Also eye-rolling.

Which calms him some, but not totally, and he keeps at you. No longer homicidal, but still incensed and stoked with verbal inertia, still all puffed up and blowing hard. Like what the great screenwriter Richard L. Breen characterized as sounding off "like a banjo player who had a big breakfast." (I just *love* that phrase.)

There is a word in Yiddish for the way this guy is coming on. The word is *broygess*. It's pronounced something like rhyming with "Boy Gus" who would be, of course, sibling to Boy George. He's all chest and flapping lips. *Broygess*. Fulla hot air and warm owl shit.

My mother, dear lady that she was, had an instant response when someone came on *broygess* with her. The offensive party would run his/her mouth and roll dem eyes, and when a spot was hit where breath had to be taken, my momma would squint at the geek and say, "Woof woof a goldfish."

I'll let that one out again:

She would thrust her head forward and say snappishly, "Woof woof a goldfish." Or maybe it was, "Woof woof, a goldfish."

I grew up with that phrase. I never questioned its accuracy, its efficacy, its logic. When someone was being a strutting and fuming pain in the ass, the only proper response was *Woof woof a goldfish*.

I'm not sure I used the phrase very much, because it seemed—in my mind—the property of the late Serita R. Ellison, but yes, every so often, out of me would pop a perfunctory woof woof a goldfish. It never got less a reaction than astonished silence. It never occurred to me that the person to whom I was addressing woof woof a goldfish was anything but stunned into sordine confusion. (Now, in the wisdom of puberty, I suspect that the addressee was simply stumped as to what the hell I was saying. Either way, it worked.)

Many years later, after the death of my mother, when I had occasion to asseverate the phrase (as Hugo winner Mark Clifton once put it), a friend asked me, "Precisely what the hell does that *mean*, 'Woof woof a goldfish'?"

"Or, possibly, 'Woof woof, comma, a goldfish,'" I replied. "Y'know, I haven't the vaguest. My mother used to say it."

So I contemplated for a while, and the best I could come up with…was that a vicious dog would go *woof woof*, and be a potential threat. But if a goldfish went *woof woof*, it would be an empty threat, because what harm could a goldfish do you, even a very large, pumped-up on steroids kind of goldfish who had possibly studied all the Sonny Chiba films and knew a lot of spiffy moves?

That was what I divined. That my mother meant to say to whoever was coming on *broygess*, that s/he was fulla hot air and warm owl shit.

But the point I'm making here is that I *used* that phrase, and it was precisely what I wanted my message to convey, even though I'd never spent a moment trying to decipher it. And so do you. You have one or more of those. Some phrase that you got from a childhood playmate, or a teacher, or your parents, or brothers or sisters, or off some long-forgotten television show.

Some phrase or more than one, that came from ingrained childhood memory, that you never examined to make sure it had the same contemporary meaning for the people to whom you'd addressed it.

Hell, I still say "nekki hokey" from *Dick Tracy* daily strips, and I say "I'm ready for Freddy" from *Li'l Abner* comics, and "in like Flynn" and "What time is it? It's Howdy Doody time!" and when I want to make a sound to frighten someone it's always the sound of that squeaking door from *Inner Sanctum*. Or, to put it a different way, the great writer Lin Yutang once wrote: "What is patriotism but the love of the food one ate as a child?"

That which forms us, unconsciously, as children, informs our opinions when we have crawled through the years to adulthood. And we seldom recognize those forces and phrases that bent and shaped us. So we do the Academic Adagio, the Deconstructionist Dip, the Theosophical Thrash, to rationalize why we love or hate or enjoy or find disappointing some book or movie or comic or tv show. Also some people, whom we accept or reject on the spot, on the instant we meet them, for mysterious "gut perceptions" about Their Manner. (For instance, Chelsea Quinn Yarbro, a very fine writer, with whom I cannot remember ever having exchanged an unpleasant word, dislikes me—and these are her precise words—"Because of your manner." There is only one response possible to such a statement, and it *ain't* woof woof a goldfish. She is absolutely entitled to have that opinion, and it's one of the few *rational* reasons for disliking a person, but when she said it to me, all I could think of saying was the retort of Raymond Chandler's Philip Marlowe, "Yeah, I get a lot of complaints about that.")

What it is about the way someone presents him/herself tins to a resonance that we hear across the decades. As if formed in the crèche by *Oberstgruppenfuehrer* Nuns who followed to the letter the instructions in the Clockwork Orange Reader of Child Behavior and Mindwash, we respond, re: Pavlov, to arts and crafts, isms and aesthetics, songs and schemes, right on order, precisely as we have since adolescence, like that robot rabbit who runs the groove at the dog track.

And that is why I must give a lashing to the multi-million-dollar dud *The Shadow* (Universal), which broke my heart, made small one of my greatest childhood idols, wasted an opportunity to bring to the big screen one of the greatest detectives ever conceived by the mind of Man, and in general pissed me off.

(And you thought I'd never get to the movie part of this, didn't you? O ye of little faith. And by the way, your pants are unzipped.)

You cannot know with what innocence of mind and spirit I went to see *The Shadow* screened. If ever there was an audience stoked to enjoy a film, I was that audience! Come, I cried, come fill me to the top with wonder and mystery and suspense and the endless enigmas that the mere name The Shadow conjures.

I'm not one of you Boomers who rattles on nostalgically about how cool it was to listen to "Old Time Radio rebroadcasts" of *The Shadow* programs ten years ago. Listen up, you GenX-come-latelies: the first movie I ever remember seeing, even before *Snow White and the Seven Dwarfs*, which was 1937, but I must've seen it at its first re-release in 1940, was Victor Jory as *The Shadow* in the fifteen-part Columbia serial. I came in late to the chapter-play, maybe part three or four, but I remember standing at the back of the old Utopia Theater in Painesville, Ohio, on a Saturday afternoon, holding my father's hand—he'd taken off a half hour from managing Hugh's Jewelry on the corner of State and Main, to walk me up the block to the Utopia for my first movie going experience—not even seated yet, waiting for my dad to show me what to do, where to sit, how to act...and looking up at that screen and seeing one of the great American actors in what wasn't one of the great American movies (but, hell, *I* didn't know that), actually live-action moving and doing what The Shadow did in my head as I listened to him every Sunday evening, sponsored by Blue Coal. Whatta rush! I *adored* The Shadow.

Six years old, I'd taught myself to read, and I was spending my allowance on *The Shadow* pulp magazine from Street and Smith, not to mention the comic, which very soon began to feature Shadow art by the legendary Bob Powell. Bret Morrison was the voice of *my* Shadow, and Grace Matthews was Margo Lane. Mandel Kramer was Shrevie, the cab driver. I *adored* The Shadow.

Years and years later, working in Hollywood, I was at Screen Gems writing *Circle of Fear* and a segment of *The Flying Nun* and a little ghosting on *Police Story*, and William Castle had bought the rights to The Shadow, and I went to him and told him I'd write the damned screenplay *for nothing*, not a centavo, zip, nada, just gimme a chance! He had hired me for *Circle of Fear*, and he was high on my work, but he laughed and said he'd already assigned the script. To Jimmy Sangster! Well, sheeeeet, I thought, Sangster is a terrific writer, but not for The Shadow. He who knows what evil llllllurks in the hearts of men is a purely American kind of folk-hero, an American taste, an American icon that no Limey, no matter how good a writer, could possibly translate to film with the proper panache and misterioso. (I make this contention about foreign directors assaying American product as a general rule of thumb. If you think I'm being irrationally nationalistic, just consider how appropriately Hugh Hudson, that great Brit Director of *Chariots of Fire*, did when he interpreted Tarzan, another purely American pop icon, in his monumentally boneheaded *Greystoke*.) But I digress. Do I digress myself? Very well then I digress myself. (I am large, I contain multitudes.)

Never got made. Sangster wrote a less than ebullient script, and the project was shelved; rights reverted, got sold to someone else, and so on and so on. Comes the announcement a few years ago that Marty Bregman had gotten a deal with Universal to develop the material yet again, and I'm weaving mist-dreams that somehow, telepathically, out-of-body intuition, ectoplasmatic pheromones, *some*thing, one of the five producers on this deal would learn of me, sense in the stillness of the night my crazed passion to write *The Shadow*, and they'd knock at my door one day and say, "Come, wee child from Painesville; come, and write the dream of your dreams!"

Stop.

We inaugurate with this column, something no other film columnist proffers: THE SECRET AGENDA. Solemn oath, hand to my heart, spit in my palm and punch it with my other fist, any time I have a background that can influence my opinion of a film, or a writer, or an actor, or *any*thing in a column, I will pause and reveal THE SECRET AGENDA. You need never fear that I'm badmouthing someone like, say, Gregory Feeley or Charles Platt, just because they are my enemies and I'd happily shoot them into outer space *sans* rocket; or that I'm praising, say, Erika Eleniak not on her acting ability (which, for a newcomer, is arresting and beguiling) but because she is the second most beautiful woman in the world. You will always know whence I come. Let Pauline Kael match *that* homage to Caesar's Wife. His first wife, Pauline, the one they don't talk about much. Good hit, lousy field.

So now you know how I went to see *The Shadow*.

Do it to me, I said.

The report: Good hit, lousy field. Special effects right out of the most fertile vineyard in your imagination (except for this stupid, dippy-looking demon-knife, a kind of Arabic *kris*, which periodically gets imbued with a simulacrum of life, and flies through the air and keeps trying to do a Lorena Bobbitt on The Shadow), but the live-action stuff is seriously Rip Van Winkle. We're talking *boe-*ring.

Like so many of these F/X shivarees, from *Explorers* to *Death Becomes Her*, from *Honey, I Blew Up the Kid* to *Solarbabies*, from *Last Action Hero* to *Star Trek: The Motionless Picture*, this is a frontrunner in the legion of the walking dead. It shambles afield, but it has no brain. It capers and jabbers, it does its little rigadoon, but it hasn't got the wit or innovation to blow itself to kingdom come. This is a stupid film, filled with breathtaking adolescent electronic and computer techniques, all in service of a story created by semiliterate children at recess time, children who cannot sit still long enough in class to learn anything. It is historically and culturally imbecile, tone-deaf and derivative, lumbering and flatulent, a waste of time and money, of energy and talent. It is a great 4th of July pyrotechnic presentation, for people who have forgotten why we celebrate the Fourth. It is a well-bedecked Christmas tree for those who think Christmas means school's out and let's go shopping.

This is yet another example of the paucity of imagination that has come to be known as The American Cinema of the '90s. At long last, after twenty-five years of dumbing-down the product for what businessmen and businesswomen perceive as the idiot teen audience, we have *this*: the perfect empty-calorie eye-candy that fools the eye 24 times a second. *The Shadow* is all flash and filigree, as Terry Southern would put it; F/X entrepreneurs run amuck; story written by know-nothing scribblers brought up on a steady diet of tv and post-music noise.

And make no mistake, it isn't the fault of the actors, who do the best they can (though why anyone would cast the glorious Jonathan Winters in a role unsuited to his talents, and then in pawky fashion not even allow him to *demonstrate* those talents, passeth understanding); nor is it the fault of the director, a certain Mulcahy who has, well, a small but identifiable ability; nor the fault of the brilliant production designer Joseph Nemec III; it is a gobbet fit only to be stuffed down the craws of the pimplebrained producers, all five of 'em, among whom there ain't a scintilla of commonsense...and the writer, David Koepp, who is oh so hot these days, oh so wooed and exulted for his scrivening on *Death Becomes Her* (cataclysmically stupid film), *Jurassic Park* (idiot plot with F/X runamuck), *Carlito's Way* (Scarface Pacino lisps again), and *The Paper* (which set back the Fourth Estate to the days of tabloids on stone tablets).

Those responsible for this mess fear producing Art.

They turn all substances to dross, and coat it with the F/X fool's gold, and dish it out in ten-second jump-cut MTV video commercials, knowing they've bastardized the audience so thoroughly that if they show enough glittery snakeskin rubies exploding, they'll pull their ten-twent-thirt million buck summer audience. Never mind that the film is a pile of rusty Kelvinator wrecks for a story, piss-yellowed bidets for emotion, drums of malodorous chemical waste for subtext, and severed rat heads for logic. These are people who were weaned on *I Love Lucy*, who think we really and truly need a film based on *The Beverly Hillbillies* or *The Flintstones* or *The Little Rascals* or *Dennis the Menace* or *Maverick* or whatever else they took to be great art when they were in swaddling.

Well, it wasn't, and they aren't, and this is yet another example of viewing the audience as mere receptors with money to be cadged and intellects to be debased. It is a stupid movie, filled with some wonderful special effects, and ordinarily I would give it the shortness of shrift it deserves. But this time they made a mistake, they fucked around with something I love.

This time they plucked the feathers off an icon not of *their* moron generation, but of mine. This time they left the environs of their own grim ghetto, and they went back in time and sullied something *I* hold dear.

And *this* time, I'm gonna ream 'em good.

Yes, gentle reader, I'm back. After three years of sabbatical in Tibet, where I acquired the power to cloud men's minds so they cannot see me, I'm back to the column. I'll tell you where I've been, and all the goodies I've brought back for you, and detail all the ways in which *The Shadow* is a disgrace (and why *The Mask* isn't, even though it's no less eye-candy) when next we meet here in my sanctum sanctorum hidden beneath Rush Limbaugh's corpulent fundament. There have been many changes since last we engaged in these hi-jinks: the Noble Publisher has turned over the editorial reins to Mine Fair Editrix; you've been polite and attentive to my compatriot Kathi Maio, who will continue with us, never fear; I've managed to accrue my very own organized hate group of Baby Weasels who knew they couldn't take me one at a time, so they merged like one of those slimey alien things in a John Campbell story; movies have gotten worse; computer bulletin boards have unleashed every rambling idiot who previously at least had to know how to spell to publish a fanzine; OJ has got hisself in deep *merde*; many good men and women have died; and I've forgotten how desperately you needed my calm and sane observations of cinema and allied visual venues.

Consider this part one of "The Return of the Omen" and I'll be back on *The Shadow*'s ass next issue. And until then, stay out of the line of fire.

Or as my momma would have said it, Woof woof a goldfish.

49 In Which the Old Man of the Sea Bites the Head off Yet Another Chicken

If you're reading this installment on or about 7 January 1995, you may lift and clink crystal champagne flutes, intone a solemn *Here's lookin' at* you, *kid*, and amaze your friends with the diurnally appropriate datum that the movies are *exactly* 101 years old today, as you take your first sip. *L'chaim!*

On 7 January 1894 (and I'd have told you this *last* year for its centenary significance, had I been here; but I was on sabbatical in Tibet, where I acquired the uncanny power to cloud mens' minds so they cannot see me, as you already know) Thomas Edison received copyright on "a moving visual image" he had titled *Fred Ott's Sneeze*, and thus, just so, the medium of the motion picture, the cinema, the movies, was born. 1894 to 1995: that's one hundred and one years. Happy birthday. *L'chaim!*

And now to work.

If you recall, in yesterday's installment, yr. faithful correspondent had copped to the secret agenda of being a stone in-love-with-*The-Shadow* kinda guy, who had lusted after the gig of writing the theatrical feature for, oh nothing important, only maybe *THIRTY GAHDAMN YEARS*...inhale...exhale...inhale...exhale...and had begun to diss the Universal Pictures's PG-13, forty-five million dollar infantile crepuscular film-fart, *The Shadow*, when time ran out and we had to cut to commercial, film at 11. So, now, back to work.

Yet let us get to the job-site by way of Enlightenment Blvd. and Arguing-From-the-Greater-To-the-Lesser Avenue. We can car-pool and avoid all the traffic snarls on the Infomercial Superhighway where apologists for fatheaded films clog the pathways of perception.

Back in May of 1994, the book critic of *New York* magazine, Walter Kirn, while in the process of reviewing a tome we need not consider here, made some devastatingly accurate observations about baby-boomers. He said, in part, they "tend to be...citizens of a sociological state whose borders are dates of birth and cultural references, whose flag shows a guitar and a TV set, and whose myth of moral superiority derives from an association with 'blameless' liberation movements. ... They see pop culture since the fifties as a kind of epic home movie that they never tire of replaying, insisting it has lessons for us all. ... They say they can't stop thinking about tomorrow, but what they really can't stop thinking about is themselves."

Kirn sideswipes the b-b brigade for its "generational arrogance" and its members as "champions of dreck" and in closing he wrote *this* eye-opener: "Nothing is inevitable, and no generation will ever change the world by watching TV and listening to lots of records."

(He probably would've resonated more purely had he tried to be a tot more *au courant* by substituting computer bulletin boards for TV, and CDs for records, but that's just bibblebibble on my part. The point he makes is irrefutable and crushingly painful to consider.)

I give you a moment to do just that. To consider.

The Shadow lies at the penultimate destination of this essay. *The Mask* (New Line Cinema) is the ultimate. Not "ultimate" in the Socratic sense of final, absolute, the last word, the apex, the pinnacle; merely ultimate in that it is the last fuel stop on this filmic hadj. The end-point to be reached through sunny side-trips and metaphoric shortcuts.

Let us pause, here at this scenic turnout overlooking the verdant valley below. Let us open the door and emerge from the sealed-off interior of our media-assault womb, this traveling prison cell that keeps us so jangled with colors and sounds and false impressions that we cannot let our minds cool, cannot take that celebrated cortical-thalamic pause to examine what it is we're being pressured into accepting as State of the Art.

(Perfect example: what the critic John Powers calls "the flying-glass school of cinema. *Lethal Weapon*, *The Last Action Hero*, *The Last Boy Scout*, *Blown Away*, *The Specialist*, and on and on, with shards protruding from your cerebellum.)

The way it used to was-been, films were made by men and women who had some familiarity with the literary landscape. Whether those good souls, talented and untalented alike, wended their way to Hollywood via the dustjacketed word, the newspaper essay, the legitimate stage, the regional theater, or from some rural or foreign cinematic venue, there was a common tongue spoken: Art.

Even those who produced nothing but *schlock*, drivel unfit for imprint on a gnat's memory, the veriest crap of woebegone idiots...even *they* could hold a conversation in the *Lingua Franca*. They understood, dimly dimly, what it was all about. Even *they*, slope-browed simulacra of Creative Intellects, even *they* knew that Ben Hecht and Joe Mankiewicz and Billy Wilder and Val Lewton and Ida Lupino dealt in some form of Art. Even *they*, lowest of the low, incapable or unwilling to go against the formidable odds when attempting to produce High Art, understood that *Treasure of the Sierra Madre* and *The 400 Blows* and *La Strada* and *King Kong*—by chance or intent—transcended the callow commercial goals set by the secret cabal of Schlock Entrepreneurs and Anal Retentive Intellectuals. Even *they*, with noses flattened against the window, looking in at Welles as he created *The Magnificent Ambersons*, at John Ford filming *Stagecoach*, at Tod Browning throwing sanity to the winds and making *Freaks*...even *they* knew how to speak the language. They were envious and defended their puny efforts with patently self-serving rationales, but they *knew* what Art was. Because it was held up for them to marvel at. It was *there*, somewhere, every day, in the flex and surge of the popular culture. Maybe not today in a movie, but at least today in a book; maybe not today in a Broadway opening, but at least today in an outspoken newspaper column. Maybe not here today, but definitely not gone tomorrow.

Today, that flex and surge is less and less apparent in popular culture. We have abrogated our debt to the past, and our hope for the future, by permitting *everything* the p.c. accolade of worthiness. So tell me, gentle reader, determined to be "new age permissive," from what university of higher education, and in precisely what rigor, did Dr. Dré get his diploma? What, exactly, is it that Sharon Stone has between her legs, possessed by at least fifty per cent of the population of the planet, that is sufficiently startling, unique, or eloquent, to convince us that this woman can act? Shouldn't the correct term be "boneheads," not "skinheads"? And maintaining the precision of form-follows-function vernacular—risking the opprobrium of the putatively aggrieved—shouldn't the homosexual opposite of "straight" not be "gay," but more correctly..."straighter"?

Everything is okay. And any objection is beaten back by artificially enhanced outrage. Bad money drives out good money; bad art seeds the landscape with a crabgrass of tolerance for *anything*, without discrimination, sans standards, and it chokes out good art. There is no continuity of memory. The young go to the theaters, and they see *The Fugitive* (at best) or *The Beverly Hillbillies*, *Dennis the Menace*, *The Flintstones*, *Super Mario Brothers*, *Maverick*, *The Brady Bunch*, *The Addams Family*, *Lassie*, or *The Jetsons* (have I missed anything, if so, fill in the blanks). They know no better. The world began for them at dawn this morning. (As one arrogant little pissant put it, at a recent San

Diego Comic-Con, as a group of older comics professionals tried to explain to him why the seminal creations of Wally Wood, Lou Fine, C.C. Beck, and Mac Raboy should be remembered and honored, "Dead guys don't count.")

(According to reports, there were a couple of people in that group who wanted to make the pissant "not count" real fast.)

The common language is now a "dead" language, no less arcane and reduced to white noise than Permian, Kipchak, Ligurian, or Ossetic. The everyday conversational of Art is now the tenebrous chatty-talk of academics and goony writers like me. No one even bothers to ask *why* the world needs a movie based on *The Brady Bunch*. Trying to quantify or contextualize the value of any given motion picture, attempting to link movies to what is happening in the world outside those dark, still rooms where something other than an immediate, compositional punch, however stylish and not boring, should be the sought chalice, becomes an exercise in profound and introspective musing. A conversation in a dead language.

The baby-boomer audience needs a feeling of movement; it needs a feeling of spectacle, even grandiloquence, hotcha style. It is bewitched by the grotesque. It is all-permitting. It sits there admiring *itself*, without a scintilla of self-criticism, unable to look at hard truths along that highway. It is devoid of conscience, otherwise how could it permit itself to be so easily manipulated, how could it permit such atrocities of random horror without squeaking a peep? The world began for this audience at dawn this morning.

It would never even *think* of asking why the world needed a live-action Flintstones flick. Out the potboiler came on the summer platter of fast-films (with fries, super-sized) and was gulped down without anyone asking if it was grilled at a temperature over 155° Fahrenheit. Gulped down, with all its *E. coli* virulence, and the system logs in another jot of poison that builds up the immunity.

Given this audience—fair game for anything idiotic if it tinkles to the memory of childhood passions—even though the memory eliminates the truth that *even when new* these were dopey ideas—disco was shit back then, and no amount of "nostalgia" grave-robbing will make it less than shit a second time around—and that goes for "How Much Is that Doggie in the Window," too—is it any wonder that *The Shadow* comes up a chipper example of The Walking Dead?

Written by baby-boomers, directed by baby-boomers, and produced by and *for* baby-boomers, a cultural icon from an earlier time cannot be permitted to sing its song in ragtime. It has to be rendered in hip-hop, or be designated hincty.

Are you still considering?

We near the penultimate point of our journey.
I shall return.

50 In Which the Playroom of the Prodigal Gives One Last Gasp

Yes, it is a mite sorrowful that I never finished the review of *The Shadow*, because I went sabbatical on film comment for the most part, with only an occasional opinion piece here or there. Peripatetic. Itinerant.

I continued going to the movies, the film review spot in *F&SF* was taken over by the most excellent Lucius Shepherd and Kathi Maio, and the world moved on. As I write this, on 4 September 2014, Lucius has passed away untimely and much to the misery of those of us who came to delight in his cinematic observations. Kathi staves on, Gordon Van Gelder will find someone new to support that ridge-pole, and I won't have to complain about the miserable state of movies in this 21st Century.

I go to the moom pitchers reluctantly these days, having been physically assaulted by *Star Trek into Darkness*, at a 3-D 200-decibel ten storey-high showing that was as close to a beating I'd taken on the Hoboken docks a lifetime ago, as I'd ever want to relive. Most "big" films these days are nothing but Marvel Comics blown up beyond sense or sensitivity. (Josh, Susan, and I made an afternoon of *Guardians of the Galaxy*, and if I were to write a review it would start:

"*Guardians of the Galaxy*—look left, look right: Not a brain in sight.")

I don't think most of you would care for my opinions of current films, so I'm as well out of the game. Every once in a while—as you'll see by looking at the entries following this apologia column that never was—I poke my head out and either lavish praise on, or excoriate, something new. But mostly, I just keep quiet. And as for that Alec Baldwin film of *The Shadow*, the most peculiar thing happened: about six months after I wrote Installment 49, I saw the movie again, on a Kleenex-box-sized screen in First Class on a flight to England. Reduced as it was, I was able to ignore the over-the-top pop art notes… and enjoyed it thoroughly.

Photograph by William Rotsler

I Saw *Ghost Rider*
Today at the Galleria

It is summat past 4:30 in the afternoon here.

Susan and I went to the Sherman Oaks Galleria, theater 6, for the 1:35PM first showing of *Ghost Rider*.

We are home now.

I saw *Ghost Rider*.

The film was written and directed by the man who wrote and directed the Daredevil film. I saw *Ghost Rider*.

Further, deponent sayeth not.

An ancillary moment of criminus behavior, witnessed by me and, thankfully, I did not have an AK-47 in my possession at the time:

The theater—this being a school day and an early showing—was three-quarters empty. Seated right below and in front of us were four enormously fat people. Not *just* overweight fat; not even morbidly or clinically fat, which is tragic; but the kind of fat that comes from being geeks who gather girth either by sitting hour-upon-hour on the sagging sofa watching endless, mindless tv, snacking on Cheetos and such provender, or in front of the idiot pc writing crap like *this* for days and nights on end. Ugly, sloppy, trailer park, gene pool pollution fat. Four of them. Not quite a family, but fuck-your-sister-and-get-a-2headed-calf kind of familial arrangement. And they kept going back again and again to the snack bar for *more* popcorn, *more* hot dogs, *more* sody pop, *more* Hot Tamales, *more* raisinets, *more* slices of pizza—I am not resorting to hyperbole. My count is imprecise, on the light side, but I actually noted *eleven* trips by the burro they had running their errands for them.

Now *none* of this is a) my business, b) of any concern to me, or c) worthy of passing along to you, were it not for this:

They had brought a tiny baby with them to this multiplex noise emporium with the sound cranked to 205 decibels. Train running over your grave loud. Steel foundry loud. 7th Avenue at high noon in Manhattan loud. I have a bad case of flu, my head is stopped up, and so I figured I wouldn't need the ear plugs I've long since made a staple of my moviegoing outside of the Writers Guild Theater where we don't allow a sound level that makes the ears bleed…and I came home with a thundering headache.

I don't *get* headaches. Never have. One of my blessings.

Pig iron foundry loud. Directly under the SST flight-path loud. Republican caucus convention loud. Impossible to enjoy a moment at a big league ballpark for all the *chaaaaarge* and amped-up rock music and we're number one shrieking loud.

That loud.

I came home with a headache.

And the baby was so tiny, under a year I'm sure, that when they passed it from fatso to fatso for two hours, the baby raised its arms into the light of the projection beam, as if the wee dear creature was supplicating for deliverance, and even compelling people behind the row of fatties to scream *doooo yoooo myyyyyynd!!??!!* several times.

And like hopeful wannabes for the road company role of Jabba the Hut, these enormously fat crap-imbibing morons—who, s'help me, sang along to the Coca-Cola ad that preceded the movie—"give back a little love"—every fucking word; and who actually applauded the *trailer* for the forthcoming Fantastic 4 sequel; and one of the younger of these slug-creatures pounded his/her fists in time to the cacophonous heart-paralyzing drumbeats of the cranked-up soundtrack, as the two Ghost Riders thundered across the desert, one *à la* hog, the other *à la* demon horse—these Tobacco Road rejects who make the redneck Okie imbeciles on *My Name is Earl* look like Rhodes Scholars—these gobbets of suppurating stupidity—passed the poor baby from hand to butter-slimy hand, while the banshee-shrieking abattoir of mayhem and slaughter on the screen reverberated at such a pitch that even rock-concert-calcified tympanic nerves had to've been shattered like Limoges.

When the lights came up, and most of the theater was emptying, they were still there, embedded in the seats, overflowing like sacks of suet stuffed into mailboxes. And the child, with eyes the size of those on a cow taking note of the descending iron maul, was upchucking over the shoulder of one of this quartet of pig-people. And, big mouth buttinski that I am, I paused as I shoved my way through them, and I said, in not my kindest tone of voice, "What the fuck is the matter with you people? If the sound in here is too awful and too damaging to an adult, can you imagine what it's doing to your baby? What kind of imbeciles are you to bring a child to a theater like this? Do you have any idea, and do you give a shit, that you're molesters, criminally endangering this baby's hearing for life?"

And Susan dragged me, forcibly, I'm telling you forcibly, drug me on away from them before I fuckin' physically attacked the cocksuckers. And yes, I know I was a buttinski, and none of my goddam business, and shut up Ellison and stop sticking your nose in where it doesn't belong…but *this anecdote*, this snapshot of the world as I live in it, is all the explanation you'll ever need as to why I just damn skippy don't go out much anymore, and why I shouldn't be *allowed* out, because one of these days I will lose it entire, and I will savage these thoughtless amoral ignorant unaware baggies of rodent blood till they disgorge their rancid swamp innards!

Now you know what a rant is.

I saw *Ghost Rider* today.

Further, deponent sayeth not.

12 Years a Slave

Rarely, in a lifetime of endless filmgoing and decades of serious cinema criticism, is one honored, privileged, rewarded by having seen a motion picture that is memorable down to one's core. Having seen *12 Years a Slave*, I cannot remember being as mesmerized, as touched, as stopped stock-still, since the night I first saw Stanley Kubrick's anti-war film *Paths of Glory*. It is that nonpareil a film, no less.

Even the dullest among us, chained to jobs and lives we detest, cherish the word and the evanescent concept of *freedom*. Above all else, what *12 Years a Slave* burns into our awareness—as no other film has achieved—is the absolute power of the slavemaster over every moment of the blacks' existence. It is a tyrannical and capricious power greater than any monarch's. For these yearning, brutalized chattel, *freedom* is a goal that will never be reached: pain and death stand in the portal.

Based on a memoir published in 1853, the story is as somber as it is historically tragic. Solomon Northrup—staunchly interpreted by Chiwetel Ejiofor—a freeborn African-American born in the Adirondack Mountains in 1807, living a genteel life with wife and two children in Saratoga Springs, New York, is gulled and cozened by Northern middlemen for Southern Slavers, kidnapped, and brutally press-ganged to a series of plantations in pre-Civil War Louisiana where his state is brought so low that even admitting he can read and write, or insisting he is not a runaway slave but a freeborn, can get him flogged to the naked bloody bone. Twelve years as a slave. A superbly reenacted chapter of a two hundred-year-long stain on American honor that today's celebrity-drunk culture of bitch-ho rap and wannabe gangsta homies not only do not comprehend, but disgrace the courage of their forebearers when they pull it as "the card." This is a film of gravitas and superior artistry. It miraculously manages to combine all the *Gone with the Wind* pastel mendacity still extant in parts of our land, with the shocking Grand Guignol gruesomeness of the *noir* reality.

    The screenplay by John Ridley, himself a Gentleman of Color, in lean, muscular, and stalwart. The direction, by Englishman Steve McQueen (whose previous films frankly gave me the creeps) is opulent yet bleak, altogether a bit finicky as if the Director has not yet fully recovered from having been bitten by the cottonmouth of self-aggrandizement, but such carps are beyond notice in a film as praiseworthy and memorable as *12 Years a Slave*.

Death To All Hollywood Award Shows!

If you are as old as primordial mud, you may remember not *that* long ago, when the Foreign Press Ass-Kissing and Suborned Jury Conclave (or whatever acronym they give themselves), the ones who give out the worthless Golden Globes every year, writhed under the burden of impartiality and selected a young woman named Pia Zadora as The Most Promising New Star of the year. Paraphrasing the glorious Jean Hagen in *Singin' In The Rain*: "A blazing comet in the Hollywood firm-uh-ment!"

If you are as old as primordial mud, you may remember only the *name* Pia Zadora.

The fact that Ms. Zadora's husband, a doting multi-billionaire, *bought* the GoldenGlober's kudos, is commonly-known industry scandal. Today, having hired themselves a coterie of the savviest PR commandos, the Golden Globe coven has sashayed itself into a position where everyone in Chitling Switch, Oklahoma actually believes their annual tv awards bash, and those trinkets which ought to be given as prizes at a carnival midway ring-toss scam, are the accurate barometer of who or what will win the equally debased Oscars.

This is a logical fallacy known as an argument *ad ignorantium*.

As a devout believer in Open Covenants, Openly Entered Into, I will not lie to you from the git-go: I do not merely *hate* all awards shows, I wish to see them beheaded, stakes driven through their black and corrupted widdle hearts, and to see the decapitated remains buried at a crossroads come midnight. Now we are on the same page.

Along about the time I matured enough to know there were no such things as *yetis*, the Loch Ness Monster, and the stork bringing babies, I gave up on the Academy Awards, the revered Oscars. It was 1952, and Cecil B. DeMille's lumbering spaz *The Greatest*

Show on Earth was christened best picture, beating out Fred Zinnemann's *High Noon*, John Huston's *Moulin Rouge*, and John Ford's *The Quiet Man*, to name only three challengers. I, and everyone in Hollywood, knew the Academy had been embarrassed into throwing the aged director a sop for his having been (correctly or otherwise) passed over for decades. But sitting in New York, watching the annual tv panegyric, I shrieked like a shrike, tore out my eyes, and swore I'd take a marlin-spike to the temple before I ever allowed myself to be taken in again with such flagrant chicanery.

Those who give the awards exchange ballots among each other's categories, provide a pasha's fortune to publicity flak-providers, logroll, solicit, and hustle shamelessly to pit every talent against every other talent, making it a transparent and debased 3-card monte scam. Phoney deified. Ass-kissing sanctified. As Bogart called it, "A Mugg's game."

There are, at rough, hardly comprehensive total presently more than seventy (70) awards ceremonies ranging from the Oscars and Golden Globes and Emmys and Grammys to the People's Choice, BAFTA, Image, and Country Music Awards. Very nice, to acknowledge outstanding work by one's peers: rent a hotel ballroom, print up brochures enumerating the honorables at-bat, have some rubber chicken and frozen peas, and get on with it. I've been to *many* such events, and have even won a plentiful share of plaques, orbs, medals and parchments…and almost without exception each ceremony was boring. That's the reason television programming should eschew all awards-giving hours-long rituals of self-aggrandizement, phoney-baloney pomp and pretense at trustworthiness.

Like World Wrestling, *The Strident Housewives of the New Jersey Marshlands*, and the chance of winning the Publishers Clearing House Sweepstakes, these *soi-disant* jubilations of achievement are phonies. Boring, bought&traded, lugubrious and endless shams that try to convince the naive and gullible that one should waste an entire tv evening just to "see what the ladies are wearing on the red carpet." I had to murder my beloved wife with an Anthony Bourdain cheese grater when she uttered those words and cozened me into exhausting five hundred years of my remaining life watching the most recent Oscar extravaganza of bad gags, false humility, inflated encomia, and dance routines that haven't been inventive since Busby Berkeley worked with Ruby Keeler.

How to better the environment, clean up the airwaves, stop this madness? Unless the gullible masses stop muttering "it's a fake" and rise with cudgel and vomit, my answer is: Armageddon.

Bram Stoker's Dracula
a previously unpublished review

Like the undead who populate this film, Francis Ford Coppola's interpretation of *Bram Stoker's Dracula* (American Zoetrope/Columbia) gives the moviegoer no peace.

In the words of Stephen King about some other film entirely, "This sonofabitch just keeps coming at you!" True, true, too too true. It's bash bash bash from first frame onward, without cessation, without diminution, without let-up. This is one rich, ripe, plump, juicy, twelve-hours-away-from-festering-on-the-vine piece of pustulent passionfruit. The colors are over the top, the sounds are over the top, the performances are so over the top they could have left the trenches and overrun the Boche at Verdun, and the screenplay by James V. Hart is Bram Stoker shrieking, "Top'a the world, Mom! Top'a the world!" Ka-boom.

So many people have said this film is a stinker, and so many people have paid so much money to see it, and so many people seem to have come away from it as ga-ga and goofy as a groundhog who's had a Fleet's enema, that it hardly seems adequate to report that your faithful columnist just simply enjoyed the demented revels of *Dracula* as he would a High Mass on Easter Sunday at Saint Patrick's Cathedral. All pomp and circumstance, all tassels and quivering breasts, all rolling eyes and tumescent cinematic appendages. This ain't no movie, folks, it's a goddam Passion Play; and as spectacle it is free of the constraints one places on works of art that are supposed to make sense.

You might as well ask a Jackson Pollock painting to convey a coherent philosophical premise.

Demand a Rothko carry a tune and hammer a nail straight.

Or cast Charlie Bronson as Lear.

What are we talking here, craziness?

This is Coppola outKenning Russell. After very nearly a hundred years of telling and retelling, the Dracula thing is verily winded. First came the novel, then the sequel, then the endless reprints, then the Lugosi template, then the Hammer films and Christopher Lee (*still* the best Vlad, for my kopecks), and the Frank Langella version based on the Broadway success, and then as far left as you could drift with it—George Hamilton in *Love at First Bite*—one of my favorite films—not to mention every other harebrained, fangily foolish, special effects-drunk vampire film that has taken a gambol down Nosferatu Lane. So what the hell is anyone complaining about with this one? How *else* could it be done, and be worth the doing?

That is to say, I think anybody who wants to do *another* vampire movie, of *any* kind, is seriously in need of deep therapy. But if you're going to crawl into those rotting raiments, if you're going to delude yourself with overweening ego that you have a way of doing it that freshly mints the coin, newly shines the doorknob, and magically revives the conceit without leaving tooth-marks, then already you're seriously deranged and little option is offered save to do it over the top precisely as Coppola has done.

As one who thinks vampire movies are mostly a bore to begin with, I tell you honestly that this sexy, splashy, rowrbazzle rendition was eye-candy of a most welcome sort. I enjoyed it, the way I'd enjoy watching, say, Pat Buchanan being messily gnawed apart by piranhas (or Fundamentalists with blunted teeth). It's a Passion Play, gang; and as a card-carrying Atheist I always enjoy watching the convoluted contortions of this kind of sexual-religious-violence mishmash. Crosses, magical wafers with the power of absolution, lopped heads, splashing blood, lip-smacking Necco masturbatory fantasies...

Gee whillikers, folks, what more could you ask for on a slow Saturday night?

Honey, I Blew Up the Baby
a previously unpublished refusal to review

There are some films one is compelled to see, dragooned into visiting, coerced into sitting through, snookered into viewing, circumstanced into exposing oneself to, taken unawares and discovering too late that one has fallen into the clutches of...that thereafter one learns one must review. One must comment on. One must voice an opinion about. One must draw its measure. One must relive, if only fleetingly, for description, its high horrible notes and loathsome venues. At such times, those of you who believe in Supreme Deities cry out, "O Lord, strike the sight from mine eyes! O God, make me to forget! O Host of Hosts, set me in a time before the occurrence!" (I now believe to my core that this is the sole benefit of Religion: that one has Someone upon whom one can call for either a quick death or blindness, or a vegetative state around which are set, like *puréed* vegetables perimetering a plate of Nouvelle Cuisine, loving relatives who think they're prominently mentioned in your will, who'll pull the plug and send you to blissful oblivion. For us Atheists, it's just suffer, suffer, suffer! Where is Ba'al, now that I needs him?)

The other night, having cleverly managed to avoid attending either the Motion Picture Academy screening or the private studio screening to which we were invited by our good friend Howard Green of Disney, after a day at Cedars-Sinai Medical Center enduring something called a Radioactive Thalium Stress Test, exhausted and needing respite, I allowed Susan to treat me to an expensive dinner at Lawry's on Restaurant Row (actually, she owed me the dinner because she lost to me in a 50-game 8-ball series on our pool table), and as a gesture of camaraderie for the spouse, said, "C'mon, there's a film at the Writers Guild Film Society, let's just shine it all on, and go relax and see something."

Thus it was, for all my maneuvering, for all my clever duck and dodge technique, for all my devious and Moriartylike planning, I found myself watching *Honey, I Blew Up the Baby* (Touchstone).

As mildly charming and amusing as *Honey, I Shrunk the Kids* (1989) turned out to be, this sequel is not mildly anything. It is magnificently what it is. Monumentally a classic of what it is. Cataclysmic in its perfection of type.

It is a mess.

It is an awful mess.

It is a magnificent, monumental, cataclysmic, perfectly formed goat-turd of a movie. Had we dropped this film on Nagasaki instead of the A-Bomb, hundreds of thousands would have lived, but we'd have had generation after generation of brain-dead slaves who would not, today, be surpassing us in every aspect of commerce and inventiveness. A nation of staring, drooling, somnambulistic drones we would have today.

This film is so outstandingly horrible that I simply refuse to review it. Won't. Won't. Won't. No amount of torture could bend me to the task. I refuse. Beat me, pillory me, take off my weenie with a cheese grater, I will *not* review *Honey, I Blew Up the Baby*.

While this volume was being prepared for publication, the author discovered this handwritten fragment of an unfinished review of *The Mask*. It amused him, and he hopes it will do likewise for you:

> "THE MASK" IS A GOODHEARTED LITTLE VILLAGE IDIOT OF A MOVIE. IT DROOLS A LOT, BUT IT MEANS NO HARM. IT MAY PISS ITSELF WHEN YOU TAKE IT OUT IN PUBLIC, BUT IT HAS THE GOOD GRACE TO LOOK CHAGRINED AT THE PUDDLE IN WHICH IT STANDS.

COPYRIGHTS, cont'd

"*Psycho*" originally appeared in *Xero*; copyright © 1960 by Harlan Ellison. Renewed, 1988 by The Kilimanjaro Corporation.

"Total Impact: *The Terminal Man*" originally appeared in *Vertex*; copyright © 1974 by Harlan Ellison. Renewed, 2002 by The Kilimanjaro Corporation.

"3 Faces of Fear" originally appeared in *Cinema* magazine; copyright © 1966 by Spectator International Inc. Copyright reassigned to Author 7 October 1980. © 1980 by The Kilimanjaro Corporation. Renewed copyright © 1984 by Harlan Ellison.

"Installment 35: In Which the Phantasmagorical Pales Before the Joys of the Mimetic" originally appeared in *The Magazine of Fantasy & Science Fiction*; copyright © 1989 by The Kilimanjaro Corporation.

"Installment 36: In Which, Darkly and Deliciously, We Travel From Metropolis to Metropolis, Two Different Cities, Both Ominous" originally appeared in *The Magazine of Fantasy & Science Fiction*; copyright © 1989 by The Kilimanjaro Corporation.

"Installment 37: In Which Not Only is No Answer Given, But No One Seems to Know the Question to Ask" originally appeared in *The Magazine of Fantasy & Science Fiction*; copyright © 1989 by The Kilimanjaro Corporation.

"Installment 38: In Which, Though Manipulated, We Acknowledge That Which All Men Seek" originally appeared in *The Magazine of Fantasy & Science Fiction*; copyright © 1989 by The Kilimanjaro Corporation.

"Installment 39: In Which We Hum a Merry Tune While Waiting for New Horrors, New Horrors" originally appeared in *The Magazine of Fantasy & Science Fiction*; copyright © 1990 by The Kilimanjaro Corporation.

"Installment 40: In Which We Scrutinize the Sedulousness to Their Hippocratic Oath of Troglodytic, Blue, Alien Proctologists" originally appeared in *The Magazine of Fantasy & Science Fiction*; copyright © 1990 by The Kilimanjaro Corporation.

"Installment 41: In Which an Extremely Nervous Fool with His Credentials Taped to His Forehead Tacks Trepidatiously Between Scylla and Charybdis Knowing that Angels and Wise Men Would Fear Even to Dog-Paddle This Route" originally appeared in *The Magazine of Fantasy & Science Fiction*; copyright © 1990 by The Kilimanjaro Corporation.

"Installment 42: In Which It Waddles Like a Duck, Sheds Water Like a Duck, and Goes Steady With Ducks, But Turns Out to be a Tortoise" originally appeared in *The Magazine of Fantasy & Science Fiction*; copyright © 1990 by The Kilimanjaro Corporation.

"Installment 43: In Which We Lament, 'There Goes the Neighborhood!'" originally appeared in *The Magazine of Fantasy & Science Fiction*; copyright © 1990 by The Kilimanjaro Corporation.

"Installment 44: In Which the Good Ship Coat-Tail-Ride Sinks, Abandoning Hundreds in Treacherous Waters" originally appeared in *The Magazine of Fantasy & Science Fiction*; copyright © 1990 by The Kilimanjaro Corporation.

"Installment 45: In Which *Tempus* Fidgets, *Fugits*, and Inevitably Omnia Revelats" originally appeared in *The Magazine of Fantasy & Science Fiction*; copyright © 1991 by The Kilimanjaro Corporation.

"Installment 46: In Which We Bend So Far Over Backwards To Be Unbiased That You Can See The Nose Hairs Quiver With Righteousness" originally appeared in *The Magazine of Fantasy & Science Fiction*; copyright © 1991 by The Kilimanjaro Corporation.

"Installment 47: In Which Artful Vamping Saves the Publisher $94.98" originally appeared in *The Magazine of Fantasy & Science Fiction*; copyright © 1991 by The Kilimanjaro Corporation.

"Installment 48: In Which the Wee Child's Icons are Demeaned" originally appeared in *The Magazine of Fantasy & Science Fiction*; copyright © 1994 by The Kilimanjaro Corporation.

"**Installment 49: In Which the Old Man of the Sea Bites the Head off Yet Another Chicken**" originally appeared in *The Magazine of Fantasy & Science Fiction*; copyright © 1995 by The Kilimanjaro Corporation.

"**Installment 50: In Which the Playroom of the Prodigal Gives One Last Gasp**" first appeared in HARLAN ELLISON'S ENDLESSLY WATCHING; copyright © 2014 by The Kilimanjaro Corporation.

"**I Saw *Ghost Rider* Today at the Galleria**" was originally posted to *Unca Harlan's Art Deco Dining Pavilion* at http://harlanellison.com/heboard/unca.php on 2 February 2007; copyright © 2007 by The Kilimanjaro Corporation.

"***12 Years a Slave***" originally appeared in *Variety*; copyright © 2013 by The Kilimanjaro Corporation.

"**Death to All Hollywood Award Shows!**" originally appeared in *Variety*; copyright © 2013 by The Kilimanjaro Corporation.

"***Bram Stoker's Dracula***" first appeared in HARLAN ELLISON'S ENDLESSLY WATCHING; copyright © 2014 by The Kilimanjaro Corporation.

"***Honey I Blew Up the Baby***" first appeared in HARLAN ELLISON'S ENDLESSLY WATCHING; copyright © 2014 by The Kilimanjaro Corporation.

"**A Few Words About *The Mask***" first appeared in HARLAN ELLISON'S ENDLESSLY WATCHING; copyright © 2014 by The Kilimanjaro Corporation.

Other Ellisonian recommendations, circa December 1988:

The Last Temptation of Christ
Betrayed
Tucker
Rocket Gibralter
Eight Men Out
Gorillas in the Mist
Another Woman
Without a Clue

HARLAN ELLISON® has been characterized by *The New York Times Book Review* as having "the spellbinding quality of a great nonstop talker, with a cultural warehouse for a mind." *The Los Angeles Times* suggested, "It's long past time for Harlan Ellison to be awarded the title: 20th century Lewis Carroll." And the *Washington Post Book World* said simply, "One of the great living American short story writers."

He has written or edited 76 books; more than 1700 stories, essays, articles, and newspaper columns; two dozen teleplays, for which he received the Writers Guild of America most outstanding teleplay award for solo work an unprecedented four times; and a dozen movies. *Publishers Weekly* called him "Highly Intellectual." (Ellison's response: "Who, Me?"). He won the Mystery Writers of America Edgar Allan Poe award twice, the Horror Writers Association Bram Stoker award six times (including The Lifetime Achievement Award in 1996), the Nebula award of the Science Fiction Writers of America four times, the Hugo (World Convention Achievement award) 8 ½ times, and received the Silver Pen for Journalism from P.E.N. Not to mention the World Fantasy Award; the British Fantasy Award; the American Mystery Award; plus two Audie Awards and two Grammy nominations for Spoken Word recordings.

He created great fantasies for the 1985 CBS revival of *The Twilight Zone* (including Danny Kaye's final performance) and *The Outer Limits*, traveled with The Rolling Stones; marched with Martin Luther King from Selma to Montgomery; created roles for Buster Keaton, Wally Cox, Gloria Swanson, and nearly 100 other stars on *Burke's Law*; ran with a kid gang in Brooklyn's Red Hook to get background for his first novel; covered race riots in Chicago's "back of the yards" with the late James Baldwin; sang with, and dined with, Maurice Chevalier; once stood off the son of the Detroit Mafia kingpin with a Remington XP-l00 pistol-rifle, while wearing nothing but a bath towel; sued Paramount and ABC-TV for plagiarism and won $337,000. His most recent legal victory, in protection of copyright against global Internet piracy of writers' work, in May of 2004—a four-year-long litigation against AOL et al.—has resulted in revolutionizing protection of creative properties on the web. (As promised, he has repaid hundreds of contributions [totaling $50,000] from the KICK Internet Piracy support fund.) But the bottom line, as voiced by *Booklist*, is this: "One thing for sure: the man can write."

He lives with his wife, Susan, inside The Lost Aztec Temple of Mars, in Los Angeles.

CHRONOLOGY OF BOOKS BY
HARLAN ELLISON®
1958 – 2014

RETROSPECTIVES:

ALONE AGAINST TOMORROW: *A 10-Year Survey* [1971]

THE ESSENTIAL ELLISON: *A 35-Year Retrospective*
(edited by Terry Dowling, with Richard Delap & Gil Lamont)
[1987]

THE ESSENTIAL ELLISON: *A 50-Year Retrospective*
(edited by Terry Dowling) [2001]

UNREPENTANT: *A Celebration of the Writing of
Harlan Ellison* (edited by Robert T. Garcia) [2010]

OMNIBUS VOLUMES:

THE FANTASIES OF HARLAN ELLISON [1979]

DREAMS WITH SHARP TEETH [1991]

THE GLASS TEAT & THE OTHER GLASS TEAT [2011]

GRAPHIC NOVELS:

DEMON WITH A GLASS HAND
(adaptation with Marshall Rogers) [1986]

NIGHT AND THE ENEMY
(adaptation with Ken Steacy) [1987]

VIC AND BLOOD: *The Chronicles of a Boy and His Dog*
(adaptation by Richard Corben) [1989]

HARLAN ELLISON'S DREAM CORRIDOR, Volume One [1996]

VIC AND BLOOD: *The Continuing Adventures of a Boy and
His Dog* (adaptation by Richard Corben) [2003]

HARLAN ELLISON'S DREAM CORRIDOR, Volume Two [2007]

PHOENIX WITHOUT ASHES
(art by Alan Robinson, and John K. Snyder III) [2010/2011]

HARLAN ELLISON'S 7 AGAINST CHAOS
(art by Paul Chadwick and Ken Steacy) [2013]

THE HARLAN ELLISON DISCOVERY SERIES:

STORMTRACK by James Sutherland [1975]

AUTUMN ANGELS by Arthur Byron Cover [1975]

THE LIGHT AT THE END OF THE UNIVERSE
by Terry Carr [1976]

ISLANDS by Marta Randall [1976]

INVOLUTION OCEAN by Bruce Sterling [1978]

NOVELS:

WEB OF THE CITY [1958]

THE SOUND OF A SCYTHE [1960]

SPIDER KISS [1961]

SHORT NOVELS:

DOOMSMAN [1967]

ALL THE LIES THAT ARE MY LIFE [1980]

RUN FOR THE STARS [1991]

MEFISTO IN ONYX [1993]

COLLABORATIONS:

PARTNERS IN WONDER:
Collaborations with 14 Other Wild Talents [1971]

THE STARLOST: *Phoenix Without Ashes*
(with Edward Bryant) [1975]

MIND FIELDS:
33 Stories Inspired by the Art of Jacek Yerka [1994]

I HAVE NO MOUTH, AND I MUST SCREAM:
The Interactive CD-Rom
(Co-Designed with David Mullich and David Sears) [1995]

"REPENT, HARLEQUIN!" SAID THE TICKTOCKMAN
(rendered with paintings by Rick Berry) [1997]

2000^X (Host and Creative Consultant
of National Public Radio episodic series) [2000–2001]

HARLAN ELLISON'S MORTAL DREADS
(dramatized by Robert Armin) [2012]

THE DISCARDED (with Josh Olson) [Forthcoming]

AS EDITOR:

DANGEROUS VISIONS [1967]

NIGHTSHADE & DAMNATIONS:
The Finest Stories of Gerald Kersh [1968]

AGAIN, DANGEROUS VISIONS [1972]

MEDEA: HARLAN'S WORLD [1985]

DANGEROUS VISIONS (The 35th Anniversary Edition) [2002]

JACQUES FUTRELLE'S
"THE THINKING MACHINE" STORIES [2003]

CHRONOLOGY OF BOOKS BY
HARLAN ELLISON®
1958 – 2014

SHORT STORY COLLECTIONS:

The Deadly Streets [1958]

Sex Gang *(as "Paul Merchant")* [1959]

A Touch of Infinity [1960]

Children of the Streets [1961]

Gentleman Junkie
and Other Stories of the Hung-Up Generation [1961]

Ellison Wonderland [1962]

Paingod *and Other Delusions* [1965]

I Have No Mouth & I Must Scream [1967]

From the Land of Fear [1967]

Love Ain't Nothing But Sex Misspelled [1968]

The Beast that Shouted Love
at the Heart of the World [1969]

Over the Edge [1970]

All the Sounds of Fear
(British publication only) [1973]

De helden van de highway
(Dutch publication only) [1973]

Approaching Oblivion [1974]

The Time of the Eye (British publication only) [1974]

Deathbird Stories [1975]

No Doors, No Windows [1975]

Hoe kan ik schreeuwen zonder mond
(Dutch publication only) [1977]

Strange Wine [1978]

Shatterday [1980]

Stalking the Nightmare [1982]

Angry Candy [1988]

Ensamvärk (Swedish publication only) [1992]

Jokes Without Punchlines [1995]

Вcе звуки страха (All Fearful Sounds)
(Unauthorized Russian publication only) [1997]

The Worlds of Harlan Ellison
(Authorized Russian publication only) [1997]

Slippage: *Precariously Poised, Previously Uncollected Stories*
[1997]

Koletis, kes kuulutas armastust maailma slidames
(Estonian publication only) [1999]

La machine aux yeux bleus
(French publication only) [2001]

Troublemakers [2001]

Ptak Śmierci (The Best of Harlan Ellison)
(Polish publication only) [2003]

Deathbird Stories (expanded edition) [2011]

Pulling a Train [2012]

Getting in the Wind [2012]

NON-FICTION & ESSAYS:

Memos From Purgatory [1961]

The Glass Teat: *Essays of Opinion on Television* [1970]

The Other Glass Teat:
Further Essays of Opinion on Television [1975]

The Book of Ellison
(edited by Andrew Porter) [1978]

Sleepless Nights in the Procrustean Bed
(edited by Marty Clark) [1984]

An Edge in My Voice [1985]

Harlan Ellison's Watching [1989]

The Harlan Ellison Hornbook [1990]

Bugf#ck! The Useless Wit & Wisdom of Harlan Ellison
(edited by Arnie Fenner) [2011]

CHRONOLOGY OF BOOKS BY HARLAN ELLISON®
1958 – 2014

SCREENPLAYS & SUCHLIKE:

THE ILLUSTRATED HARLAN ELLISON (edited by Byron Preiss) [1978]

HARLAN ELLISON'S MOVIE [1990]

I, ROBOT: THE ILLUSTRATED SCREENPLAY (based on Isaac Asimov's story-cycle) [1994]

THE CITY ON THE EDGE OF FOREVER [1996]

MOTION PICTURE (DOCUMENTARY):

DREAMS WITH SHARP TEETH (A Film About Harlan Ellison produced and directed by Erik Nelson) [2009]

ON THE ROAD WITH HARLAN ELLISON:

ON THE ROAD WITH HARLAN ELLISON (Vol. One) [1983/2001]

ON THE ROAD WITH HARLAN ELLISON (Vol. Two) [2004]

ON THE ROAD WITH HARLAN ELLISON (Vol. Three) [2007]

ON THE ROAD WITH HARLAN ELLISON: HIS LAST BIG CON (Vol. Five) [2011]

ON THE ROAD WITH HARLAN ELLISON: THE GRAND MASTER EDITION (Vol. Six) [2012]

AUDIOBOOKS:

THE VOICE FROM THE EDGE: I HAVE NO MOUTH, AND I MUST SCREAM (Vol. One) [1999]

THE VOICE FROM THE EDGE: MIDNIGHT IN THE SUNKEN CATHEDRAL (Vol. Two) [2001]

RUN FOR THE STARS [2005]

THE VOICE FROM THE EDGE: PRETTY MAGGIE MONEYEYES (Vol. Three) [2009]

THE VOICE FROM THE EDGE: THE DEATHBIRD & OTHER STORIES (Vol. Four) [2011]

THE VOICE FROM THE EDGE: SHATTERDAY & OTHER STORIES (Vol. Five) [2011]

THE WHITE WOLF SERIES:

EDGEWORKS 1: OVER THE EDGE & AN EDGE IN MY VOICE [1996]

EDGEWORKS 2: SPIDER KISS & STALKING THE NIGHTMARE [1996]

EDGEWORKS 3: THE HARLAN ELLISON HORNBOOK & HARLAN ELLISON'S MOVIE [1997]

EDGEWORKS 4: LOVE AIN'T NOTHING BUT SEX MISSPELLED & THE BEAST THAT SHOUTED LOVE AT THE HEART OF THE WORLD [1997]

EDGEWORKS ABBEY OFFERINGS (Edited by Jason Davis):

BRAIN MOVIES: THE ORIGINAL TELEPLAYS OF HARLAN ELLISON (Vol. One) [2011]

BRAIN MOVIES: THE ORIGINAL TELEPLAYS OF HARLAN ELLISON (Vol. Two) [2011]

HARLAN 101: ENCOUNTERING ELLISON [2011]

THE SOUND OF A SCYTHE *and 3 Brilliant Novellas* [2011]

ROUGH BEASTS: *Seventeen Stories Written Before I Got Up To Speed* [2012]

NONE OF THE ABOVE [2012]

BRAIN MOVIES: THE ORIGINAL TELEPLAYS OF HARLAN ELLISON (Vol. Three) [2013]

BRAIN MOVIES: THE ORIGINAL TELEPLAYS OF HARLAN ELLISON (Vol. Four) [2013]

BRAIN MOVIES: THE ORIGINAL TELEPLAYS OF HARLAN ELLISON (Vol. Five) [2013]

HONORABLE WHOREDOM AT A PENNY A WORD [2013]

AGAIN, HONORABLE WHOREDOM AT A PENNY A WORD [2014]

BRAIN MOVIES: THE ORIGINAL TELEPLAYS OF HARLAN ELLISON (Vol. Six) [2014]

HARLAN ELLISON'S ENDLESSLY WATCHING [2014]

8 IN 80 BY ELLISON (guest edited by Susan Ellison) [2014]

Made in the USA
Middletown, DE
25 October 2014